SEWING CLOTHES

ELEVATE YOUR SEWING SKILLS

Sewing Clothes—Elevate Your Sewing Skills

Landauer Publishing, www.landauerpub.com, is an imprint of Fox Chapel Publishing Company, Inc.

This book is a collection of new and previously published material. Portions of this book have been reproduced from Time Life's The Art of Sewing series, under license by New Design Originals.

Noted Contributors to Time Life's The Art of Sewing Series:
Gretel Courtney, fashion instructor and author of *The Butterick Sewing Machine Handbook*
Annette Feldman, knit and crochet designer and author of *Crochet and Creative Design*; *Annette Feldman's Needlework for the Home*; *Handmade Lace and Patterns*; *Knit, Purl, and Design*; *The Big Book of Afghans*; *The Big Book of Small Needlework Gifts*; *The Needlework Boutique*; *Beginner's Needlecraft*; *Fun with Felt*; and *Needlework for the Home*
Tracy Kendall, costumer and author of *The Fabric & Yarn Dyer's Handbook*
Jo Springer, home sewing writer and consultant and author of *Pleasure of Crewel*
Erica Wilson, graduate of the Royal School of Needlework in England, teacher, and author of *Erica Wilson's Embroidery Book* and *Erica Wilson's Needlepoint*
Toni Scott, teacher of needlework and quilting techniques and author of *The Complete Book of Stuffedwork* and *Basic Sewing*

Sewing Clothes—Elevate Your Sewing Skills Project Team:
Editor: Diana Kern
Designer: Matthew Hartsock
Photographer: Joi Mahon and Amelia Johanson
Proofreader & Indexer: Jean Bissell

Paperback ISBN 978-1-63981-048-2
Hardcover ISBN 978-1-63981-107-6

Library of Congress Control Number: 2024935674

Credits and Sources
Photos: Page 47 Designer Joi Tweed Suit M7280 Photo by McCall Pattern Company; Page 60 Frog Closure Design by Joi. Photo by Mike Yamin Threads #225 Spring 2024; Page 66 Designer Joi Wool Coat M7666 Photo by McCall Pattern Company ; Page 73 Designer Joi Bias Strap Gown M7568 Photo by McCall Pattern Company; Page 134 Designer Joi Lace Skirt M7048 Photo by McCall Pattern Company; Page 142 Knit top and Sereflex Thread Photo provided by Mettler Thread; Page 143 Overlock Stitch Photo provided by BERNINA ; Page 178 Embroidery Sleeve Blouse by Joi. Photo by Jack Deutsch for *Threads* magazine; Page 180 Designer Joi White Cotton Lace Dress M7318 Photo by McCall Pattern Company; Unless otherwise stated all garments and photos were created by the Author Joi Mahon.
Acknowledgements: DeeDee Johnson Burnt Fabric Flower Design page 75. Amelia Johanson for smocking the fabric used on page 53. Amelia Johanson for YoYo project and photography on page 168. Bernie Frisch for crocheting the cuffs on page 51. Amelia Johanson for project and photo on page 77. Amelia Johanson for photos on pages 174, 180, and 182.

We are always looking for talented authors. To submit an idea, please send a brief inquiry to acquisitions@foxchapelpublishing.com.

Note to Professional Copy Services:
The publisher grants you permission to make up to six copies of any patterns in this book for any customer who purchased this book and states the copies are for personal use.

Printed in China

SEWING CLOTHES
ELEVATE YOUR SEWING SKILLS

A Master Class in Finishing, Embellishing, and the Details

Joi Mahon

Author of
*Ultimate Illustrated Guide
to Sewing Clothes*

Landauer Publishing

CONTENTS

ADDITIONAL RESOURCES

 Here, you will find a QR code that links to additional resources, such as template downloads, patterns, videos, and other free items. These should further enhance the techniques and projects shared here. Make sure to check out my website www.designerjoi.com for compatible fabrics and free tutorial videos that also compliment the projects, especially in Chapters 8 and 9.

Additionally, you will want to check out my previous book, *Ultimate Illustrated Guide to Sewing Clothes*. While this book is all about techniques, embellishments, and ends with several complete projects, the earlier title will teach you more about pattern fitting, the basics of garment sewing, fabric basics, and much more. If you would like to learn with me every week, check out my free Facebook Live on my page Designer Joi Mahon. And for even more learning and often specialized and individual learning, join my subscription club, Perfect Pattern and Fit Club. You can find all these resources and so much more on my website www.designerjoi.com.

INTRODUCTION

Welcome to *Sewing Clothes—Elevate Your Sewing Skills*. I mean, who doesn't want to take their sewing to the next level? This book is all about the "lost arts" of sewing—those skills and techniques that define a quality garment that are often bypassed in quick sew fashion. We all enjoy making a quick one-hour garment, but I didn't want you to miss out on the tried-and-true techniques that I teach and use in my sewing studio every day. They are presented here in a handy and easy-to-follow reference guide with fresh and modern designs and approachable fashion projects. I am all about making sewing fun, easy, but with amazing results!

Sewing doesn't have to be time consuming or overly complicated, but as with any skill, it requires an investment of time and practice to become proficient and achieve quality results. In addition, you must decide if the garment you are making is a fast-food version, which is quick and may cut corners (hacks), or a gourmet version that you will savor and invest your time and energy.

It can be difficult to distinguish between various sources that are for Sewing Education or for Sewing Entertainment. Both have a purpose, but the results can be quite different. These days, we are inundated with an almost infinite and overwhelming number of ideas for creating new projects and techniques to "improve" our sewing due to the influence of social media. Quick reels and video clips are often clever and entertaining to watch, and sometimes even feature some really good ideas. However, they often skip the technical steps and skills needed to achieve the featured results and provide viewers with a false sense of knowledge. So how can you tell the difference and decide what technique or source is really going to help you?

LET'S TALK ABOUT MY SEWING FORMULA

*My formula combines **appropriate fabric selection**, **the correct pattern**, **a perfect fit**, and **quality sewing techniques**.*

The result should equal a well-designed and expertly sewn garment. Each of these skills and techniques work together to produce the eye-catching designs we all aspire to create. You may excel in one area and be deficient in another. I have encountered many sewers with technical excellence who are not able to select the right fabric or pattern to best represent their abilities. I have also encountered excellent pattern fitters who have poor technical skills. If you came to me, like many of my students in live classes have done, and asked, "Joi, will you give me the basics of what I need to know to design and sew a garment?" I would give you this book as a reference. I would also tell you it is going to take you more than an hour to learn. Each chapter contains what I feel are some of the "lost arts" of sewing—solid foundational skills to elevate your sewing, based on what I have done throughout my sewing career. I could not include everything, but I did work carefully with my editor, Amelia, to hand-select content that we felt were the next steps to elevate your sewing. I would encourage you to take one project or technique at a time and practice it until you are confident in your abilities and then move on to another.

It takes time to learn and practice to make those skills stick. We all have limited time, so I encourage you to skim through the book to get a feel for all the fun topics and lessons. Then, go back and read cover to cover. Invest in a good bookmark because you can read a few pages and work on one design exercise and then resume at your convenience. I am so excited for you to elevate your sewing and design skills! Post pictures of your projects on the Designer Joi Facebook page to share. Happy sewing!

— Designer Joi

Sioux City, Iowa

TIME LIFE THE ART OF SEWING SERIES

Although the originals are out of print, you can use this QR code to access them as ebooks in all their original, colorful, funky style.

Critical to the success of my first book, *Ultimate Illustrated Guide to Sewing Clothes*, as well as to this new second title, has been the ability to access and repurpose excellent material from the Time Life The Art of Sewing series, the rights to which are now owned by my publisher. Now highly sought-after collector's items, this 1974 series propelled sewing fashion into the modern world for home and small-scale sewists like me.

Created by a team of expert designers, winners of the Vogue Fabric Award, and teachers at the most prestigious fashion and design schools in the world, such as the Fashion Institute of Technology and Parsons School of Design, these books are an invaluable resource, and it was a pleasure giving this content new life within these pages. From The Art of Sewing collection, I carefully hand-selected and curated the styles and techniques that have stood the test of time, and that today's sewists would love to learn and customize with their own modern, personal touches.

THE ART OF SEWING SERIES INCLUDED THE FOLLOWING TITLES:

Restyling Your Wardrobe	*Exotic Styling*	*The Custom Look* (aka *The Professional Look*)
Boutique Attire	*Making Home Furnishings*	
Basic Tailoring	*Novel Materials*	*The Classic Techniques*
Creative Design	*Shortcuts to Elegance*	*Traditional Favorites*
Decorative Techniques	*Separates that Travel*	*The Personal Touch*
Delicate Wear		*The Sporting Scene*

"The illustrations are clear, and even though the projects look sophisticated, they almost assume the reader can't thread a needle. Everything is explained from the very beginning in great detail. The 'delicate wear' one for instance demonstrates every conceivable hand stitch and seam, every knitting, lace, and crochet stitch you might need, as well as all the diagrams for pattern pieces, etc. 'The Making of Home Furnishings' goes into such detail about cutting and sewing a set of loose covers and blinds, one could not really go wrong."
—*Threads* magazine on the complete The Art of Sewing series

"A unique and surprising series. By virtue of the narrow task at hand, its instructions are thorough. If you find this for sale, get it."
—David Page Coffin, longtime *Threads* magazine editor and author of many sewing titles, including *Shirtmaking: Developing Skills for Fine Sewing*, on *Basic Tailoring* from The Art of Sewing series

CHAPTER 1

TECHNIQUES THAT ENHANCE

The perfection of a custom garment is on display even in its tiniest detail. The essentials of such crafting, or how the garment is carefully cut out and then sewn together, enhance both visible—such as the mitered corner or faultlessly finished bound buttonholes—and invisible—such as the interfacing and precise marking—details. Pockets and zippers created with detailed workmanship take minutes to sew, yet elevate and enhance any garment for a more professional, polished look. Any technique can elevate your sewing when created with care and appreciation for the finished results. Try to step away from pattern hacks and cutting corners to achieve fast fashion—a common mindset in society. In this chapter, we will explore the steps taken to master some popular sewing techniques that go beyond basic pattern instructions. As a result, your custom designer clothing will elevate from a quick fix to a gourmet project that you will treasure for years to come.

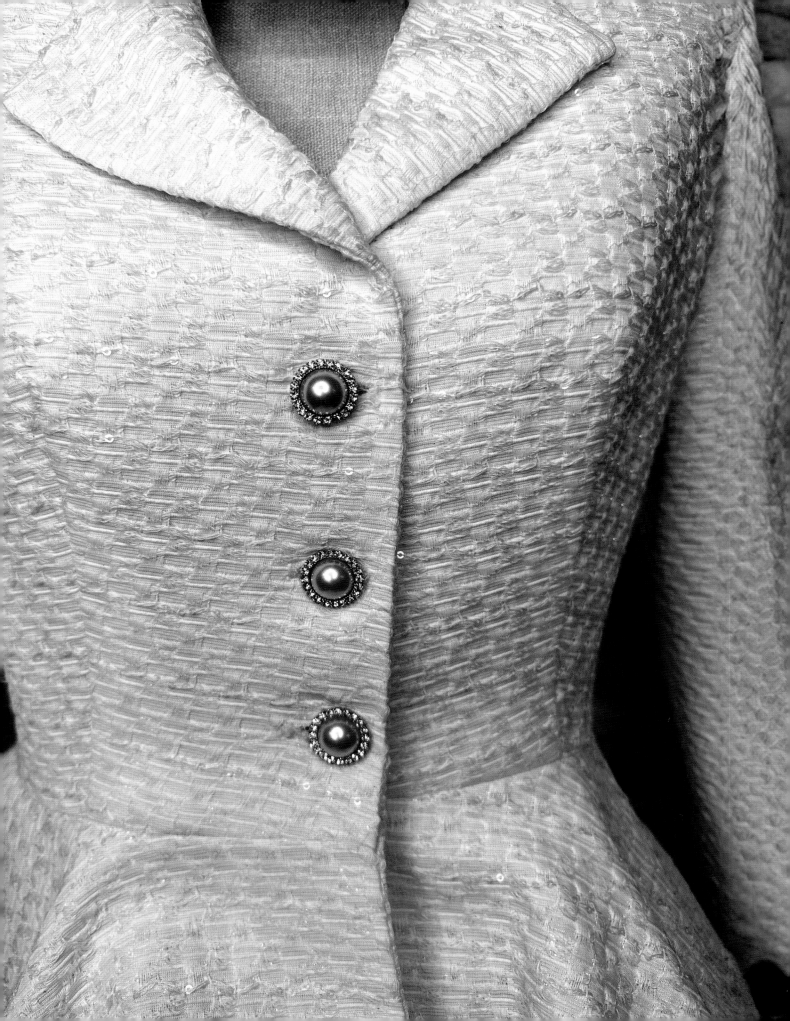

ZIPPERS

Traditionally, zippers are placed in the front, back, or side seam of most garment patterns. Zippers come in a variety of shapes, sizes, and materials, but unlike the conventional zipper—which reveals a telltale bulge and stitching—the invisible zipper is set into the seam with the aid of the zipper foot. This zipper is barely visible. Of course, the centered and lapped application are also widely used in many garments. The key to choosing your zipper is to evaluate your fabric, the thickness of the seam, and the style of the garment for the best selection. With a little creativity, these closures can be added not only for function, but decorative application, too.

INVISIBLE ZIPPER

Preparing the Garment for the Zipper (A)

1. Place the right half of the garment back on a flat surface, wrong side up.
2. Lay the closed zipper on top of the garment along the markings for the center back seam line, positioning it so that the zipper tab falls ⅝″ (1.6 cm) below the neckline edge.
3. Mark the position of the zipper tab and the bottom end of the zipper with pins, then set the zipper aside.
4. Mark the position of the pins with a horizontal running stitch (page 195) and remove the pins.
5. Run a line of basting stitches along the seam line marking of the garment section between the horizontal markings made in Step 4. This line indicates exactly where the zipper will be inserted.
6. Repeat Steps 1–5 on the left half of the garment back.

Preparing the Zipper (B)

7. Open the zipper and lay it face down on your ironing board. The inside edges where the zipper coils are located will be folded over a fraction of an inch toward you.
8. With the tip of your iron, press the inside edges of the zipper flat so the folded over coil edge is turned toward the other side.

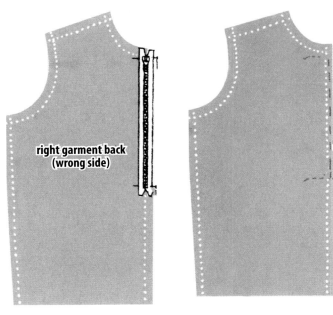

right garment back
(wrong side)

left garment back
(wrong side)

(A)

DESIGNER TIP

You can add zippers to areas of the pattern even if the instructions don't call for one. Simply mark your pattern where the zipper will be added. Cut the pattern apart and make sure to add seam allowance to either side of the new seam for inserting the zipper.

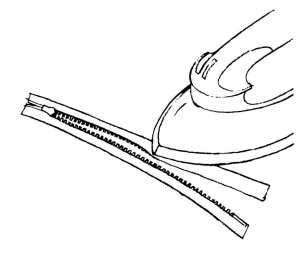

(B)

Attaching the Zipper to the Right Half of the Garment (C)

9. Place the right half of the garment back on a flat surface, wrong side down.
10. Place the open zipper face down on the garment back so the top and bottom ends of the coils are aligned with the horizontal basted markings made in Step 4. The coils of the left half of the zipper should be flush against the vertical basted markings made in Step 5.
11. Pin and baste the zipper to the garment. Remove the pins.

Stitching the Zipper to the Right Half of the Garment (D)

12. Assemble the special zipper foot and attach it to your machine, following your machine instructions.
13. Making sure that the zipper coil feeds into the right-hand groove of the zipper foot (as you face it), stitch the zipper to the garment beginning at the neck edge and continuing until the zipper foot touches and is stopped by the pull tab. Then, stitch backward a few stitches before removing the garment from the machine. Remove all bastings and the adhesive basting tape, if used.

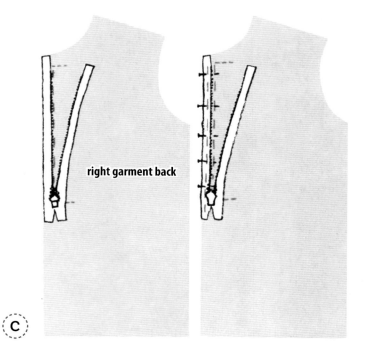

right garment back

C

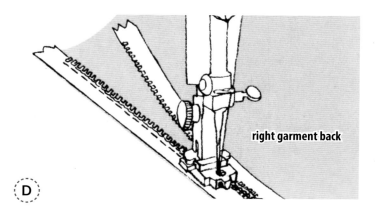

right garment back

D

Attaching the Zipper to Left Half of the Garment (E)

14. Place the left half of the garment back on a flat surface, wrong side down.

15. Place the remaining free side of the zipper tab face down on the left garment back so the top end of the coil is aligned with the horizontal basted marking made in Step 4. The coiled edge should be flush against the vertical basted markings made in Step 5.

16. Pin and baste the zipper to the garment. Remove the pins.

Stitching the Zipper to the Left Half of the Garment (F)

17. Making sure that the zipper coil feeds into the left-hand groove of the zipper foot (as you face it), stitch the zipper to the garment beginning at the neck edge and continuing until the zipper foot touches and is stopped by the pull tab. Then, stitch backward a few stitches before removing the garment from the machine. Remove all basting and the adhesive basting tape, if used. Close the zipper before proceeding to the next step.

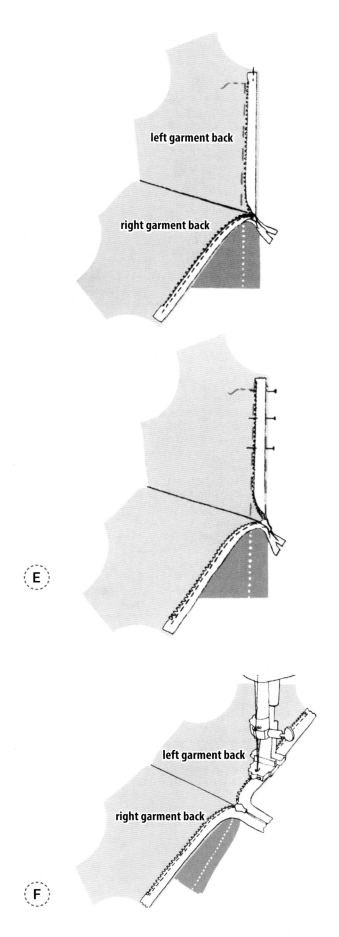

left garment back

right garment back

E

left garment back

right garment back

F

Finishing the Center Back Seam (G)

18. With the zipper closed, fold the garment along the center back seam, wrong side out.

19. Lift the bottom unstitched end of the zipper so that it is kept free of the seam allowances below the zipper.

20. Pin and baste closed the center back seam of the garment, overlapping by ¼″ (0.6 cm) the line of machine stitching that holds the zipper to the garment. Continue down to the bottom of the garment. Remove the pins.

21. Adjust the zipper foot so the needle is just outside the groove at the right edge of the foot.

22. Stitch closed a portion of the center back seam. It may begin where the basted line made in Step 20 begins, ending at the bottom end of the zipper tape. It may also be stitched from the hem toward the zipper tape. Stitch as close as possible to the machine stitching that holds the zipper to the garment. Secure the start of the stitching by pulling the bottom thread through with a pin and tying a knot. If you have difficulty getting your machine close enough to the machine stitching, close this part of the seam by hand with a few tiny running stitches; end with a fastening stitch (page 243).

23. Replace the zipper foot with the presser foot and stitch closed the rest of the center back seam.

Finishing the Invisible Zipper (H)

24. Machine stitch the bottom ends of the zipper tape to the seam allowances beginning about 1¼″ (3.2 cm) from the bottom. Do not sew into the garment itself.

25. Remove the basting, press the seam open, and turn the garment right side out. The zipper will be hidden inside the seam.

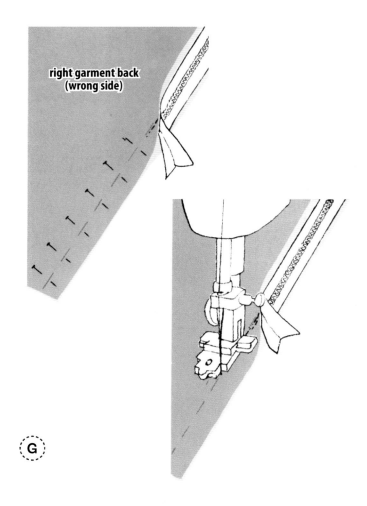

right garment back (wrong side)

G

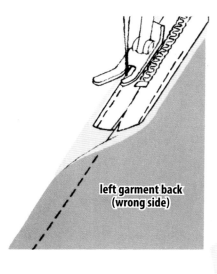

left garment back (wrong side)

garment back

H

CENTERED ZIPPER

Determining the Length of the Zipper Opening (A)

1. Pin the center back seam (white) of the garment closed after the garment has been fitted and all darts and other seams have been sewn and pressed.
2. Place the open zipper face down on the center back seam line so the zipper's top stop is ¼″ (0.6 cm) below the markings for the neck seam line.
3. Mark the position of the top and bottom stops of the zipper on the center back seam line with chalk or a pin. Then re-mark, using a horizontal running stitch (page 195); extend these marks across the two center back seam allowances.

Preparing the Seam (B)

4. Baste (red) the center back seam from the bottom of the garment pieces to the marking for the bottom stop; remove the pins. Machine stitch (blue) and remove the basting.
5. Baste closed the remainder of the center back seam, stitching on the seam line marking from the bottom stop to the neck edge.
6. After pressing open the center back seam, lay the garment on the right back and extend the seam allowance of the right back so that it lies flat.

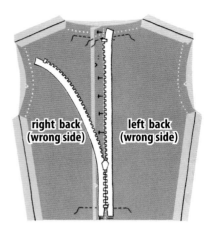

A

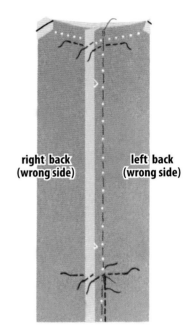

B

Basting the Zipper to the Garment (C)

7. Place the open zipper face down on the extended right back seam allowance with the top stop at the horizontal marking made in Step 3 and the teeth flush against the center back seam. Pin the left tape to the back seam allowance.

8. Baste the zipper tape to the extended seam allowance, using short stitches placed ¼" (0.6 cm) from the teeth and remove the pins.

9. Close the zipper and turn the garment right side out.

10. Hold the zipper inside the garment so it's centered on the seam; pin it across both center back seam allowances.

11. Hand baste along both sides of the zipper ¼" (0.6 cm) from the center seam line, catching all layers—the garment fabric, the seam allowance, and the zipper tape. Remove the pins.

Stitching the Zipper (D)

12. Turn the garment wrong side out.

13. Slide the right side of the fabric—the side that will be visible when the garment is completed—into the machine and using a zipper foot, stitch down the right-hand side of the zipper, just outside the basting line, from the neck edge to ⅛" (3.2 mm) below the bottom stop marking.

14. Continue stitching across and up the left side of the zipper to the neck edge. Snip open the center seam basting, remove all other bastings, and press.

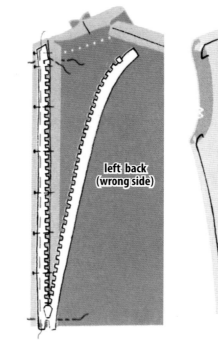
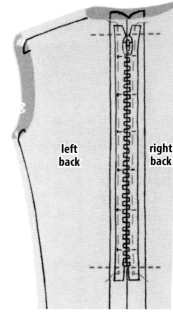

left back (wrong side)

left back

right back

C

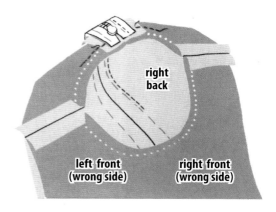

right back

left front (wrong side)

right front (wrong side)

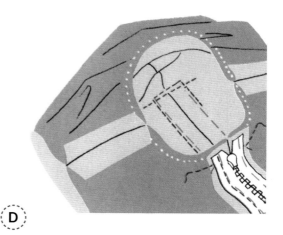

D

LAPPED ZIPPER

Preparing the Side Seam for the Insertion of the Zipper (A)

1. If your pattern does not provide an extra-wide seam allowance of 1″ (2.5 cm) for the side zipper, add it to the side seam as you cut out the fabric.
2. With wrong sides facing out, pin closed the left side seam (white), then mark (green) the length of the zipper as shown for the centered zipper, Section A, Steps 1–3 (page 15).
3. Baste (red) the side seam from the hemline up to the marking for the bottom stop; remove the pins. Machine stitch (blue), then remove the basting.
4. Baste closed the remainder of the side seam directly on the seam line marking from the bottom stop to the waistline edge.

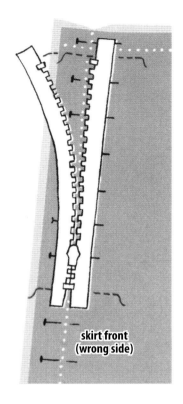

skirt front
(wrong side)

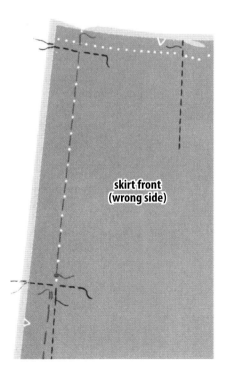

skirt front
(wrong side)

Sewing the Zipper to the Garment Back (B)

5. Press open the side seam.

6. Lay the garment down on the back section and extend the back seam allowance so it lies flat.

7. Place the open zipper face down on the extended back seam allowance, with its top and bottom stops at the horizontal markings made in Section A, Step 2. The teeth should be flush against the closed side seam. Pin the left tape to the back seam allowance.

8. Baste the zipper tape to the extended back seam allowance close to the teeth. Work from the bottom of the zipper tape to the top, machine basting with a zipper foot or using shorthand stitches. Remove the pins.

9. Close the zipper and fold the back seam allowance under the garment along the line of basting made in Step 8, thus causing the zipper to flip up.

10. Pin together all layers of the fabric: the front seam allowance, the skirt front and back, and the back seam allowance.

11. Using a zipper foot, machine stitch along the narrow strip of folded seam allowance from the bottom of the zipper tape to the top. Remove the pins.

Sewing the Zipper to the Garment Front (C)

12. Turn the garment right side out.

13. Hold the zipper inside the garment so it lies flat on the seam. Pin in place across both seam allowances.

14. Hand baste ½″ (1.3 cm) from the side seam up the skirt from the bottom stop marking to the top edge, sewing through all layers: the front, the front seam allowance, and the zipper tape. Remove pins.

15. Turn the garment wrong side out.

16. Slide the garment front, wrong side down, under the zipper foot. Beginning at the side seam and following a line ⅛″ (3.2 mm) outside the marking for the bottom stop made in Section A, Step 2 (page 15), stitch across the bottom and up the length of the zipper to the top edge of the garment. Then, snip open the side seam basting, remove all other bastings, and press.

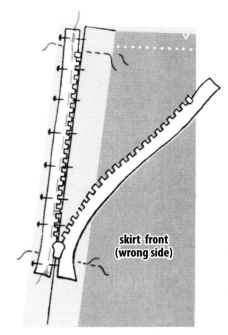

skirt front
(wrong side)

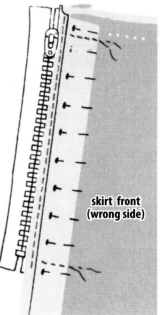

skirt front
(wrong side)

B

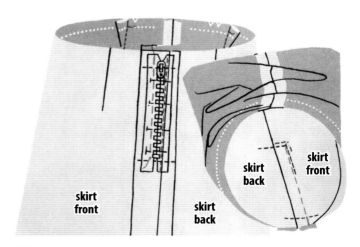

skirt front

skirt back

skirt back

skirt front

C

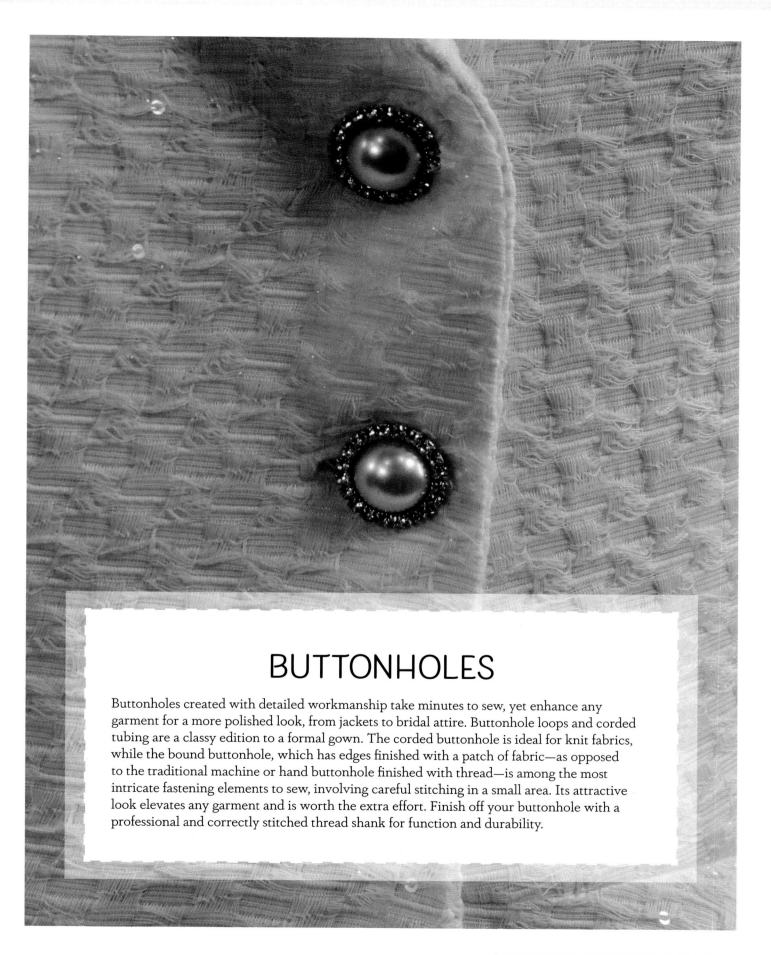

BUTTONHOLES

Buttonholes created with detailed workmanship take minutes to sew, yet enhance any garment for a more polished look, from jackets to bridal attire. Buttonhole loops and corded tubing are a classy edition to a formal gown. The corded buttonhole is ideal for knit fabrics, while the bound buttonhole, which has edges finished with a patch of fabric—as opposed to the traditional machine or hand buttonhole finished with thread—is among the most intricate fastening elements to sew, involving careful stitching in a small area. Its attractive look elevates any garment and is worth the extra effort. Finish off your buttonhole with a professional and correctly stitched thread shank for function and durability.

CORDED BUTTONHOLES FOR WOVENS AND KNITS

1. Complete the garment following your pattern instructions, but do not remove the line of basting marking the center front.
2. To determine the width for the buttonholes, measure the diameter and thickness of your button and add the two figures.
3. With the right-front garment section wrong side down, mark a guide for the outer edge of the buttonholes by basting a line of stitches ⅛″ (3.2 mm) outside and parallel to the center front line.
4. Using the buttonhole width determined in Step 2, mark a guide for the inner edge of the buttonhole by basting a line of stitches inside and parallel to the line made in Step 3.
5. Using your paper pattern as a guide for the number and spacing of the buttonholes, baste a horizontal center line for each buttonhole between and perpendicular to the two vertical lines of basting made in Steps 3 and 4.
6. Insert a pin in line with the basted center line of each buttonhole, 1½″ (3.8 cm) inside the inner buttonhole edge. The pin heads must face away from the buttonhole markings.
7. For each buttonhole, cut a 10″ (25.4 cm) length of cording from buttonhole twist thread of the same color as your regular thread.
8. Fold one piece of the cording in half and place the loop around the head of one of the pins. Then, arrange the cording parallel to, and above and below, the centerline marking of the buttonhole.
9. Holding the cording straight, run machine zigzag stitches on one side of the buttonhole over the cording, following the directions accompanying your machine. Sew from the inner edge marking (Step 3); do not sew into the cording.
10. Make a bar tack at the outer edge of the buttonhole, sewing over but not into both the top and bottom parts of the cording.
11. Stitch the second side of the buttonhole, sewing over but not into the cording.
12. Finish the second end of the buttonhole with a bar tack, stitching over but not into both the top and bottom parts of the cording. Remove the pin.
13. Pull the cut ends of the cording until the loop is flush with the second bar tack. Clip the excess cording close to the first bar tack.
14. Repeat Steps 8–13 to work the remaining buttonholes.

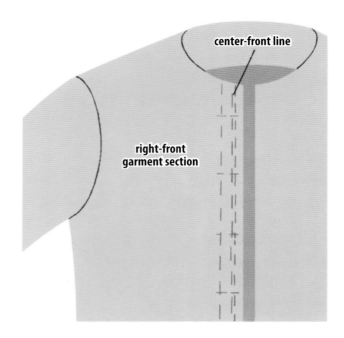

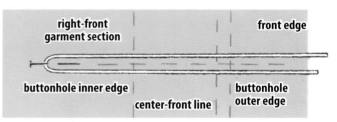

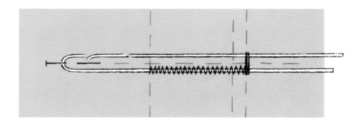

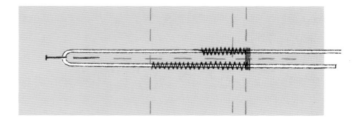

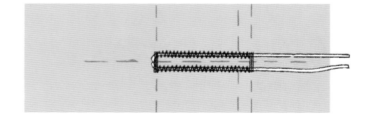

BOUND BUTTONHOLES

Interfacing the Buttonhole Area (A)

1. Cut the interfacing from special interfacing fabric, using the pattern piece provided, or measure the entire buttonhole area and cut an interfacing that is 2″ (5.1 cm) longer and 2″ (5.1 cm) wider.

2. Pin the interfacing to the wrong side of the garment section, aligning its outer edge either with the fold line that shows where the facing will be folded over when the garment is completed (as shown in the drawing), or with the seam line that shows where the facing will be stitched to the garment—whichever your pattern indicates. Make sure the interfacing extends 1″ (2.5 cm) above and below the buttonhole area.

3. Baste the edges to hold the interfacing in place. Remove the pins.

Marking the Buttonhole **Placement** Lines (B)

4. Lay the pattern piece showing the placement of buttonholes over the interfacing. Pin it to the garment. Slip carbon paper face down under the pattern piece, then transfer the markings for the center front line and each buttonhole to the interfacing with a tracing wheel. Remove the pattern piece.

5. To locate the outer placement line for positioning the outside edges of the buttonholes, measure ⅛″ (3.2 mm) from the center front line toward the garment opening along each buttonhole line. Mark these points with chalk. Then, using a ruler, draw a solid chalk line connecting the marks.

6. To locate the inner placement line for positioning the inside edges of the buttonholes, measure the desired width of each finished buttonhole opening—as determined by the diameter of your button—from the outer placement line toward the side seam of the garment along each buttonhole placement line. Mark these points with chalk, then draw a solid chalk line connecting the marks.

7. To mark the location of the placement lines on the interfacing and the outside of the garment, use one thread color to baste along the inner, outer, and buttonhole placement lines. Use another thread color to baste along the center front line.

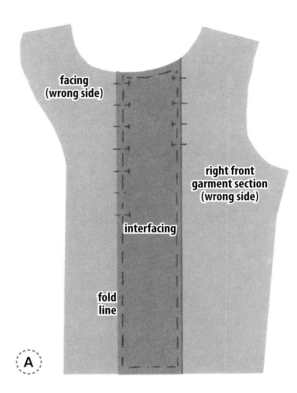

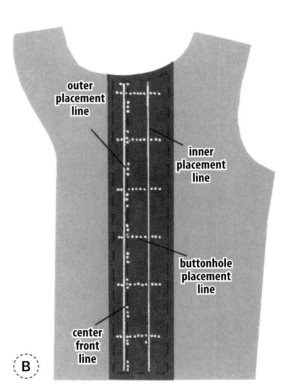

Preparing the Patch (C)

8. For each buttonhole, make a binding patch from the fabric that was left over after cutting out the garment itself. Each of the patches should measure 2″ (5.1 cm) along the lengthwise grain of the fabric and be at least 1″ (2.5 cm) wider than the desired width of the finished buttonhole.

9. Fold each patch in half crosswise with the wrong sides together and mark the center line of the patch with a row of basting stitches on the fold.

10. To mark the upper- and lower-fold lines of each patch, make a parallel row of basting stitches ¼″ (0.6 cm) above and another row ¼″ (0.6 cm) below the center line.

11. Fold the patch along the upper-fold line, wrong sides together, and pin.

12. Machine stitch halfway between the center line and the upper fold line. Stitch slowly, slipping out the pins as you go. The stitching must be straight and even to ensure a professional- looking buttonhole.

13. Fold and pin the patch along the lower fold line, wrong sides together, then machine stitch halfway between the center line and the lower fold line. These two rows of stitching, ¼″ (0.6 cm) apart by the upper- and lower-fold lines, will create two tucks that will form the visible bound edges of the finished buttonhole.

14. Remove the upper- and lower-fold line bastings but leave in the basting stitches along the center line of the patch.

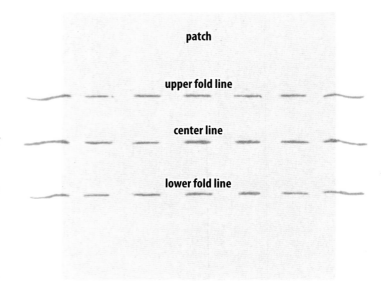

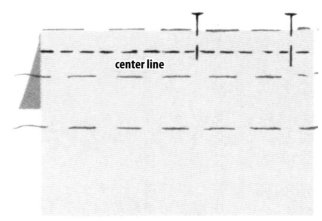

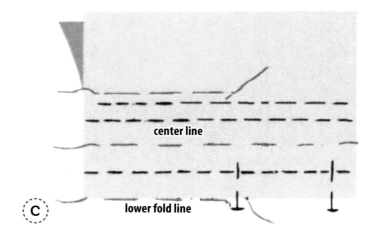

Attaching the Patch to the Garment (D)

15. Turn the garment wrong side down and place a patch, wrong side up, on one buttonhole. Spread the patch open so that the basted center line is visible, then match the basting to the buttonhole placement line, Let the ends of the patch extend ½ inch (1.27cm) beyond the inner and outer placement lines.

16. Pin the patch to the garment, checking again to be sure that the center line on the patch exactly matches the buttonhole placement line.

17. Baste over the center line of the patch to fasten it to the interfacing and garment fabric. Remove the pins.

18. Fold the top of the patch down so that the upper row of stitching made in Section C, Step 12, is visible, and place a pin at each end of the patch inside the outer and inner placement lines.

19. Replace the presser foot on your machine with a zipper foot. Insert the machine needle at the inside edge of the pin at the outer placement line. Turn the machine wheel by hand to make one stitch backwards over the pin. Remove the pin and stitch forward just below the original line of stitching until you reach the second pin.

20. Turning the wheel again by hand, make one stitch over the second pin, slip it out, and secure the thread with two backstitches.

21. Shift the top patch upward and out of the way. Fold the bottom of the patch up so that the lower row of stitching made in Section C, Step 13, is visible. Pin and stitch as described in Steps 18–20, sewing just outside the visible stitching. Remove the bastings from the patch.

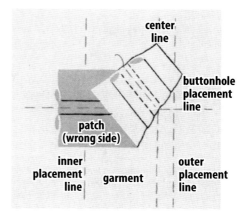

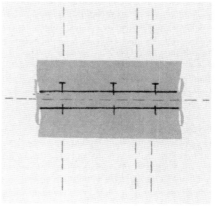

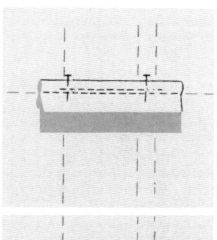

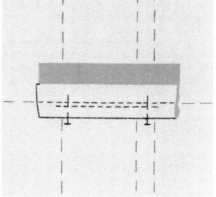

D

Opening the Buttonhole (E)

22. Spread the patch open, using the row of basting stitches on the buttonhole placement line as your guide, and cut the patch in half with small, sharp-pointed scissors.

23. Turn the garment wrong side up. To open the buttonhole from the interfacing side, make a ¼″ (0.6 cm) long cut at the center of the buttonhole, parallel to the visible rows of machine stitching, midway between them. Be sure to cut through the interfacing, lining or underlining, and garment fabric.

24. Make diagonal cuts through all the fabric layers from the center cut to each of the four corners of the buttonhole. Cut up to (but not through) the ends of the machine stitching. Make sure to keep the edges of the patch on the opposite side of the garment out of the way of the scissors.

25. Turn the garment wrong side down and, with your fingers, push the edges of the patch and the triangles of fabric at each end of the buttonhole through the opening to the wrong side of the garment.

26. Turn the garment wrong side up and make sure that the little triangles formed by the diagonal cuts in Step 24 are pushed completely through the buttonhole opening. Press the edges of the patch flat with an iron.

Completing the Buttonhole Patch (F)

27. To hold the buttonhole in shape while you make the finishing stitches, turn the garment wrong side down and baste the visible bound edges of the buttonhole together with diagonal basting stitches.

28. Turn the garment wrong side up so that the buttonhole patch is visible.

29. Fold over one side of the patch along the outer placement line.

30. Fold the garment and interfacing back along the outer placement line so the underside of the patch extends away from the folded garment.

31. Machine stitch parallel to the outer placement line from about ⅛″ (3.2 mm) above to ⅛″ (3.2 mm) below the two visible rows of stitching, making sure to catch the little triangles.

32. Fold the opposite side of the patch along the inner placement line and repeat Step 31.

33. Complete all the other buttonholes called for by your pattern to this stage. Remove all basting stitches except those marking the center front line of the garment and those holding the lips of the buttonholes together.

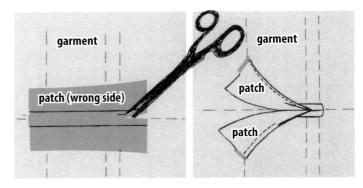

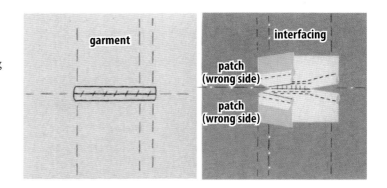

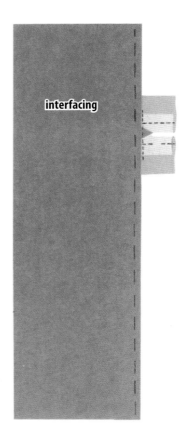

Finishing the Buttonholes (G)

34. Fold the facing wrong side down over the interfacing along the fold line or the seam line and pin it down.
35. Baste the facing to the garment around each buttonhole. Insert pins through the fabric at each corner and at the center of one buttonhole. Turn the garment wrong side up. Follow the pin markings and cut open the facing as in Section E, Steps 23–24. Remove the pins.
36. Tuck under the top and bottom edges of the cut and the triangles at either side. Sew the edges with tiny hemming stitches.
37. Repeat Steps 35–36 at all other buttonholes and remove all bastings.

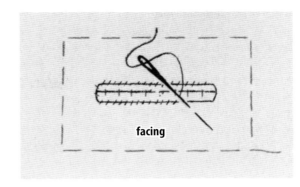

facing

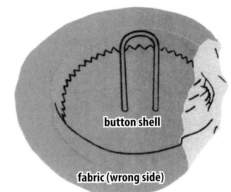

button shell

fabric (wrong side)

(G)

BUTTON SHANKS

1. Using a strand of knotted buttonhole twist, make a small stitch in the fabric at the point where the center of the button is to fall. Insert the needle through one of the holes on the underside of the button and pull the thread through.
2. Hold a toothpick or large needle between the buttonholes and pull the thread over it as you point the needle down into the other hole. Then, make two or three stitches across the match; in case of a four-hole button, make two rows of parallel stitches across the match.
3. Remove the match and pull the button up, away from the fabric to the top of the thread.
4. Wind the thread tightly five or six times around the loose threads below the button to create a thread shank.
5. End by making a fastening stitch (page 243) in the thread shank.

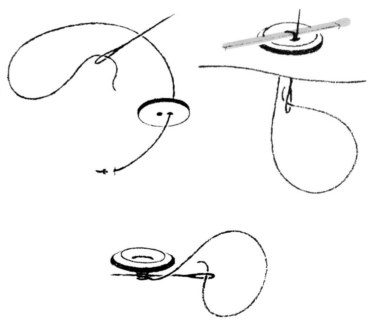

CONTINUOUS BUTTONHOLE LOOPS

Marking the Position for the Loops (A)

1. Run a line of basting to mark the center-front seam line on the right garment front.
2. Place the garment front wrong side down on a flat surface.
3. Measure the length of the portion of the seam line along where the loops will be made.
4. Make a length of corded tubing (page 57) equal to at least four times the length measured in Step 3. Do not finish the ends of the tubing.
5. Center a button on the basted seam line at the point where the top loop should be.
6. Form a sample loop with the corded tubing around the button.
7. Mark the outer edges of the loop, where it crosses the seam line, with chalk.
8. Mark the distance from the basted seam line to the outer curve of the loop with a pin. Set aside the tubing and the button.
9. Run a line of basting through the pin marker parallel to the basted seam line. Remove the pin.
10. Measure the interval between the two marks made in Step 7 and mark off as many intervals as necessary along the basted seam line.

Attaching the Loops (B)

11. Baste the interfacing, if any, to the wrong side of the garment front.
12. Place one end of the tubing, seamed side up, between the top two marks and form a loop. Make sure the outer curve of the loop meets the basting line indicating the depth of the loop, and that the outer edges are aligned with the horizontal chalk marks. Pin.
13. Continue to make and pin loops between the marks down the garment edge. Make sure the folds of the loops extend ½″ (1.3 cm) into the seam allowance, as shown, and the outer curves meet the basting line.
14. Baste the loops to the garment front ¼″ (0.6 cm) outside the seam line. Remove the pins.
15. Machine baste at six stitches to the inch the loops to the garment front ¹⁄₁₆″ (1.6 mm) outside the seam line. Then, run another line of machine basting just outside the first line.
16. Remove all the hand bastings.

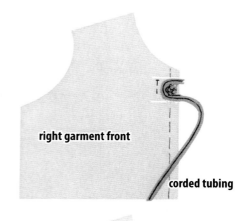

right garment front

corded tubing

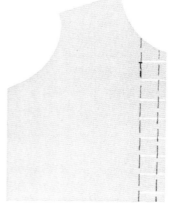

(A)

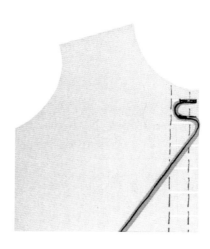

(B)

Attaching the Facing to the Garment (C)

17. With the wrong sides out, pin the facing to the garment front. Baste and remove the pins.
18. Resetting the machine to the normal 12 stitches to the inch, machine stitch the facing to the garment front. Stitch from the garment side. just inside the machine bastings that hold the loops in place. Remove the basting.
19. Trim the seam allowance of the facing to ⅛″ (0.3 cm).
20. Trim the ends of the tubing between the seam allowances to ⅛″ (0.3 cm).
21. Trim the garment front seam allowance to ⅜″ (0.9 cm).
22. Press the trimmed seam allowances toward the facing.

Finishing the Loops (D)

23. Turn over the assembled garment front so the garment front and the facing are wrong side down and the facing is extended away from the garment.
24. Machine stitch along the edge of the facing as close as possible to the seam so the seam will lie flat. Make sure to stitch through the seam allowances beneath the facing.
25. Turn the facing to the inside and press. The loops, held between facing and garment, should extend beyond the pressed edge.

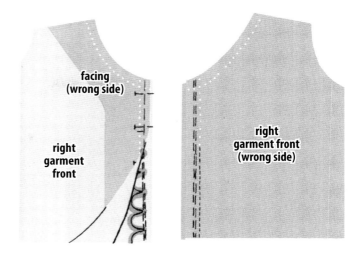

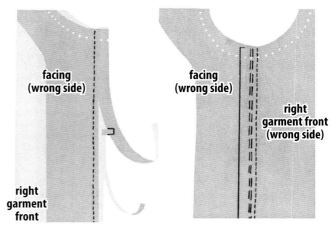

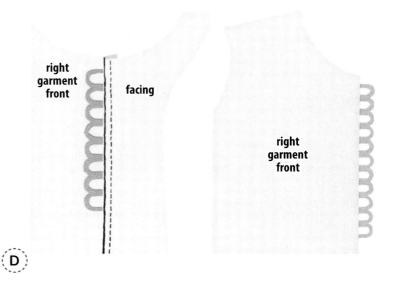

PLAIN TUBING

Preparing and Sewing the Tubing (A)

1. To determine the length of tubing you will need, add 4″ (10.2 cm) to the total called for by your pattern or project.
2. To cut out and join the fabric strip that will form the tubing and encase the cord, follow the instructions for making plain cording (page 68, Steps 2–14).
3. Leaving ½″ (1.3 cm) of cord free at one end, fold the fabric strip wrong side out around the cord and pin the edges together at 1″ (2.5 cm) intervals. Leave half of the cord free at the other end.
4. Using a zipper foot, machine stitch the strip to the cord, as shown. Make sure to stitch ¹⁄₁₆″ (1.6 mm) beyond the bottom edge of the cord.
5. Pivot and stitch in at an angle toward the cord.
6. Stretching the strip slightly and removing the pins as you go, stitch straight down the length of the strip. Keep the zipper foot close to the cord, but not right up against it. End by backstitching.
7. Trim the seam allowances to ⅛″ (0.3 cm).

Turning the Tubing Right Side Out (B)

8. To turn the tubing right side out, grasp the loose ½″ (1.3 cm) of cord left at one end of the tubing in Step 4. Pull the enclosed cord out of the tubing with one hand as you work the tubing over the free half of the cord with the other hand.

Finishing the Tubing (C)

9. Trim off the corded tubing at both ends so the cord and the tubing are even.
10. Pull back the tubing at each end and trim off ¼″ (0.6 cm) of the cord.
11. Tuck in the raw edges of the tubing at each end and close the ends with a slip stitch.

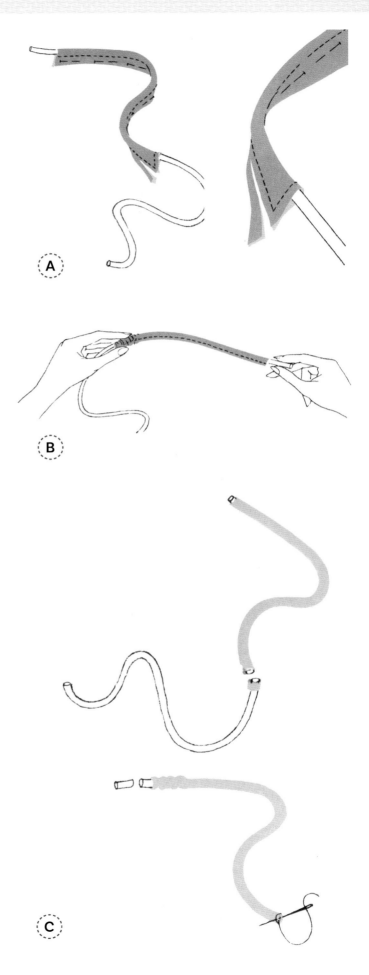

A

B

C

POCKETS

Pockets are both decorative and functional and can enhance any garment, from pants and suit coats to athletic and wedding attire. Pockets were once considered to be a separate item but have now developed into a repertoire of classic sewing techniques.

The appliqué or patch pocket is one of the most common types of pockets. Although easy to make, care in positioning is necessary to determine the most flattering and functional placement. Consider making your patch pocket into a shape other than the basic square, such as a heart or scalloped edge. It is usually made from the same fabric as the garment, however, using contrasting fabric creates an added visual interest.

The inseam pocket is stitched inside the garment seams and is made of lining fabric that is meant to be invisible on the outside of the garment. It is constructed as a complete unit and then fastened to the side seam, or sometimes to the waist based on the pattern design. A matching facing made from fashion fabric can be used on the outermost edge for complete blending from the fashion side of the garment. Pocket bag fabric is usually made from cotton, but pockets can be made from a variety of fabrics as long as they're lightweight. Flesh tone hues provide the most inconspicuous application, especially in lighter color garments.

The discreet, flat welt is one of the more elegant variations on this clothing essential. In this version, all but the top edge of the pocket, or welt, is entirely hidden inside the garment. Welt pockets are best suited for garments made from firmly woven fabrics that do not fray easily. To achieve this pocket, take special care to precisely mark all pattern markings, and to accurately cut and stitch when making the little triangles at the end of each pocket opening, as illustrated on page 32.

FLAT WELT POCKETS

Cutting Out the Welt Interfacing (A)

1. Using half of the welt pattern, cut a medium-weight interfacing that extends ⅝" (1.6 cm) beyond the pattern fold line.

Attaching the Interfacing (B)

2. Cut the welt from the garment material and pin the interfacing to the wrong side of the welt, matching the seam lines and other pattern markings.
3. Baste the left, upper, and right edges of the interfacing to the welt just inside the seam lines. Remove the pins.
4. Just outside the fold line, attach the interfacing to the welt with small running stitches, about six to an inch. Use thread that's the same color as the garment and pick up only a thread of the welt fabric.
5. Trim the seam allowance of the interfacing on the seam line of the three basted sides.
6. Hand stitch the interfacing to the welt along the three basted sides with a catch stitch (page 242), picking up a few threads on the interfacing and then a thread or two on the seam allowances of the welt. No stitches should show on the visible side of the finished welt. Remove the bastings.

Stitching and Folding the Welt (C)

7. Fold the interfaced welt along the fold line, wrong side out.
8. Pin and baste the folded welt along the seam lines at left and right. Remove the pins.
9. Machine stitch the welt seams at left and right, starting at the fold line and continuing to the upper edge. Remove the bastings.
10. Grade the seam allowances at both ends by trimming the seam allowance on the interfaced half of the welt to ¼" (0.6 cm) and the seam allowance on the non-interfaced half to ⅛" (0.3 cm).
11. Turn the welt right side out and push the corners out with closed scissors. Press.
12. Baste together the unstitched side of the welt (top in the picture) ⅝" (1. 6 cm) from the raw edges.
13. Trim the basted edge ¼" (0.6 cm) from the bastings.
14. If it is called for by your pattern, apply decorative topstitching or edge.

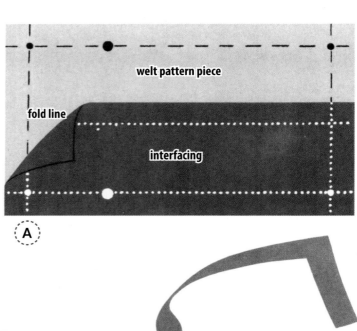

A

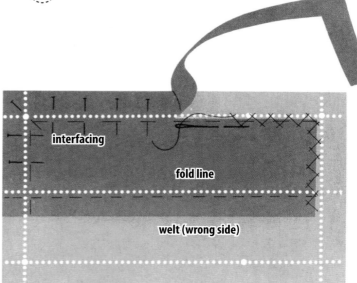

B

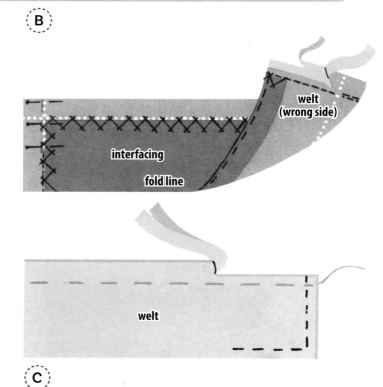

C

Attaching the Welt to the Garment (D)

15. Unless you have already done so, run lines of basting stitches on the garment along the pattern markings or the stitching lines and the slash line for the pocket opening.
16. Pin the welt to the right side of the garment—the side that will be visible when the garment is finished—matching the basting made in Step 12 to the marking for the lower stitching line.
17. Baste the welt to the garment just below the basting made in Step 12 and remove the pins.
18. Machine stitch the welt to the garment between the two lines of basting. Remove both lines of basting.

Lining the Pocket (E)

19. Unless you have already done so, run lines of basting stitches on the pocket lining along the pattern markings for the stitching lines and the slash line for the pocket opening.
20. With the larger part of the pocket lining at the top, place the lining wrong side up on the garment, matching the lower stitching line of the lining to the machine stitching on the welt made in Step 18.
21. Pin the lining to the garment along the basted upper stitching lines and to the welt along the basted lower stitching lines. Be sure to match the ends of the basted markings on lining and garment.
22. Baste along the upper and lower stitching lines, then remove the pins.
23. Machine stitch the upper stitching line through pocket lining and garment; machine stitch the lower stitching line through pocket lining, garment and the two layers of welt fabric. Reinforce both ends of the stitching lines with backstitches. Do not machine stitch along the ends. Remove the bastings.
24. Using small, sharp scissors, cut lining and garment along the basted slash line, first to the apex of the triangular marking at one end and then to the apex of the triangular marking at the other.
25. Carefully clip along the triangle sides toward the ends of the stitching lines, cutting up to—but not into—the machine stitches made in Step 23.

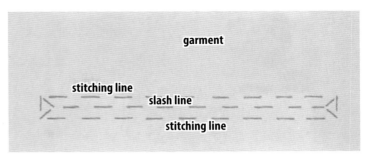

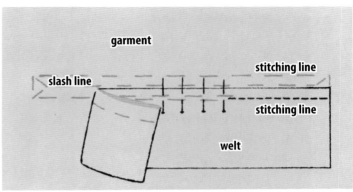

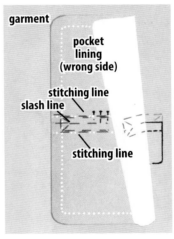

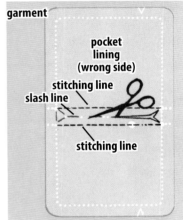

Forming the Pocket (F)

26. Turn the garment wrong side out and pull the upper and lower sections of the pocket lining through the slash.
27. Flip the upper pocket lining down over the lower pocket lining.
28. Finish the slashed edges of the upper pocket lining and garment fabric with overcast stitches (page 243).
29. Smooth the pocket lining down and press the overcast seam upward.
30. Flip both sections of the pocket lining up and overcast the seam edges of the lower pocket well and garment fabric as in Step 28. Press the seam edges downward.

Finishing the Pocket (G)

31. Turn the pocket lining sections down again and pin them together along the sides and bottom, matching seam lines and other pattern markings.
32. Baste, making sure to stitch to the lining the little triangles of lining and garment material formed at each end when you slashed the pocket opening in Step 24. Remove the pins.
33. Push the garment fabric out of the way so it lies above and to the left of the pocket lining. Working with the wrong side of the lower pocket lining up, machine stitch along the sides and bottom, being sure to catch the little triangles. Remove all bastings.
34. Trim the seam allowance to ¼″ (0.6 cm).
35. Overcast the raw seam edges as in Step 28.

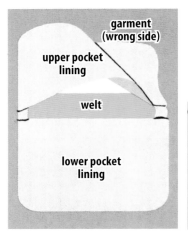

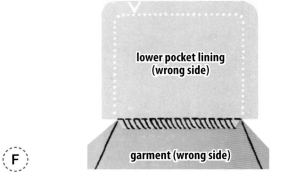

F

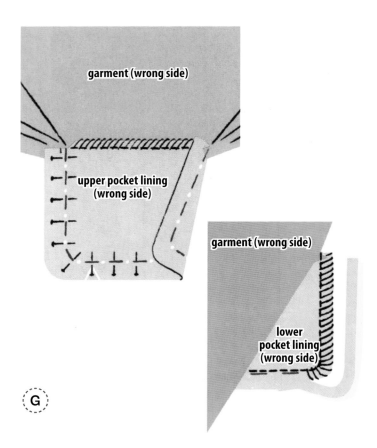

G

Finishing the Welt (H)

36. Turn the garment right side out. Press the welt upward and pin the ends of the welt to the garment. Baste and remove the pins.

37. Slip stitch (page 244) the welt ends to the garment, picking up only a thread of the garment fabric close to the welt and sliding the needle through the fold of the welt. Remove the basting and press.

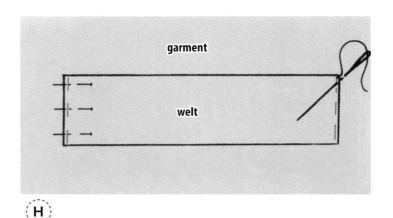

H

APPLIQUÉ PATCH POCKETS

Preparing the Pocket (A)

1. Run a basting stitch (temporary longer stitches) around all sides of the pocket on the seam lines usually ⅝″ (1.6 cm) from the edge, and along the top hem fold line.

2. With the pocket section wrong side up, fold down the top hem edge ¼″ (0.6 cm) and press.

3. Machine stitch close to the folded hem edge and press again.

Finishing the Hem Edge (B)

4. Turn the pocket over so the wrong side is facing down. Fold the hem over along the hem fold line toward the front and press.

5. Pin and baste the hem to the pocket section just outside the basted seam line. Remove the pins.

6. Machine stitch along the three seam lines just outside the basted markings. Begin at the folded hem edge and stitch down to the end of the side seam, then stitch across the bottom of the pocket and up the other side seam to the top folded edge. Remove all bastings.

7. Trim the two corners of the hem edge diagonally.

8. Trim both side seam allowance of the hem only to ¼″ (0.6 cm).

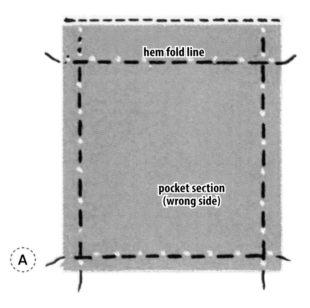

A

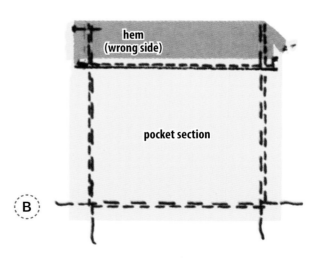

B

Completing the Pocket Section (C)

STRAIGHT POCKETS

9. A. On pockets with straight bottoms, turn the pocket section wrong side up, turn over the hem and press. Then fold in the side seam allowances just beyond the line of machine stitching made in Step 6 and press. Fold up the bottom seam allowance and press.

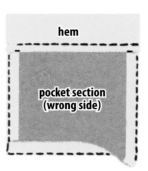

hem

pocket section (wrong side)

POINTED POCKETS

B. On pockets with pointed bottoms, turn the pocket section wrong side up, turn over the hem and press. Then, fold up the two bottom seam allowances that form the point just beyond the line of machine stitching made in Step 6 and press. Fold in the side seam allowances and press.

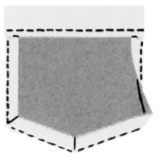

ROUNDED POCKETS

C. On pockets with rounded bottoms, turn the pocket section wrong side up, turn over the hem and press. Notch the curves at ½″ (1.3 cm) intervals. Fold in the seam allowances just beyond the machine stitching made in Step 6 and press. Overlap the notched segments where necessary and press.

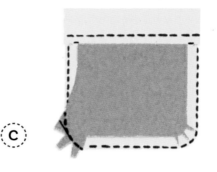

C

Stitching the Pocket to the Garment (D)

10. If your pattern has not instructed you to do so yet, baste a placement line on the right side of the garment- the side that will be visible when the garment is completed. With the wrong side of the pocket facing down, place the pocket on the right side of the garment. Align the edges of the pocket with the basted placement lines on the garment.

11. Pin the pocket to the garment at each corner and at 1″ (2.5 cm) intervals.

12. Baste the pocket along the side and bottom edges about ¼″ (0.6 cm) from the edge. Remove the pins.

13. Try on the garment and adjust the position if necessary.

14. A. For an invisible finish, hand stitch the pocket to the garment with a slip stitch along the side edge.

B. To add strength and give a visible finish, machine stitch the pocket to the garment close to the edge. Add an additional line of decorative topstitching further in on the pocket.

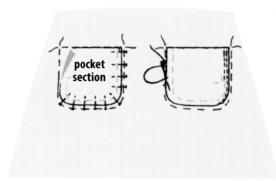

pocket section

D

DESIGNER TIP

If your fabric allows (test on a sample first), lightly spray temporary embroidery spray adhesive on the wrong side of the pocket. This will dissolve or steam away and will aid in holding the pocket to the garment while positioning and pinning.

INSEAM POCKETS

Preparing the Pocket Section (A)

1. On the right-hand pocket section—cut out of lining, not garment fabric—run a line of basting stitches (green) along the pattern markings (white) for the seam and placement lines.
2. If your pattern includes a marking at the waistline for aligning the pocket with the pants, re-mark it with a vertical running stitch (page 195).
3. Re-mark with a horizontal running stitch the pattern markings for the bottom of the pocket opening.

Preparing the Facings (B)

4. Cut a right-hand pocket facing from the garment fabric, using the facing pattern piece, and run a line of basting stitches along the pattern markings for the seam lines.
5. If your pattern includes a marking at the waistline for aligning the pocket with the pants, re-mark it with a vertical running stitch.
6. Re-mark with a horizontal running stitch the pattern markings for the bottom of the pocket opening.
7. Fold over the long unnotched edge of the facing along the basted seam line and press.
8. Trim the pressed edge to ¼″ (0.6 cm) and trim the excess fabric from the bottom corner. Remove the basting from the pressed edge.
9. Cut a rectangular facing strip from the garment fabric, according to the measurements on your pattern guide sheet.
10. With the facing strip wrong side up, fold over one long edge ¼″ (0.6 cm) and press.

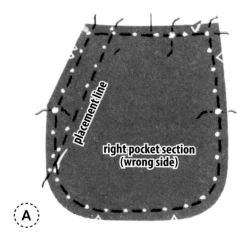

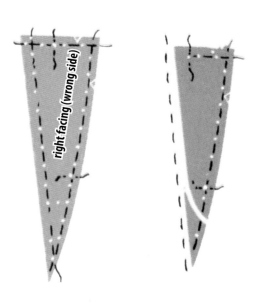

Stitching the Facings to the Pocket (C)

11. Place the right-hand pocket section wrong side down and lay the facing wrong side down on it. Pin the facing to the pocket section along the basted seam line, matching the notches and the running stitch markings.

12. Baste the facing to the pocket section ¼" (0.6 cm) outside the seam markings. Remove the pins.

13. Pin and baste the facing to the pocket along the folded edge made in Step 7. Remove the pins.

14. Machine stitch close to the folded edge. Remove the basting from the folded edge only.

15. Place the facing strip wrong side down on the pocket, lining up the folded edge made in Step 10 with the basted placement line on the pocket section.

16. Pin and baste the facing strip to the pocket section along the folded edge. Remove the pins.

17. Machine stitch close to the folded edge. Remove the bastings from the folded edge.

18. Turn the pocket section over wrong side up and pin the pocket section to the facing strip along the outer seam-line markings.

19. Baste ¼" (0.6 cm) outside the seam markings. Remove the pins.

20. Trim the facing strip so that it is even with the pocket section around all edges.

Sewing the Pocket (D)

21. Fold the pocket in half lengthwise wrong sides together, matching the pattern markings and the horizontal running stitches that mark the pocket opening.

22. Pin and baste the pocket together along the basted seam line from the horizontal running stitch that marks the bottom of the pocket opening (Step 6) to the bottom of the folded edge. Remove the pins.

23. Machine stitch the basted seam ¼" (0.6 cm) outside the seam markings.

24. Clip into the seam allowances at the horizontal markings for the bottom of the pocket opening, cutting to the stitching line.

25. Trim the seam allowances to ⅛" (0.3 cm), cutting from the bottom fold to the clip made in Step 24.

26. Notch around the curve. Then remove all basting from the stitched seam.

27. Turn the pocket wrong side out and press the stitched seam flat.

28. Machine stitch on the seam markings from the clip to the bottom folded edge. Reinforce the seam at the clip by going forward three stitches, back three, then forward to the seam end.

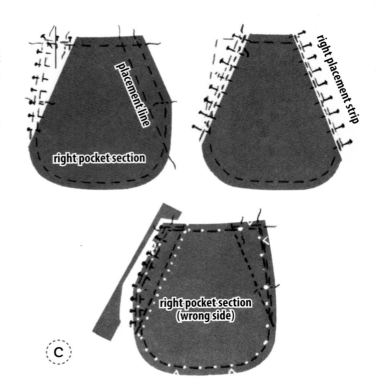

placement line

right placement strip

right pocket section

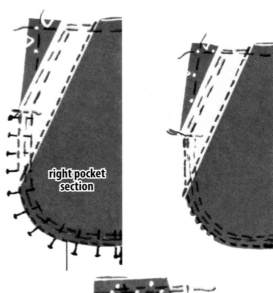

right pocket section (wrong side)

C

right pocket section

right pocket section (wrong side)

D

Attaching the Pocket to a Pair of Pants (E)

29. Complete the pants up to the point at which both front sections have been stitched together at the crotch, the zipper has been inserted, and the outer pants leg seams have been stitched up to the pattern markings for the pocket opening.

30. Lay the pants front wrong side down and lay over it the back section wrong side up. Fold down the upper portion of the pants back as far as the bottom of the pocket opening.

31. With the right-hand pocket wrong side out, lay it down on the right-hand pants front, matching the notches of the open side edges. The number of notches on the upper part of the pocket (two in this diagram) will correspond to the number of notches on the pants front opening.

32. Push the underneath side of the pocket out of the way.

33. Pin only the upper side of the pocket to the pants front along the side seam line. Insert the first pin at the very bottom of the seam opening. Pin next at the notches and at the intersection of the side seam line with the waist seam line, then at ½″ (1.3 cm) intervals in between.

34. Baste the pocket to the pants just outside the side seam line and remove the pins. Machine stitch along the seam line. Remove the basting.

35. Press open the seam to the bottom of the pocket opening.

36. Fold the pocket over so that it lies outside the pants and lift up the folded-down pants back.

37. Pin the remaining unstitched side of the pocket to the open portion of the pants back along the side seam line. Pin first at the very bottom of the opening, then at the notches and the intersection of the side seam line with the waist seam line, and finally at ½″ (1.3 cm) intervals in between.

38. Baste the pocket to the pants back along the seam line. Remove the pins.

39. Machine stitch the seam. Remove all bastings except the basted marking along the waist seam line. Press open the stitched seam.

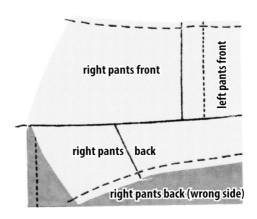

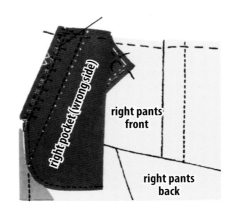

DESIGNER TIP

Instructions are similar for attaching a side seam pocket in skirts and dresses. Follow your pattern guide and omit the instructions for sewing the crotch curve in pants.

Finishing the Pocket (F)

40. Open the right pants section so it lies flat, wrong side down, and turn the pocket toward the pants front. Press the front pocket seam flat.

41. Pin along the pressed seam to hold it flat and baste ⅜″ (0.9 cm) from the edge.

42. Pushing the rest of the pocket and the pants back fabric out of the way, place the pants front under the machine presser foot. Topstitch the front pocket opening seam ¼″ inch (0.6 cm) in from the folded edge, from the waist to the bottom of the pocket opening.

43. Pull the threads to the inside of the pocket and tie them off. Remove the basting.

44. At the waistline, align the front edge of the pocket with the vertical running stitch and pin.

45. Pin the pants front to the folded pocket along the waist seam-line markings, then baste just outside the seam-line markings. Remove the pins.

46. Reinforce the bottom of the pocket opening by machine stitching at right angles to the side seam through all layers of the fabric from the end of the topstitching made in Step 42 to just beyond the side seam. Stitch forward, then backward, then forward again, then pull the threads through to the wrong side of the garment and tie them off. Press.

47. Repeat Steps 1–46 on the left pocket section, facing, and strip.

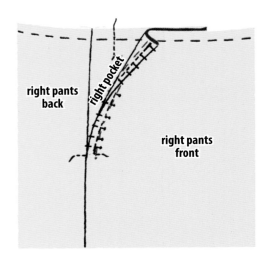

right pants back

right pocket

right pants front

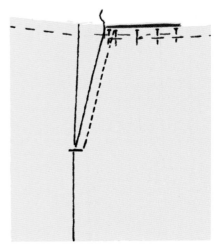

(F)

POLISHED EDGES

The final touches to a garment are often applied to the outer edges from necklines to hemlines. A well-made waistband, for example, will lay flat without wrinkling or buckling and it has a soft roll at the top edge. The secret to this look is the interfacing and care in marking the band. Mitered corners not only look sharp, but they reduce bulk and help areas, such as the artful slit of a kick pleat or the sleeve vent. These areas of a garment can be further enhanced by adding a bias binding complete with a mitered edge.

SHAPED WAISTBAND

Preparing the Interfacing (A)

1. If the waistband and interfacing (dark gray) are cut from the same pattern piece, fold the interfacing in half lengthwise and mark a center fold line with chalk.
2. **A.** Cutting ¼″ (0.6 cm) above the center fold line, trim away the long part of the interfacing that has no pattern notches.
   B. If the interfacing has not been cut from the same pattern piece, make sure that it is the same length and ¼″ (0.6 cm) more than half the width of the waistband.

Attaching the Interfacing (B)

3. Place the interfacing on the wrong side of the waistband, lining it up with the notched edge. Pin together, matching the notches and pattern markings (white).
4. Baste (red) the interfacing to the waistband along the notched side and both ends. Remove the pins.
5. Hand stitch (black) the interfacing to the waistband ⅛″ (3.2 mm) above the center fold line, using thread the same color as the fabric. Make ½″ (1.3 cm) stitches on the interfacing side, but do not stitch through the waistband material; pick up only a thread of the waistband fabric.
6. Trim the interfacing close to the bastings along the three outer edges. Do not trim along the center fold line.

Sewing the Waistband (C)

7. Fold the waistband in half lengthwise, wrong side out.
8. Pin along the seam markings around the corner of the waistband, from the lap line to the folded edge. Baste and remove the pins.
9. Machine stitch (blue) along the seam markings and trim the lap line around the corner to the folded edge.
10. Pin the other end of the waistband together. Baste along the end seam markings and remove the pins.
11. Machine stitch along the end seam markings, beginning at the corner where the end and long seam markings intersect—not at the edge of the fabric.
12. Clip into the seam allowance diagonally at the lap line, cutting close to but not into the stitching.
13. At the lapped end, trim the seam allowance to ¼″ (0.6 cm) and trim both corners diagonally.
14. Trim the seam allowance at the other end of the waistband to ¼″ (0.6 cm) and trim diagonally at the folded edge.

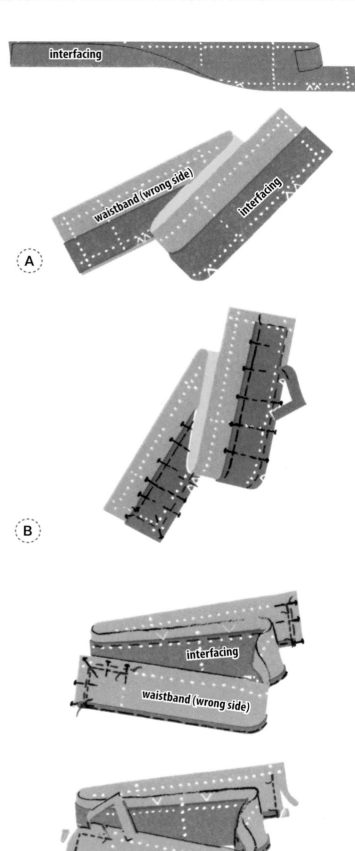

Sewing the Waistband to the Garment (D)

15. Turn the waistband and the garment right sides out.
16. Pin the long-notched edge of the waistband to the garment along the waist seam-line markings, matching notches and seams. Be sure the sides of the waistband and garment fabric that will be visible in the finished garment are facing each other.
17. Baste along the waist seam-line markings. Remove the pins, and then machine stitch.
18. Trim the garment seam allowance to ⅛" (3.2 mm). Trim the waistband seam allowance to ¼" (0.6 cm). Trim the seam allowance of the long-unstitched waistband edge to ¼" (0.6 cm).

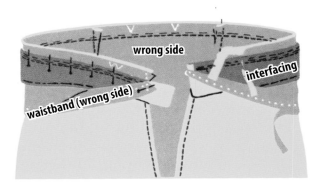

D

The Final Touches (E)

19. Turn over the long, unstitched edge of the waistband to the inside of the garment.
20. Fold under the unstitched edge along the seam markings and pin it to the garment, then baste and remove the pins.
21. Hand stitch the folded edge of the waistband to the garment with a slip stitch (page 244). Do not stitch into the garment fabric but pick up only a few threads of the seam allowance. Remove all bastings and press.

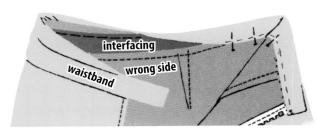

E

ELASTIC CASING

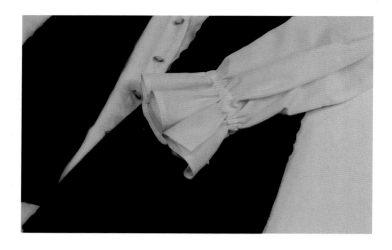

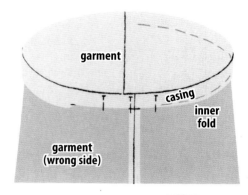

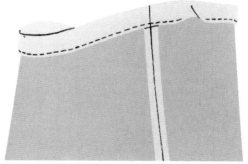

Making the Casing (A)

1. To determine the depth for the casing, measure the width of the elastic you plan to use. Then, add ¼″ (0.6 cm) for clearance and ¼″ (0.6 cm) for the seam allowance.
2. With the garment wrong side out, turn up the garment edge that you are putting the elastic in by the amount determined in Step 1. Press.
3. Turn under the raw edge ¼″ (0.6 cm), and pin at 1″ (2.5 cm) intervals.
4. Baste near the inner folded edge and remove the pins.
5. Machine stitch as close as possible to the inner folded edge, leaving open a 2″ (5.1 cm) wide space to insert the elastic. Remove the basting.
6. Press the casing lightly.

Inserting the Elastic (B)

7. To determine the length of the elastic, put the elastic around the appropriate body area and stretch it until it is both secure and comfortable. Allow 1″ (2.5 cm) for joining the ends.
8. Cut the elastic to the length you determined in the previous step.
9. Attach a small safety pin to one end of the elastic. Insert the pinned end of the elastic into the open space you left in the casing and work it through the casing. Remove the pin.
10. Overlap the ends of the elastic and stich securely.
11. Finish machine stitching the opening in the inner folded edge of the casing.

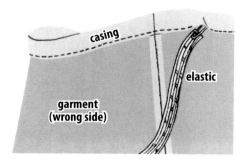

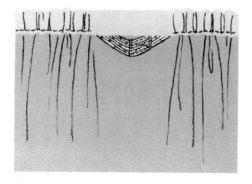

MITERING OUTSIDE CORNERS WITH BIAS

1. To attach bias binding around an outside corner—such as at the intersection of the hemline and front opening of a jacket or hem—first attach one side of the binding to the garment along one of the sides that forms the corner. Follow the directions for attaching single or double bias binding if using purchased binding or create your own following the steps on pages 69–70.

2. End the stitching at the basted corner marking or, for double bias binding, at a distance from the corner equal to the finished width of the binding.

3. At the corner, fold the unattached portion of the binding diagonally up to the end of the machine stitching.

4. Fold the unattached portion of the binding again, aligning the fold with the garment edge.

5. For a single bias binding, line up the fold line of the binding with the basted markings on the garment, as shown. For a double bias binding, line up the outer cut edges of the binding with the other garment.

6. Pin the binding to the garment along the binding fold line.

7. Machine stitch along the fold line, beginning at the garment edge. Remove the pins.

8. Turn the binding right side up to form the miter.

9. Turn the garment to the other side.

10. Fold the unattached edge of the binding over the garment edge. At the corner, re-form the diagonal fold.

11. Finish attaching the binding to the garment, following the instructions for attaching single or double bias binding.

12. Slip stitch the outside and inside folds of the miter if desired.

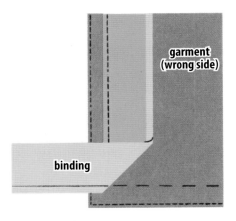

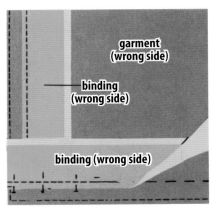

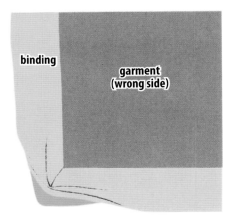

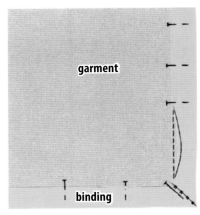

FACED SLIT WITH MITERED CORNERS

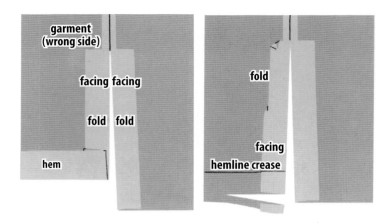

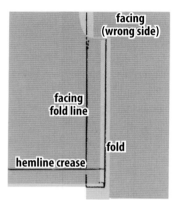

Preparing the Facing and Hem (A)

1. Following your pattern instructions, finish the garment except for the slit and hem.
2. With the garment wrong side out, press open the seam above the slit. Fold back the slit facings along the fold lines and continue pressing down to the garment edge.
3. Turn up the hem of the garment along the hemline and press.
4. Unfold the hem and trim the hem allowance so that it is the same width as the slit facing.
5. Fold under the edge of the facing ¼" (0.6 cm) and press.
6. Fold out the facing, as shown.
7. Turn up the raw edge of the hem ¼" (0.6 cm) and press.

A

Marking the Seam Line (B)

8. Turn up the corner of the facing diagonally so the fold crosses the point where the hemline crease and the slit facing fold line meet. Match the creases on the folded-up corner with those on the garment underneath.
9. Unfold the corner. The diagonal crease left by the fold will become the seam line for the mitered corner.

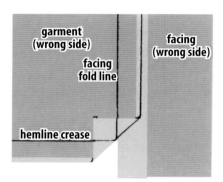

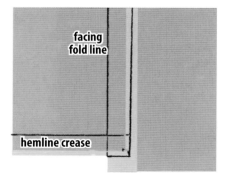

B

Closing the Seam (C)

10. Refold the corner as shown and, as you do so, push the hem under the facing to form a triangle.
11. Align the folded outer edges of the facing and the hem and pin them together.
12. Pin the facing and hem together along the crease made in Step 9.
13. Baste just below the crease and remove the pins.
14. Machine stitch along the crease and remove the basting.
15. Cut off the corner to within ¼″ (0.6 cm) of the seam.
16. Clip the corner of the seam allowance diagonally.
17. Press open the seam.

Finishing the Facing and Hem (D)

18. Turn up the facing and the hem. Push out the mitered corner with your fingers.
19. Using a needle, gently pull out the tip of the corner.
20. Make a ⅛″ (3.2 mm) diagonal clip on the upper corner of the facing.
21. Make a ¼″ (0.6 cm) clip in the top edge of the facing where it meets the seam allowance.
22. Turn under the top edge of the facing ¼″ (0.6 cm) and pin.
23. Pin the side edge of the facing and top edge of the hem to the garment.
24. Sew the folded edge of the facing and the hem to the garment using a slip stitch (page 244). Remove the pins and press.
25. Repeat Steps 3–24 on the other side of the slit.

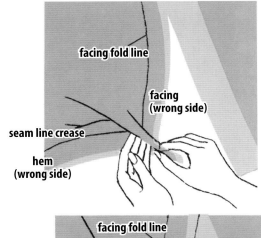

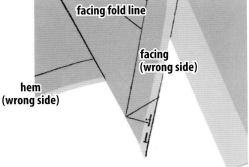

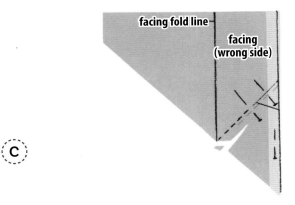

C

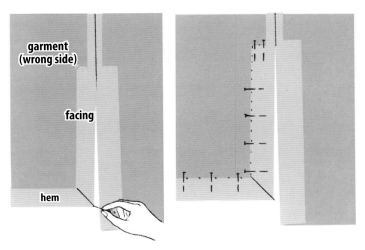

D

CHAPTER 2

EDGE FINISHINGS AND EMBELLISHMENTS

Whatever the material or inspiration, boutique clothes are simple designs transformed by techniques that create one-of-a-kind fashions that will be the statement pieces of your wardrobe. The attractiveness of silken thread woven into a custom fringe, or a classic crochet edge binding adds character to an otherwise simple garment. Smocking has the effect of changing the fabric's texture, giving it a degree of elasticity along with enhancing the visual appeal. This technique looks classy and modern when featured on the cuff of a sleeve or the neckline of a blouse. The couture passementerie braid is associated with classy, high-end fashion, adorning the edge of a tailored jacket along with handmade corded tubing and the Chinese ball button for an even more custom embellishment. Top it all off with a custom fabric flower hand cut petal by petal for ultimate cohesiveness in design and details. These embellishments will take your sewing to a whole new level.

SILKY FRINGE

Preparing the Garment (A)

1. Measure the edge you plan to fringe and figure out how many separate clusters of fringes—spaced ⅜″ (0.9 cm) to ½″ (1.3 cm) apart—the edge can hold. To weave the top, you must have an even number of evenly spaced clusters.

2. Use a dressmaker's awl or a sharp knitting needle to punch holes along the garment edge at the interval determined in Step 1. Place the holes just inside a rolled hem, but ¼″ (0.6 cm) inside a folded edge.

Forming the Strands (B)

3. Determine how much fringing material you will need by first deciding how long you want the finished fringe to be and adding 2″ (5.1 cm) for weaving the top.

4. Multiply the figure found in Step 3 by the number of strands you plan to use in each fringe cluster. Then, double the result and multiply by the number of holes made in Step 2 to obtain the total number of inches (cm) of fringing material required.

5. Cut out a rectangle of cardboard the length found in Step 3 and about 12″ (30.5 cm) wide.

6. Starting at one end of the rectangle, wind the fringing material around the cardboard to make a cluster of the desired number of strands.

7. Starting at one end of the rectangle, wind the fringing material around the cardboard to make a cluster of the desired number of strands.

8. Without cutting the fringing material, skip a space on the cardboard and wind the next cluster.

9. Repeat Step 7 until you reach the opposite end of the rectangle.

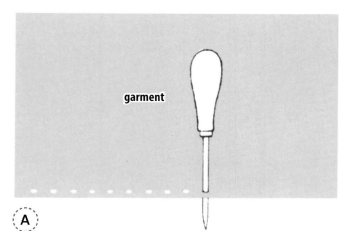

garment

A

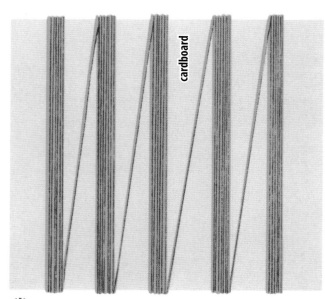

cardboard

B

Mounting the Fringe (C)

10. Insert the top blade of a pair of scissors between the endmost cluster and the bottom edge of the cardboard. Cut the fringing material along the edge and slide it off the cardboard.

11. To attach the cut fringe cluster to the garment edge, insert a crochet hook from the wrong side of the fabric through the first hole made in Step 2. Center the cluster on the tip of the crochet hook.

12. Pull the hook through the hole to form a small loop on the wrong side of the garment.

13. Catch the loose strands of the cluster that are still on the right side of the garment on the tip of the hook.

14. Pull the strands completely through the loop to create a firm knot.

15. Repeat Steps 10–14 with each of the clusters of fringes remaining on the cardboard. If necessary, repeat Steps 6–8 and then Steps 10–14 until the garment edge is completely fringed.

Preparing the Fringe (D)

16. With the garment wrong side down, center the fringed edge on an ironing board or other firm, flat surface into which you can insert pins.

17. Beginning at the left side of the fringed edge, tie the first two clusters together with an overhand knot. Tighten the knot as close to the garment edge as possible without puckering the fabric.

18. Tie the next two clusters together loosely, then insert a straight pin into the knot.

19. As you tighten the knot, use the pin to slide the knot into position at the same distance from the garment edge as the knot tied in Step 17. Remove the pin.

20. Repeat Steps 18 and 19 to knot pairs of fringe clusters across about 10″ (25.4 cm) of the garment edge.

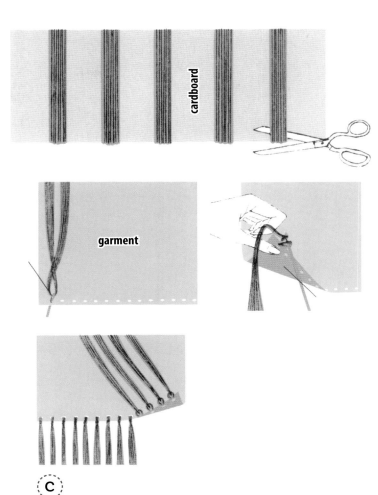

C

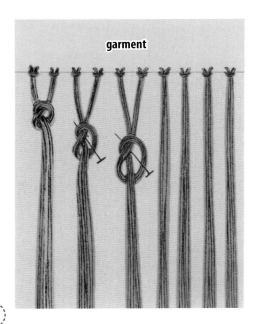

D

Weaving the Fringe (E)

21. Divide each knotted unit in half below the knot and insert a pin to keep the segments separated.

22. To create the first row of weaving, start at the left side of the fringe clusters and pass the right half of the first fringe (shown here in blue) over the left half of the second fringe about ½" (1.3 cm) below the mounting knot. Insert a pin below the point where the segments meet.

23. Pass the right half of the second fringe over the left half of the third fringe and insert a pin. Continue across the row, weaving and pinning pairs of adjacent segments.

24. To weave the second row, first pick up the original right half of the first fringe—which is now the third segment from the left side—and pass it under the adjacent or fourth segment about 1" (2.5 cm) below the mounting knot. Insert a pin below the point where the segments meet.

25. Pick up the fifth segment from the left edge, pass it under the sixth segment and insert a pin. Continue across the row, weaving and pinning pairs of adjacent segments.

26. To weave the third row, first pick up the original right half of the first fringe—which is now the fourth segment from the left side—and pass it over the adjacent or fifth segment about 1½" (3.8 cm) below the mounting knot. Insert a pin below the point where the segments meet.

27. Pick up the sixth segment from the left edge, pass it over the seventh segment, and insert a pin. Continue across the row, weaving and pinning pairs of adjacent segments.

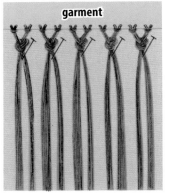
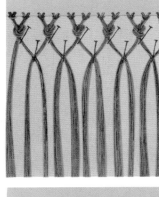
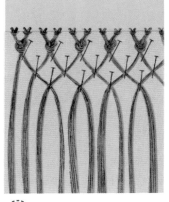
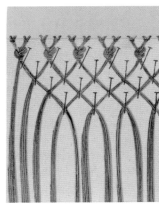

E

Finishing the Fringe (F)

28. To finish the woven top of the fringe, first pick up the original right half of the first fringe—which is now the fifth segment from the left side—and tie it to the sixth segment with an overhand knot positioned 2 or 3" (5.1 or 7.6 cm) below the mounting knot.

29. Knot the seventh segment to the eighth, inserting a pin as in Steps 18 and 19 to position the knot; repeat across the row.

30. If your garment edge is wider than 10" (25.4 cm), repeat Steps 18 and 19, plus Steps 21–29 for each 10" (25.4 cm) width.

31. To weave the four segments that remain untied at each side of the fringe, pick up the first segment on the left side. Pass the first segment under the second segment and over the third segment, then tie it to the fourth segment 2 or 3" (5.1 or 7.6 cm) below the mounting knot, inserting a pin to make it even with the others.

32. Tie together the two remaining untied segments at the left edge of the garment, inserting a pin to position the knot.

33. To finish the right edge, turn the garment wrong side up; repeat Steps 31 and 32.

34. Trim the ends of the fringe evenly to the desired length with sharp scissors.

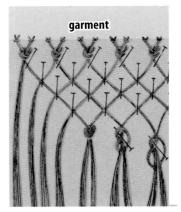
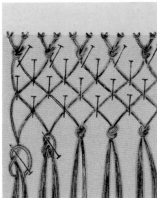

F

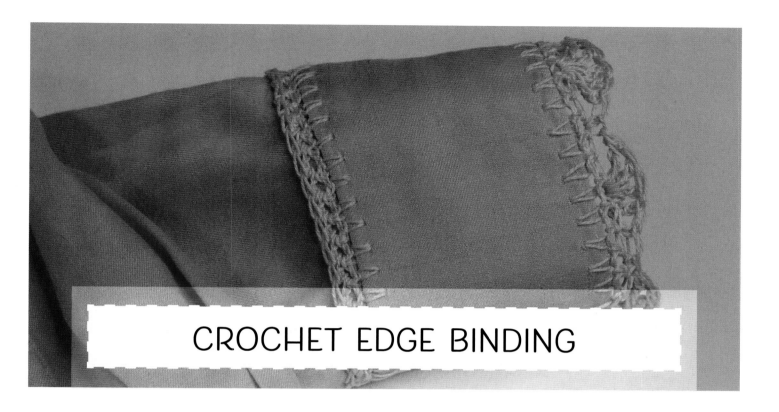

CROCHET EDGE BINDING

Preparing the Edges

1. Trim the edges to be bound along the seam line markings.

2. Place the garment wrong side down. Depending on the effect desired, mark a guideline $\frac{3}{16}$ to $\frac{1}{2}''$ (0.5 to 1.3 cm) from the edge for making slits. Mark garments made of leather, suede, or imitation suede by lightly scoring a line with a stylus. Use chalk for garments made of felt or non-ravel fabrics.

3. To make slits through which to crochet the binding, place the garment wrong side down on a piece of heavy cardboard.

4. Position the cutting edges of the slit cutter on the guide near one end. Hold the tool at a right angle to the garment and hammer down on the end until you have pierced the material. (If you don't have a slit cutter, an awl may be substituted).

5. To punch the next series of slits, position the cutting edges of the tool along the guideline with the last prong inserted in the last slit punched, and continue along the length of the guideline.

6. At the corners, punch the slits up to, but not beyond, the intersection of the guidelines. If necessary, insert several prongs of the cutter into previously punched slits. On the second side forming the corner, place the cutting edges of the tool on the guideline one slit width away from the intersection.

7. Bind the edges, following the instructions on the next page for a single crochet binding.

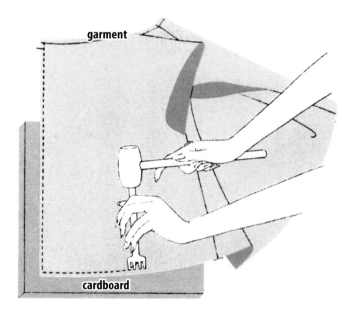

garment

cardboard

Starting a Binding with Single Crochet Stitches

8. **A.** Prepare needle for crochet with a chain stitch.
Form a loose slip knot around the crochet hook, about
1″ (2.5 cm) from the end of the yarn. Grasp the yarn
attached to the ball with the tip of the hook and pull
the yarn through the slip knot with the tip of the
hook, as shown.

   B. Hold the hook in your right hand, similar to a
pencil. Place the yard from the ball around the left
little finger, then up and over the left index finger.
Grasp the free end of the yarn between the thumb and
middle finger of the left hand.

9. With the finished side of the garment toward you,
make one single crochet stitch in each slit along the
garment edge. Treat each slit as though it were a stitch
in a foundation chain.

10. If you are binding an edge that is not continuous,
make the first single crochet stitch at one end of the
row of slits. Start to bind a continuous edge at an
unobtrusive point along the garment edge, such as at
the center back of the collar, neckline, or hem.

11. At the corners, make three single crochet stitches in
the corner slit. Then make one single crochet stitch in
each slit along the next edge.

12. **A.** If you are binding a continuous edge, continue to
make one single crochet stitch in each remaining slit
in the garment. Repeat Step 11 at corners. Complete
the first round by making a slip stitch in the first single
crochet stitch of the round, as shown.

   B. If you are working a noncontinuous edge, complete
the first row by making one single crochet stitch in
each remaining hole or slit in the garment. Chain one,
as shown, and turn.

Finishing a Binding with Single Crochet Stitches

13. **A.** Work a second round by making one single crochet
stitch in each stitch of the first round. At the corners,
make three single crochet stitches in the corner stitch
of the previous round. Complete the round by making
a slip stitch in the first single crochet stitch of the
round. Fasten off.

   B. Make a second row of single crochet stitches and
fasten off by cutting the yarn from the ball, leaving a
2″ (5.1 cm) long end. Pull this end through the loop on
the hook to secure it and weave it through one or two
nearby stitches.

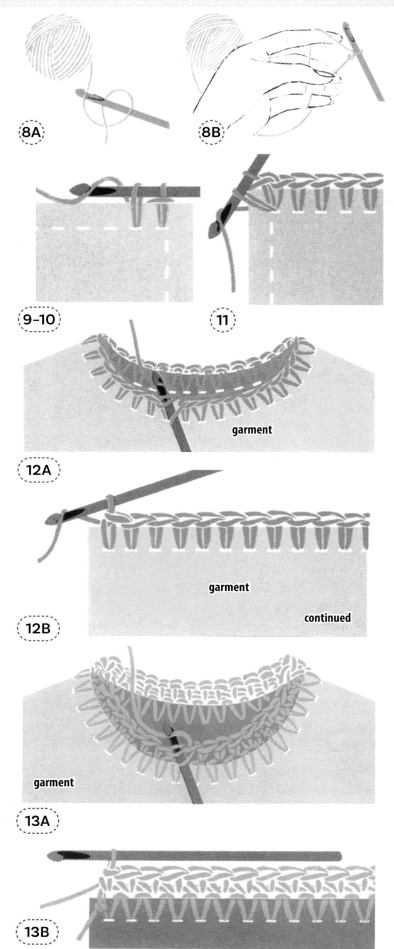

8A

8B

9–10

11

garment

12A

12B

garment

continued

13A

garment

13B

HONEYCOMB SMOCKING

Preparing the Fabric (A)

1. If you're smocking part of a garment without a pattern, first be sure the crosswise and lengthwise threads of your fabric are at right angles to each other. Snip the fabric, snag a crosswise thread with a pin, and pull the thread gently until it shows as a puckered line. Trim along this line. If the piece of fabric has no selvage edge, repeat along a lengthwise edge.

2. Using an L square, align the other two edges of the rectangle with the two straightened edges and trim.

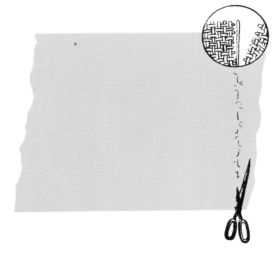

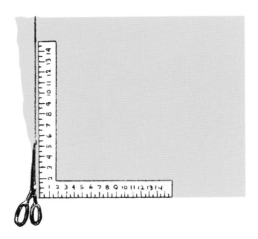

(A)

Making the Grid Pattern (B)

3. Place the fabric wrong side down on a flat surface.
4. Set the L square at the top left corner of the fabric about 1″ (2.5 cm) in from either edge. Lightly mark a row of equally spaced pencil dots ¼ to 1″ apart (0.6 to 2.5 cm), depending on the pattern effect you want; mark the dots along both outside edges of the square.
5. Move the L square down so the top corner is aligned with the second dot down and mark off another horizontal row of dots.
6. Carefully continue marking evenly spaced rows of dots until the grid pattern covers the piece of fabric to be smocked.

Making the First Smocking Pleat (C)

7. Using a knotted thread, insert the needle from underneath the fabric through the first dot at the top left of the grid pattern. Pull the thread through.
8. Pointing the needle to the left and holding it horizontally, make a tiny stitch underneath the next dot to the right, pushing the needle under the dot from right to left.
9. Make a similar tiny stitch underneath the first dot.
10. Pull the thread taut to form a pleat.

> **If You Are Left-Handed...**
> Follow the instructions in Steps 7–9, beginning at the top right corner and working from right to left with the needle pointing to the right.

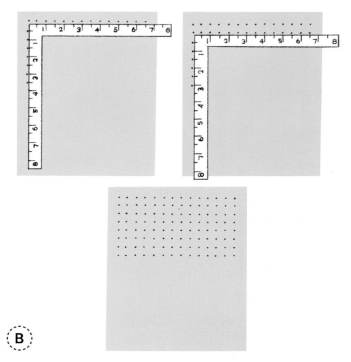

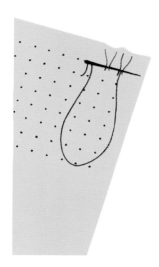

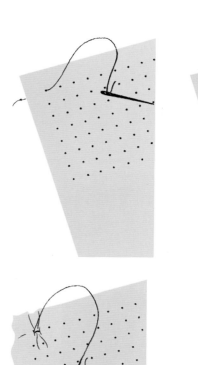

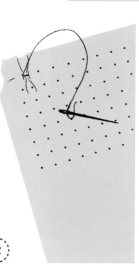

Forming the First Row of Smocking Pleats (D)

11. Pointing the needle down, insert it through the fabric as close as possible to the stitch, holding the first smocking pleat made in Section C as shown, and bring it out through the dot directly below the right-hand side of the pleat—the second dot from the edge.

12. Make a tiny stitch underneath the next dot to the right, as shown.

13. Make a similar tiny stitch underneath the dot to its left—the one through which the needle emerged in Step 11. Pull the thread taut.

14. Pointing the needle up, insert it through the fabric as close as possible to the stitch, holding the smocking pleat made in Step 13 as shown, and bring it out through the dot above—that is, the third dot in the first row. Pull the thread taut.

15. Repeat Steps 8–14 working across rows 3–4, 5–6, etc. Make sure the last stitch is made according to the instructions in Step 8.

Forming the Second Row of Smocking Pleats (E)

16. At the end of the first row of work (using the first two rows of dots), turn the work around so the pleats are nearest you. Pointing the needle down, insert it through the fabric as close as possible to the last smocking stitch holding the pleat at the left (at the right if you are left-handed).

17. Skip the dot in the row above the pleat and bring the needle up through the first dot in the next row as shown.

18. Repeat Steps 8–14 across the row, beginning with the next dot to the right.

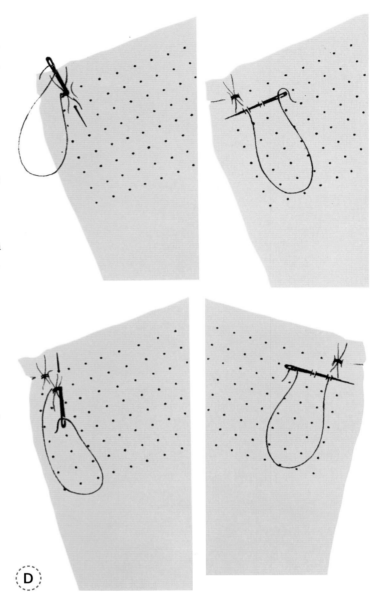

D

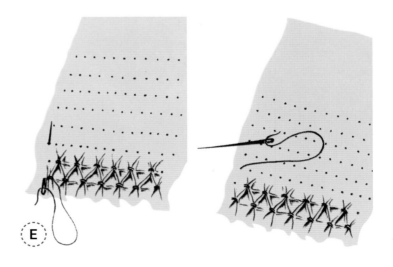

E

Finishing the Smocking Pattern (F)

19. Finish the smocking with small fastening stitches through the last pleat on the wrong side of the fabric.

Setting the Smocking Pleats (G)

20. Pin the finished smocking to the pad of an ironing board. Holding the iron about ½″ (1.3 cm) above the fabric; steam it for 20 seconds. Do not touch the pleats directly with the iron.

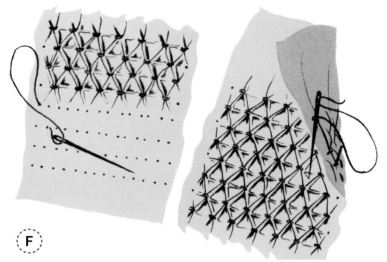

F

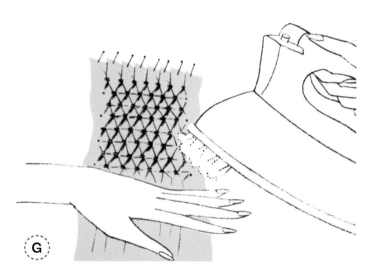

G

PLACING THE PATTERN

Once your smocking panel is complete, place the pattern piece on the smocked panel. Baste around the pattern to plot out the design prior to cutting. Once you're happy with the design layout, make sure to anchor any area of the smocking by pinning, basting in place, or using a narrow strip of fusible interfacing about 1"(2.5 cm) wide. Lightly fuse the interfacing so it will hold the pleats on either side of the cutting line.

CORDED TUBING & CHINESE BALL

Making the Tubing (A)

1. To determine the length of tubing you will need, add 4″ (10.2 cm) to the total called for by your pattern or project.

2. To cut out and join the fabric strip that will form the tubing and encase the cord, follow the instructions for making plain cording (page 68, Steps 2–14).

3. Cut a piece of cord that is twice the length of the strip.

4. Leaving ½″ (1.3 cm) of cord free at one end, fold the fabric strip wrong side out around the cord, and pin the edges together at 1″ (2.5 cm) intervals. Leave half of the cord free at the other end.

5. Using a zipper foot, machine stitch the strip to the cord, as shown. Make sure to stitch $\frac{1}{16}$″ (1.6 mm) beyond the bottom edge of the cord.

6. Pivot and stitch in at an angle toward the cord

7. Stretching the strip slightly and removing the pins as you go, stitch straight down the length of the strip. Keep the zipper foot close to the cord but not right up against it. End by backstitching.

8. Trim the seam allowances to ⅛″ (3.2 mm).

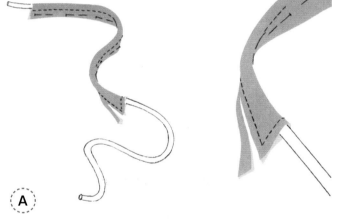

(A)

DESIGNER TIP

Select a fabric that has a slightly smooth finish, such as a silk sateen. This will allow for ease in turning the tube inside out. The corded tubing can also be created without the cording for a flat finish. An alternate tubing choice is soutache braid, which comes in a variety of sizes, shapes, and colors. This can also be substituted for a Couture Passementerie Braided Trim, featured on page 62.

Turning the Tubing (B)

9. To turn the tubing right side out, grasp the loose ½″ (1.3 cm) of cord left at one end of the tubing in Step 4, and pull the enclosed cord out of the tubing with one hand as you work the tubing over the free half of the cord with the other hand.

> **Alternate:** If making a flat tubing, a tube turner tool easily turns the tube inside out.

Finishing the Ends (C)

10. Trim off the corded tubing at both ends so the cord and the tubing are even.
11. Pull back the tubing at each end and trim off ¼″ (0.6 cm) of the cord.
12. Tuck in the raw edges of the tubing at each end and close the ends with a slip stitch.

Making the Buttons (A)

1. Make a 16″ (40.6 cm) length of corded tubing, but do not finish the ends.
2. Lay the tubing, seamed side down, on a flat surface. Hold down 2″ (5.1 cm) of the tubing at the left-hand end. Make a counterclockwise loop over the tubing near the end.
3. Holding the first loop in place, make another counterclockwise loop that overlaps the lower end of the first one.
4. Slip the long end of the tubing under the short end.
5. Bring the long end up in a counterclockwise motion and lay it over the right side of the second loop made in Step 3.
6. Holding the loops in place, weave the long end through the second loop and the lower part of the first loop, as shown.
7. Weave the long end under the upper-left side of the first loop and pull it through.
8. Pull the loose ends of the tubing from both sides, easing the loops closed without tightening them completely.
9. Hold the loose ends of tubing below the knot with one hand and carefully pull the knot closed with the other hand so the knot is shaped into a ball. As you do so, adjust the knot loops so they're even.

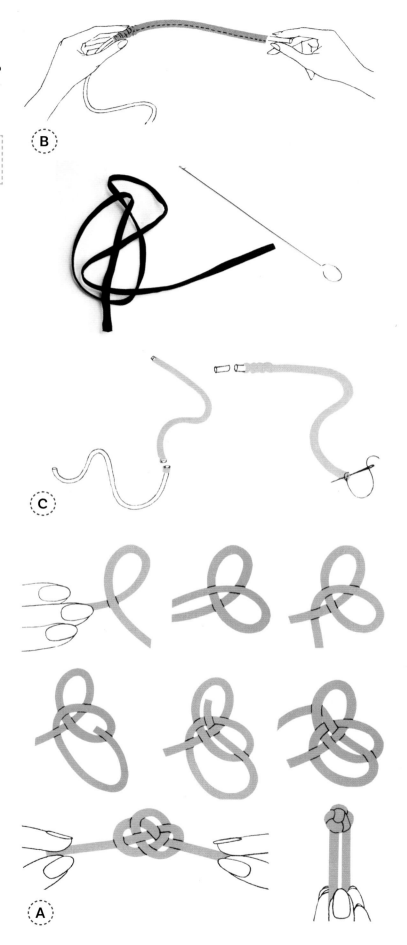

Finishing the Buttons (B)

10. Clip the ends of the tubing to ¼″ (0.6 cm).
11. Pull back the tubing on each end and trim off about ¼″ (0.6 cm) of the cord.
12. Hand stitch one end of the tubing to the bottom of the button. On the other end, tuck the raw edges inside the tubing.
13. Sew the loose end of the tubing over the attached end by hand.

Attaching the Buttons (C)

14. Using a double strand of knotted thread that is the same color as the garment fabric, take a small stitch in the fabric at the point where the center of the button is to fall. Insert the needle through the bottom of the button at its center and pull the thread through.
15. Angle the button away from the fabric with your thumb and make two or three small stitches joining the button and the fabric.
16. Wind the thread several times tightly around the stitches below the button to create a thread shank. End by making a fastening stitch (page 243) in the thread shank.

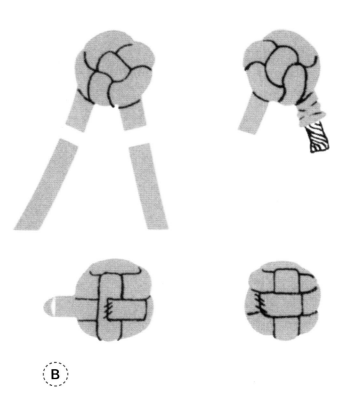

FROG WITH A BALL BUTTON

Making the Button Loop on the Left Half of the Frog (A)

1. Make a 6' (2 yd or 1.8 m) length of corded tubing following the instructions on page 57, but do not finish the ends.

2. For the left half of the frog, cut a 40" (1 m) piece of tubing.

3. Make a Chinese ball button with the tubing following the instructions on page 58, Steps 2–9. Hold down about 3" (7.6 cm) of the tubing as you start so the button will be formed near the end.

4. Along both fronts of the garment where the frog will be attached, run a line of basting to mark the center front line.

5. Pin the right garment front over the left front, matching the center front lines.

6. Place the tubing on the garment so the Chinese ball button is positioned on the center front line of the right front (as shown) and the ends extend over the left front.

7. Lay the long end of the tubing over the short end so they cross about ½" (1.3 cm) from the end of the right front.

8. Holding the crossed ends in place, pick up the tubing and turn it over so the seamed side is up. Hand stitch the short end of the tubing to the long end with a small fastening stitch. Keep the needle threaded and do not cut the thread, so you can readily attach the other loops as they are formed.

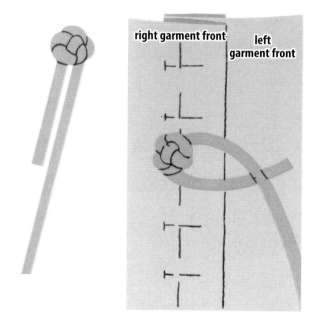

right garment front   left garment front

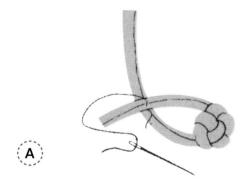

(A)

Completing the Left Half of the Frog (B)

9. To form the top loop of the frog, make a clockwise loop of the desired size with tubing. Bring the end of the loop over the tubing so it is next to the attached end of the first loop. Secure the loop with a fastening stitch.

10. To form the side loop, make another clockwise loop of the desired size—not necessarily the same as the top loop. Bring the end of the loop under the tubing so it is next to the left side of the top loop. Secure the loop with a fastening stitch.

11. To form the bottom loop, make a clockwise loop the same size as the top loop. Place the end of the tubing next to the attached end and secure it with a fastening stitch. Cut the thread.

12. Trim both ends of the tubing to ¼" (0.6 cm)

13. Pull back the tubing on both ends and trim off about ¼" (0.6 cm) of cord. Tuck in the ends of the tubing and close them by hand stitching.

14. Turn the frog half over wrong side down and stitch the loops together on the upper side with small stitches.

Making the Right Half of the Frog (C)

15. Pin the left half of the frog on the left garment front. Make sure the ball button is on the center front line of the right front.

16. With the seamed side down, loop one end of the remaining piece of tubing around the ball button so the short end is under the long end. Adjust the ends so they cross the same distance from the button as the loops on the left half.

17. Make the right half of the frog following the instructions for the left half (Steps 8–14).

18. Button the frog and position it on the garment fronts with the button on the center front line. Pin frog in place.

19. Leaving the two inner loops free so the frog can be buttoned, hand stitch the three outside loops to each garment front.

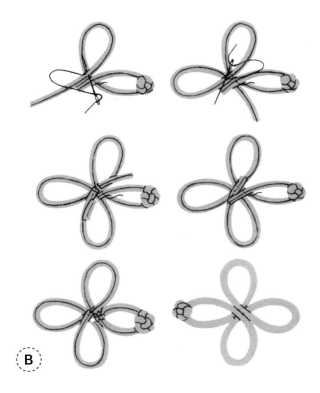

B

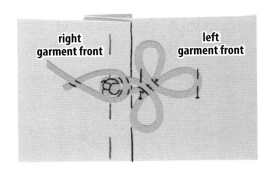

right garment front | left garment front

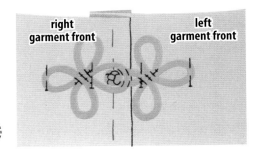

right garment front | left garment front

C

COUTURE PASSEMENTERIE BRAIDED TRIM

Preparing the Garment Pattern (A)

1. Make a duplicate of the section of the garment pattern you want to trim by inserting dressmaker's carbon, carbon side down, between the pattern and heavy brown paper. If the garment pattern piece is to be laid out and cut on the fold of the fabric, make a mirror-image duplicate pattern and tape it to the pattern piece before copying the section onto the brown paper.

2. Using a tracing wheel, trace all pattern markings onto the brown paper. Remove the carbon pattern piece.

Making the Passementerie Pattern (B)

3. With a pencil, draw the interlocking loops for the desired passementerie on the brown paper, adapting the design to the garment outline. If the passementerie will be used on adjacent garment sections to form one continuous design, make sure the drawn pattern touches the seam line between the sections.

4. When you're satisfied with the design and its placement, draw in a second line, close to the first, to indicate the width of the tubular braid you plan to use.

5. Draw over the pencil lines with a dark indelible non-smudging pen. Erase the pencil lines.

6. Cut out the design area, leaving about a 1″ (2.5 cm) margin around its perimeter.

7. To determine how much braid you need, lay a string along the lines of the design. Cut off the string needed to cover the design and measure it.

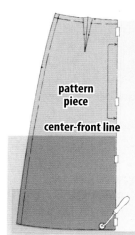

pattern piece

center-front line

A

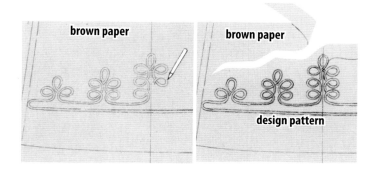

brown paper

brown paper

design pattern

B

Preparing the Tubular Braid (C)

8. Thread a size 7 darning needle with a single strand of hard, coated cotton thread (such as glace, waxed quilting cotton, or Seralene brand) that's the same color as the braid and knot the end. Insert the needle into the braid about ½″ (1.3 cm) from the end and draw the needle through.

9. Whip the braid by tightly wrapping the thread around the braid four or five times.

10. Push the needle through the whipped section and trim off the fuzzy end of the braid close to the whipping.

Forming the First Loop (D)

11. Without cutting the thread, place the whipped end of the braid on one of the loops of the drawn design at the point where two sets of lines intersect.

12. Shape the braid to match the loop with the whipped end on top at the point where the braid crosses. The top surface of the work will be the wrong side of the finished passementerie.

13. Pick up the loop, holding it securely between your thumb and forefinger.

14. Anchor the whipped end by pushing the needle (the thread is shown here in red) down through both layers of braid and then up again a short distance away.

15. Place the loop on the drawn design again and push the needle down through both layers of braid one more time and then through the brown paper. Bring the needle up again a short distance away.

16. Bring the needle straight across the loop, then push it down into the braid and through the paper.

17. Bring the needle up again through the paper and braid midway between the stitches made in Steps 15 and 16.

18. Bring the needle straight across the loop and push it down through the braid and paper to make a crisscross with the thread and securely anchor the braid to the paper. Do not cut the thread.

19. Form a second loop on the paper, pressing the braid with your fingers to make the curve lie flat. Bring the needle up and down and up again through the two layers of braid, then make a crisscross of threads by repeating Steps 16–18.

20. Continue forming the design with the braid, stitching it into position on the brown paper as you proceed.

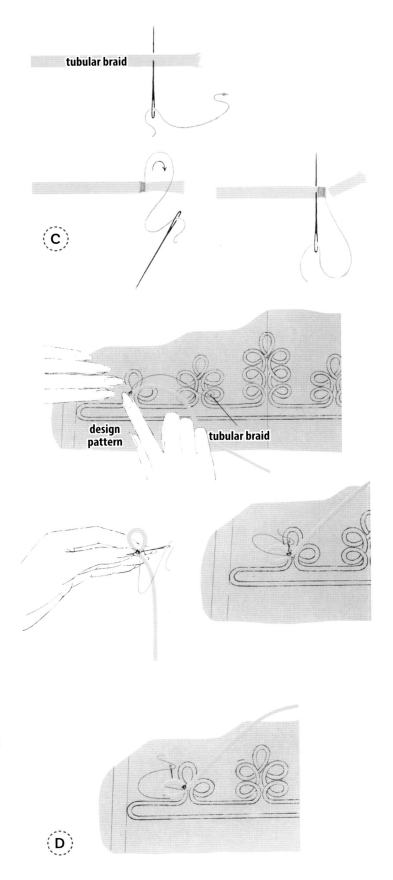

tubular braid

C

design pattern

tubular braid

D

Forming the Design (E)

21. Continue forming the design with the braid, stitching it into position on the brown paper as you proceed.

22. Where it is not possible to make a crisscross stitch, use ½″ (1.3 cm) running stitches (page 195) to hold the braid onto the paper.

23. To determine where to finish off the braid, work the design to within a few inches of the end. Place the braid on the design and insert a pin at the point where the working braid overlaps the whipped end.

24. At the pin, whip the braid, following Steps 8–10. Cut off the excess.

25. Finish stitching the braid onto the pattern by pushing the needle down through both of the whipped ends and the brown paper.

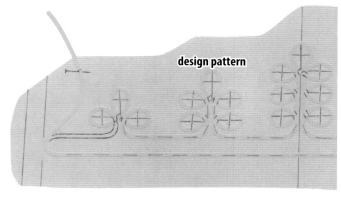

E

Sewing the Passementerie (F)

26. Using tiny fastening stitches (page 243), sew the whipped ends to the braid underneath on both sides of the whipping.

27. Without cutting the thread (shown here in black), push the needle through the inside of the braid to the point where the first and second loops touch and sew their edges together with tiny fastening stitches.

28. Continue fastening the braid at points where two edges touch.

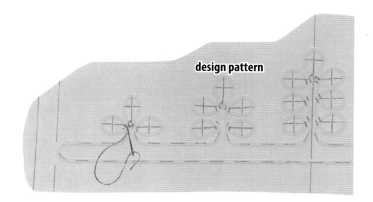

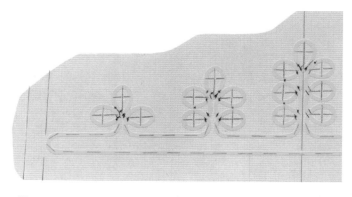

F

Attaching the Passementerie to the Garment (G)

29. Turn over the brown paper and lightly press it with a steam iron.

30. To detach the passementerie from the brown paper, cut the tacking stitches from the underside. The fastening stitches will keep the loops of the design in place.

31. Arrange the passementerie as desired on the finished garment and use tiny slip stitches (page 244) to sew the design in place. If the garment calls for a lining, stitch the passementerie in place before adding the lining.

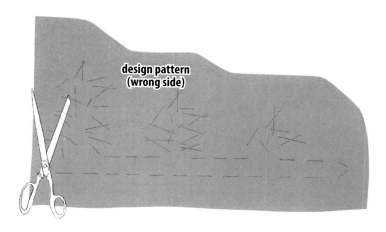

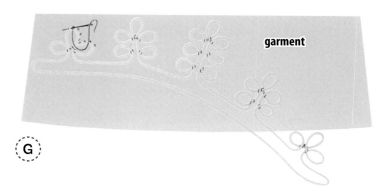

DECORATIVE EDGE TRIMMING

Preparing the Garment Piece (A)

1. Place the garment piece wrong side up on a flat surface and trim the edge ⅛″ (3.2 mm) below the hemline marking.
2. Turn the edge up along the hemline marking and press.

Attaching the Trim (B)

3. Place the trim wrong side up on the garment piece, aligning the nondecorative edge of the trim with the turned-up edge of the hem. Pin at 3″ (7.6 cm) intervals until you reach a corner.
4. At the corners, pin the trim so the outer decorative edge lies flat and the inner, nondecorative edge bunches up as shown.
5. Baste the trim to the garment piece through all three layers—the trim, the turned-up hem, and the garment itself—until you reach a corner. Skip over the bunched-up trim and continue basting along the next edge. Remove the pins.
6. Clip diagonally across the bunched-up trim to the corner, cutting up to but not into the decorative edge. Cut away the excess trim along the clip until the two sides meet diagonally without overlapping.

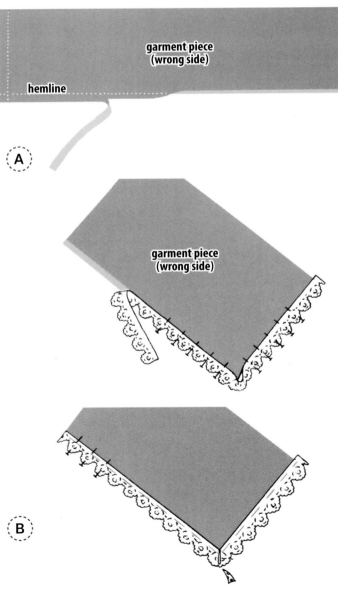

garment piece
(wrong side)

hemline

A

garment piece
(wrong side)

B

Finishing the Trim (C)

7. Hand stitch the cut edges of the trim together on the wrong side with a small whip stitch, which is similar to the overcast stitch except that it catches both edges of the fabric.

8. To finish off the end of the trim, where necessary, turn the end under ⅛″ (3.2 mm) and secure it with a small stitch.

9. Turn over the garment piece so it is wrong side down and machine stitch the trim to the garment piece as close to the edge as possible. Remove the basting.

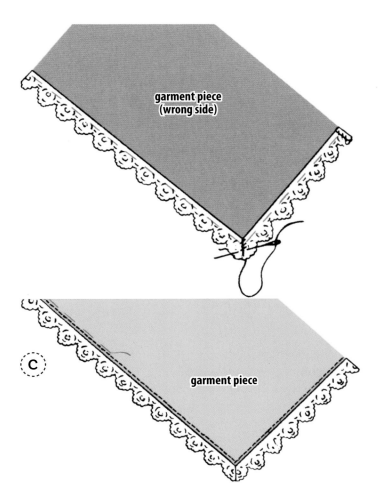

garment piece
(wrong side)

garment piece

C

BIAS BINDING

Cutting the Fabric Strips for the Binding (A)

1. To determine the total length of the binding strip you will need, measure all edges to be bound. Add 12″ (30.5 cm) to this figure.
2. Fold the fabric diagonally so a crosswise edge is aligned with a lengthwise (selvage) edge and the wrong sides are together. Pin the edges.
3. Cut along the folded edge. Remove the pins and the top piece of fabric.
4. Determine the number of fabric strips you will need to make the total length of binding required, adding ½″ (1.3 cm) for seam allowances on every strip.
5. To mark the strips, draw chalk lines parallel to the diagonal edge. For a single bias binding, each strip should be twice the desired finished width, plus ½″ (1.3 cm) for seam allowances. For a double bias binding, each strip should be six times the desired finished width.
6. Trim off both selvages.
7. Cut out the strips along the chalk lines.

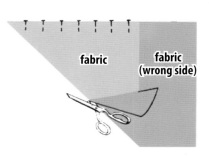

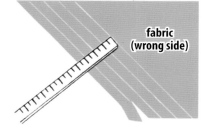

A

Joining the Bias Strips (B)

8. Mark a ¼″ (0.6 cm) seam allowance with chalk on the ends of each strip.
9. Place two strips together, wrong sides out, so they form a V. Align the seam lines and pin.
10. Machine stitch and remove the pins.
11. Repeat Steps 8–10 as many times as necessary to make one long strip of the length required.
12. Press open the seams and trim the extended points of the seam allowances.
13. Cut off one end of the strip at a right angle to the sides.
14. Measure the length you determined in Step 1 and cut off the other end of the strip. Again, make the cut at a right angle to the sides.

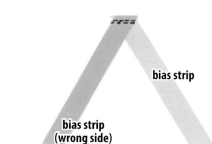

B

Finishing the Binding (C)

15. **A.** For a single bias binding, place the strip wrong side up on the ironing board. Fold down each side ¼″ (0.6 cm) and press.

    B. For a double bias binding, fold the strip in half lengthwise with the wrong sides together. Fold over the two long cut sides slightly less than one-third the width of the strip. Press.

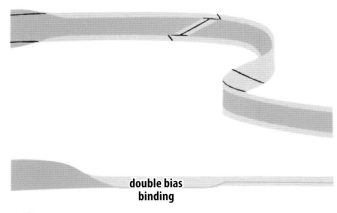

ATTACHING SINGLE BIAS BINDING

1. Stay stitch any raw garment edges to be bound ⅛″ (3.2 mm) inside the seam line markings. Trim off the seam allowances along the seam lines.

2. Mark a guideline for the binding by running a line of basting stitches around each garment edge to be bound. Baste at a distance from the edge slightly less than the finished width of the binding.

3. To attach the binding with decorative topstitching, place the garment wrong side up, as shown. To attach the binding with invisible slip stitching, place the garment wrong side up.

4. Make a bias strip or cut commercial bias tape to the length required.

5. Unfold one side of the binding. Place the binding, wrong side up, on the garment, with the unfolded side next to the edge.

6. Align the fold line of the binding with the basted marking on the garment. Pin. On straight edges, hold the binding taut as you pin.

7. Ease the binding slightly around outward curves and stretch it slightly around inward curves.

8. Baste around curves just outside the fold line of the binding. Remove the pins from the basted areas.

9. Machine stitch along the fold line. Remove the pins and the bastings.

10. Turn the garment to the other side and extend the unattached folded side of the binding.

11. Turn the unattached folded side over the garment. To finish with topstitching, align the binding just beyond the stitching made in Step 9. To finish with slip stitches, align the binding with the machine stitching. Pin.

12. Attach the binding to the garment with topstitching or with slip stitches. Remove the pins. Press.

double bias binding

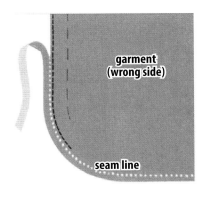

garment (wrong side)

seam line

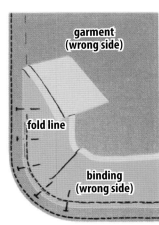

garment (wrong side)

fold line

binding (wrong side)

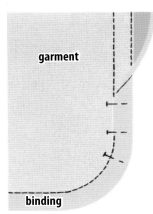

garment

binding

ATTACHING DOUBLE BIAS BINDING

1. Stay stitch any raw garment edges to be bound ⅛″ inside the seam line markings. Trim off the seam allowances along the seam lines.
2. Make a bias strip for the double bias binding (pages 68–69).
3. Place the garment wrong side down. Unfold the cut edges of the binding. Place the binding on the garment, aligning the cut edges with the garment edge.
4. Pin the binding to the garment along the fold line. Along straight edges, hold the binding taut as you pin.
5. Ease the binding around outward curves and stretch it around inward curves.
6. Baste around the curves. Remove the pins from the basted areas.
7. Machine stitch along the fold line. Remove the pins and the basting.
8. Place the garment wrong side up and extend the unattached side of the binding.
9. Turn the unattached side of the binding over the garment edge and align it with the machine stitching made in Step 7. Pin.
10. Attach the binding with a slip stitch (page 244). Remove the pins. Press.

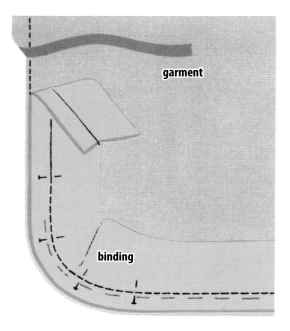

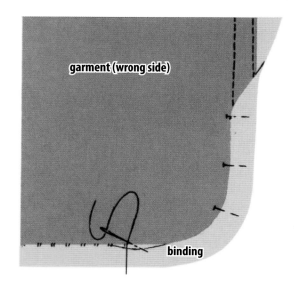

MITERING AN INSIDE CORNER WITH BIAS BINDING

1. To attach bias binding around an inside corner, such as on a square neckline, first stay stitch any raw edges ⅛″ (3.2 mm) inside the seam line markings. Trim off the seam allowances along the seam lines.

2. Baste a guideline around the inside corner. Baste at a distance from the edges slightly less than the finished width of the binding.

3. Stay stitch around the corner just outside the basted guideline. Remove the basting.

4. Clip the corner diagonally up to the inner stay stitching.

5. Spread the fabric so the two garment edges form a straight line. Attach one side of the binding along the entire edge, following the directions for attaching single or double bias binding, depending on the type selected.

6. At the corner, re-form the garment to its original shape.

7. Turn the binding right side up along one side of the corner, creating a diagonal fold. Press the fold.

8. To create the miter, turn the binding right side up along the other side of the corner. Insert a pin near the inner stitched edge of the binding to hold the overlapped fabric in place. Do not pin through the garment fabric.

9. Turn the garment to the other side.

10. Pull the excess binding material through the slit in the garment fabric.

11. Fold the unattached edge of the binding over the garment edge. At the corner, reform the diagonal fold of the miter.

12. Finish attaching the binding to the garment, following the instructions for attaching single or double bias binding.

13. Slip stitch the outside and inside folds of the miter, if desired.

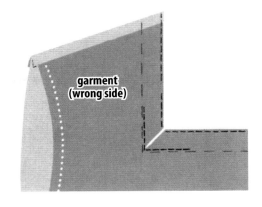

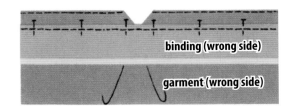

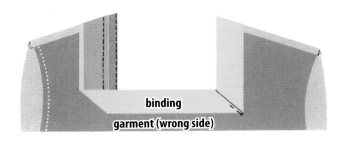

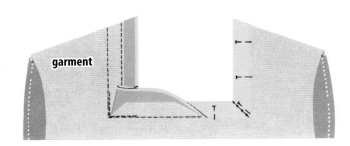

MITERING AN OUTSIDE CORNER WITH BIAS BINDING

1. To attach bias binding around an outside corner, such as at the intersection of the hemline and front opening on a jacket, first attach one side of the binding to the garment along one of the sides that forms the corner. Follow the directions for attaching single or double bias binding, depending on the type selected.
2. End the stitching at the basted corner marking or, for double bias binding, at a distance from the corner equal to the finished width of the binding.
3. At the corner, fold the unattached portion of the binding diagonally up to the end of the machine stitching.
4. Fold the unattached portion of the binding again, aligning the fold with the garment edge.
5. For a single bias binding, line up the fold line of the binding with the basted marking on the garment, as shown. For a double bias binding, line up the outer cut edges of the binding with the other garment edge.
6. Pin the binding to the garment along the binding fold line.
7. Machine stitch along the fold line, beginning at the garment edge. Remove the pins.
8. Turn the binding right side up to form the miter.
9. Turn the garment to the other side.
10. Fold the unattached edge of the binding over the garment edge. At the corner, reform the diagonal fold.
11. Finish attaching the binding to the garment, following the instructions for attaching single or double bias binding.
12. Slip stitch the outside and inside folds of the miter, if desired.

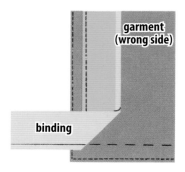
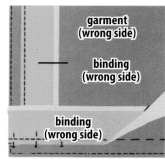
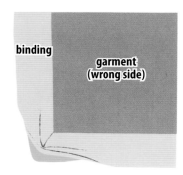
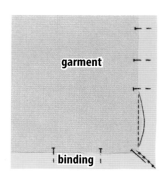

ENDING BIAS BINDING AT A GARMENT OPENING

1. To attach a bias binding that will end at a garment opening, such as a neck opening, attach one side of the binding to the garment, following the instructions for attaching single or double bias binding, depending on the type selected. Be sure to leave ½" (1.3 cm) to ⅝" (1.6 cm) of binding extending beyond the garment edges at the opening.
2. Turn the garment to the other side and fold each extended end of the binding over the garment edge at the opening. Pin.
3. Fold the unattached side of the binding over the garment edge. Finish attaching the binding, following the instructions for attaching single or double bias binding.

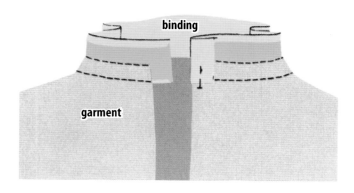
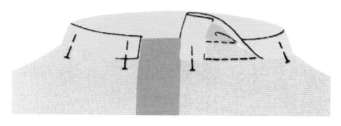

BIAS STRAPS

Stitching the Strap (A)

1. To determine the length of each strap, measure a strap on a slip or bra that fits you comfortably. Then add 2″ (5.1 cm) for adjusting. Double this amount so that you can make two straps at the same time.
2. To determine the width of the strap, double the desired finished width. Then add ½″ (1.3 cm) for the seam allowance.
3. Cut a bias strip (page 68), using the length determined in Step 1 and the width determined in Step 2.
4. Fold the bias strip in half lengthwise with the wrong side out. Pin along the raw edges.
5. Baste with long, loose stitches and remove the pins.
6. Machine stitch ¼″ (0.6 cm) in from the raw edge, stretching the fabric as you stitch. Remove the basting.
7. Trim the seam allowance to ⅛″ (3.2 mm).

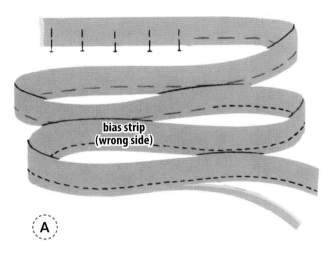

bias strip (wrong side)

A

Turning the Strap (B)

8. **A.** To turn a wide strap right side out, pin a safety pin to one edge of one end. Insert the pin into the same end.
B. Work the safety pin through the strap. Remove the pin.

9. **A.** To turn a very narrow strap right side out, use a large tapestry needle with a double strand of sturdy thread knotted at the end. Take a small stitch into the seam allowance at one end of the strap. Then, to anchor the thread firmly, pass the needle between the two strands of thread, as shown, and pull on the thread tightly.
B. Insert the end of the needle into the same end. Work the needle through the strap. Cut the thread.

10. Cut the strap in half.

Attaching the Straps (C)

11. Pin one end of each strap to the garment front at the pattern markings.

12. Pin the other ends of the straps to the garment back at the pattern markings.

13. Try on the garment and adjust the length of the straps so they fit comfortably.

14. Trim the end of each strap, leaving ½″ (1.3 cm) for seam allowance.

15. Sew the straps to the garment, following your pattern instructions.

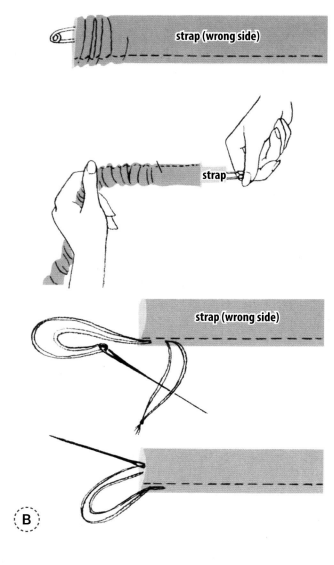

strap (wrong side)

strap

strap (wrong side)

B

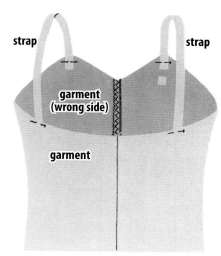

strap   strap

garment
(wrong side)

garment

C

DESIGNER TIP

If you have a metal tube turner with a latch hook top, you can turn the tube using this too.

CUSTOM FABRIC FLOWER
WITH BURNT EDGE ACCENT

A handmade fabric flower featuring matching self-fashion fabric is the ultimate custom clothing accessory. Certainly not something you would find in a retail store, these matching flowers are made petal by petal to match any detail on your garment creating a variety of looks, from elegant and classy to fun, sporty, and whimsical. Fabric flowers are easy to make and the combinations are limitless. These embellishments will take on the characteristics of their fabric, adding to the variety of looks. Often, fabric flowers are made by simply gathering a segment of ribbon or lace, but this twist on the traditional gathered flower adds another layer of interest. This style of adornment features a burnt edge, which is not only functional by preventing raveling, but is also decorative.

Synthetic fabrics are ideal for this technique. Fabrics such as taffeta, organza, lace, tulle, satin, suiting, and lining that feature nylon, polyester, or blends of fibers work best. Of course, experiment with a variety of fabrics. If you chose a natural fiber, then a narrow, hand-rolled hem will prevent raveling.

Flower Making Supplies

Supplies to create the burnt edge flower include threads to match, wool felt, felt or buckram scrap, small tea light candle, spray water bottle, and optional pin back to make them removable. Decorative elements, such as pearls, buttons, beads, or brooches for adorning the flower centers, add personality and can be found in your sewing stash, jewelry box, or a local antique or resale shop.

Preparing the Flower Petals (A)

1. Cut out several layers of squares in a few different sizes that you determine. Next, cut the squares down into circles. Hand cut, or trace a pattern onto fabric and cut. The more layers, the more bulk your flower will have. You can cut from all the same fabric and colors, but mix things up by blending alternating layers of laces and tulles with the solids, satins, and taffetas to add more depth and interest to the design. Cut the squares into descending sizes with a couple of each size for each layer.

Creating the Burnt Edge (B)

2. Take each individual petal layer and lightly singe the edges in the candle fire until you have the desired effect. Hold each circle with tweezers to protect your fingers and be careful and prepared by having a spray bottle of water handy. Synthetic fibers melt very easy, so you only want to catch the very edge of the petal to cause it to darken. A light burnt edge all the way around is best to create the effect without creating an excessively deep burnt edge. Make a few practice flowers to master your technique. It all gives a lovely effect when layered.

Shaping the Flower (C)

3. Cut a small circle of felt or buckram to attach all layers to the bottom. Layer the singed circles biggest to smallest in a stack. Alternate the satins and laces, or whichever accent fabrics you are using, every layer or every couple of layers.

Finishing the Flower (D)

4. Hand stitch these layers together beginning at the bottom with the biggest petals and attaching each additional petal to the one previously added.

5. Once all layers are together, make a decorative center by adding pearls, rhinestones, a self-fabric covered button, or a blingy brooch for the center. These elements may be sewn on or glued depending on where you are placing them and how you want it to look.

6. Add a pin or clip to the back if you want the flower to be removable. If desired, you can also add leaves made from a single petal piece that is gathered and sewn to the bottom layer.

> **Note:** Fabric flowers should not be washed in the washing machine. Instead, hand wash lightly only if needed. The burnt edges may fall away if added to water.

4" Circle — 3" Circle — 2 ½" Circle

Cut two circles from each fabric.

A

B

C

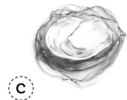

D

FASHION YOYO

Fabric manipulation, whether a recognized shape or abstract gathered section of a garment, adds great interest to any design. The traditional fabric yoyo has been included in projects from brooches and bags to quilts and jewelry. However, adding this classic embellishment as an inset to a garment or decorative hemline creates a fanciful and unexpected creative twist to edge finishings and embellishment. Sewn here in a classic plaid sleeve inset or elevated to a high-end couture design featuring a silk fabric with rhinestones, pearls, or buttons to accent, whatever your look, this resourceful use of fabric scraps finds purpose in any wardrobe. Yoyos are best sewn by hand and are a great project to take when you're on the go, but joining them to fabric, and joining them together, is easily done with a tiny machine zigzag.

Making the Yoyo Pattern (A)

1. To make the pattern for a circular yoyo patch, first decide how large you want the finished circle to be—usually between 1¼–3″ (3.2–7.6 cm) in diameter and add ¼″ (0.6 cm) for the hem. Double this figure.

2. To make the circle, trace a template, use a compass, or tie one end of string to a pushpin and insert the pin into the center of a piece of cardboard or stiff paper at least as long and as wide as the diameter determined in Step 1. Tie the other end of the string to a pencil. Pull the string taut and adjust its length to equal half the diameter obtained in Step 1.

3. Draw a circle on the cardboard or paper and cut it out along the drawn line.

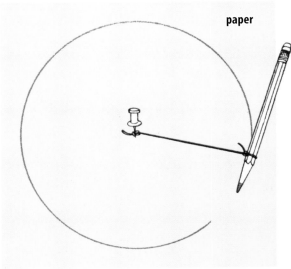

paper

(A)

Making the Patch (B)

4. Using the circle for a pattern, trace around the outside edge with a lead or chalk pencil to draw as many patches as you need onto the desired fabric. Cut out the fabric circle.

5. Thread a needle with button or carpet thread and make a double knot at the end.

6. With the fabric wrong side up, turn up a ¼" (0.6 cm) hem all around one circle, taking ¼" (0.6 cm) long running stitches ⅛" (3.2 mm) inside the fold as you go. Start stitching from the hemmed side of the circle and end on the unhemmed side without breaking the thread.

7. Pull on the needle end of the thread to draw the hem together and gather the circle into a flat double patch.

8. Stitch together the first and last gathers of the hem to anchor it, then tie off the thread inside the patch.

9. Repeat Steps 5–8 to make the desired number of yoyo patches.

Joining the Patch (C)

10. Fold each patch in half and mark the ends of the fold with a chalk pencil.

11. Place two patches together, top sides out and align the chalk marks.

12. Tack stitch the patches together at one set of matching chalk marks.

13. Tack additional patches to the first pair, one at a time, to make a row of the desired length.

Connecting the Rows (D)

14. To make even rows of connecting patches, match the bottom center of each patch on one row with the top center of each pattern on the adjacent row. Tack the rows together where the patches meet.

15. To make half-drop rows with staggered side edges, fit the upper edges of each patch in one row into the spaces between the bottom edges of each patch in the adjacent row. Tack the rows together where they meet.

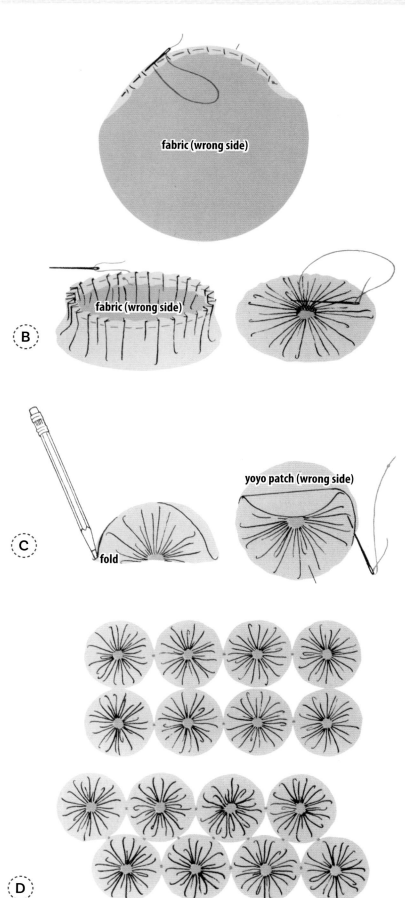

fabric (wrong side)

B

fabric (wrong side)

C

fold

yoyo patch (wrong side)

D

Joining Yoyos by Machine

1. Set your machine for a 2.0 width and a 0.6 length. Place two yoyos right sides together (gathered side to gathered side) and place under your machine foot. Pierce your needle through both yoyos very close to the folded edge.

2. Anchor your stitch, then zigzag stitch so the needle goes off the side of the yoyos to the right, then back onto the edge of the yoyos to the left for four or five stitches. Anchor your stitching by tying off or taking several stitches to fix the stitch.

3. Remove and trim tails. Open the yoyos and finger press.

4. For a short sleeve, continue until you've joined five in a row. Make two rows. Then, use the same technique to join the two rows of yoyos. Repeat to make a panel for a second sleeve. To see how to add incorporate the yoyo sleeve to a garment, turn to page 205 in Chapter 8.

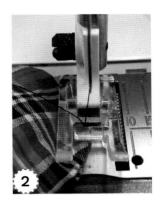

CHAPTER 3

BEADING, BEADS, AND SEQUINS

Not only for formal attire, beads and sequins adorn fashion from a formal gown to a basic handbag. These adornments are an inexpensive way to enhance any garment.

There are infinite possibilities along with a myriad of bead styles, textures, and colors to choose from. Strings of beads are easily formed into a design with needle and thread, then fastened to the project with various stitches. Beads can be anchored directly onto a project or finished individually and then attached to a project like an appliqué providing flexibility of attaching at the beginning or ending of a design.

This soothing pastime is a great creative outlet, and what might look intimidating is created simply with a needle, thread, and decorative beads. You'll be rewarded with your effort when you finish your next beaded design.

BEAD BASICS AND SUPPLIES

TYPES OF BEADS

Beads for apparel should be of the highest quality and come in all shapes and sizes. Glass, wood, crystal, and gemstones are the best options because they're durable. Glass is the best choice to prevent melting. Better quality beads will have color added in the bead development process. Lesser quality may have a painted-on finish. A painted-on finish may iron off with the heat of an iron and transfer to areas of the garment, so avoid these. While they may be purchased in the same area of the hobby store, craft beads are not recommended for apparel because of this.

With beads, the higher the number, the smaller the bead. Some popular beads include:

- **Seed Beads:** Tiny round beads that come in a plethora of colors.
- **Bugle Beads:** Long skinny rectangular beads also available in a wide assortment of colors.
- **Crystals:** Diamond shaped with beautiful reflection of light.
- **Paillette:** Round flat sequin often sewn under a seed bead or crystal.
- **Sequin:** Small flat metallic disks sewn in rows, or under a crystal. These melt and turn dull under high heat, so avoid steam and pressing from the top of the garment.
- **Pearls:** An opaque rounded bead made in the soft tissue of a mollusk.
- **Gemstones:** Stones in all shapes, sizes, and colors, such as purple amethyst, black obsidian, green jade, and teal turquoise, to name a few.

BEADING SUPPLIES, NEEDLE AND THREAD

Beading requires minimal supplies, but selecting the right needle and thread can impact how well your beads affix to the garment and their longevity.

Hand sewing needles specific for beading are thin, narrow, and small enough to pass through the hole in the bead. The thread is also added to the needle, and it must all pass through the bead without forcing it through, causing the bead to break. Longer needles allow you pick up more beads in a single stitch, but shorter needles may be quicker to stitch with. Test a variety to find what's more comfortable for you.

Thread selection is important for beading. There are a variety of bead threads available on the market under various brand names. Threads such as 100% cotton or 100% polyester aren't strong enough. Glass beads are sharp on the inside and the friction of the thread passing back and forth can cut through the thread, so durability is key. Many bead threads are made from nylon and synthetic blends.

Other materials useful in beading include size 14 steel crochet hook for tambour-like application, a spool holder for use with crochet hook, beading frame, and, if applicable, a stabilizing material like organza for stabilizing or transferring designs and fusi-knit interfacing to stabilize the back side of the fabric.

Preparing the Fabric

The beaded design will either be stitched onto the pattern piece for the garment—the partially assembled garment— or it will be stitched onto a mesh or netting to create an appliqué that will be stitched to the garment. The instructions listed here are for woven fabrics, but beads can be added to a variety of materials. When beading a knit or stretch fabric, simply apply a fusi-knit or other interfacing to the back side of the fabric. Making a sample is a smart way to test the fabric, interfacing, and thread for durability.

1. **A.** If using a beading hook, arrange the pattern pieces for your project on the wrong side of the fabric, leaving a rectangle of fabric with margins at least 1″ (2.5 cm) wide outside the edges of each piece you plan to bead. Pin the pattern pieces to the fabric.

2. **A.** Using dressmaker's carbon and a tracing wheel, transfer all the pattern markings to the wrong side of the fabric. Also transfer the cutting lines for each piece you plan to bead. Remove the patterns.

3. **A.** Cut out a rectangle around each piece you plan to bead, leaving fabric margins 1″ (2.5 cm) wide outside the cutting lines. Measure the dimensions of each rectangle.

4. **A.** Follow your pattern or project instructions to cut out the other sections.

5. **A.** Draw the outline of your design on paper, then transfer the design to the wrong side of the fabric with dressmaker's carbon and a pencil. Make sure the design lines do not cross seam lines.

1. **B.** If using a size 14 crochet hook for beading, cut out and mark the pattern pieces for your project, following your pattern or project instructions.

2. **B.** Draw the outline of the design you have chosen for your beading on paper.

3. **B.** To make the pattern for the net fabric backing, draw a rectangle around the design, leaving margins at least 1″ (2.5 cm) wide outside the design area.

4. **B.** Using the pattern that you made in the preceding step, cut out a rectangular piece of net fabric with holes smaller than the beads you plan to use.

5. **B.** Use dressmaker's carbon and a pencil to transfer the design onto the net fabric. Cut out the fabric backing.

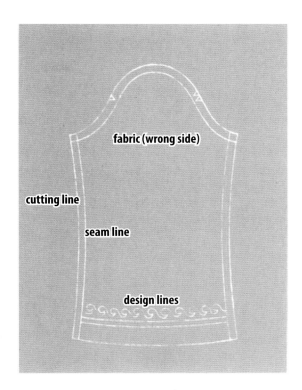

fabric (wrong side)

cutting line

seam line

design lines

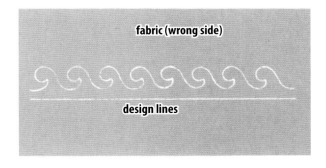

fabric (wrong side)

design lines

DESIGNER TIP

Trace your pattern piece onto silk organza and place the design outline on the organza. Baste all around the outer edge of the organza to the wrong side of your fashion fabric. This will eliminate marking your fashion fabric and will add a layer of interlining.

THE BEADING FRAME

Beading frames are the optimal solution for securing the fabric surface being embellished and are also ideal when making appliqués that aren't formed directly on the fabric or garment. There are many ready-made options available in the marketplace today in a variety of sizes and styles. A traditional round embroidery hoop for hand sewing is a simple, inexpensive style to begin with. With a quick internet search, you will find hands-free, floor-standing models, table-mounted frames with an attached light and magnifying glass, tabletop frames with a tilt function, and more. Many are very affordable, and it's recommended to use a frame that has a stand or can be elevated for best results. With a little creativity, you can also make a frame from pieces of wood, or even a decorative picture frame can be used, as long as you can tightly attach the fabric. The key is to anchor the fabric secure and taught. This frame technique resembles the highly regarded haute couture tambour beading technique.

Preparing the Beads

6. To determine approximately how many beads you will need, first lay string along the lines of the design. Cut off the string needed to trace the design and measure its length in inches, then divide that figure by the width of one bead.

7. If using single beads, first unwind a length of beeswax-coated beading thread of a matching or neutral color from its spool and—without cutting it—thread it through a slender beading needle, then string the beads onto the thread. Skip to Step 11.

8. If using already-strung beads, restring them onto a beeswax-coated thread of a matching or neutral color. To do this, first unwind a length of coated thread and—without cutting it—tie a loose knot at the end.

9. Insert the end of the thread on which the beads are strung through the loop of the knot and tighten the knot around the thread.

10. Carefully slide the beads over the knot and along the beeswax-coated thread to the spool. Do not restring more than two strands at a time.

DESIGNER TIP

If the piece of fabric beading is too small to fit into your frame, hand baste the fabric onto a larger piece of fabric, such as silk organza, that can be trimmed away after beading. You can also cut away the larger fabric behind the area being beaded. Once the beading is complete, remove the basting stitches and remove the support fabric.

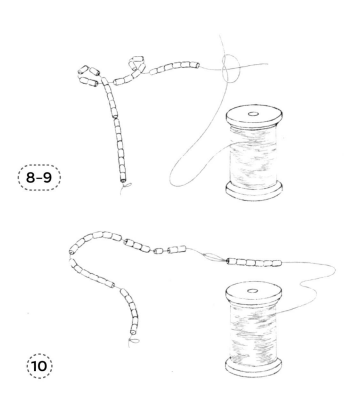

8–9

10

Anchoring the Thread

11. If your frame doesn't include a stand, elevate the frame so you can work from underneath the fabric. Place the spool of thread on the nail at the edge of the beading frame or on a spool holder next to the frame.

12. With your right hand, push the tip of a beading hook or a size 14 steel crochet hook down through the fabric (shown in cross section) at the right-hand end of the design line.

13. With your left hand, bring the beaded thread around the edge of the frame and underneath the fabric. Loop it over the hook 2″ (5.1 cm) from the end.

14. Draw the tip of the hook up through the fabric, turning the hook slightly so it doesn't catch on fabric threads. Pull the end of the beaded thread through.

15. Push the hook down through the fabric again, slightly to the left of the point from which the thread last emerged and loop the thread underneath the fabric over the tip of the hook.

16. Draw the hook back up, pulling a small loop of thread through the fabric.

17. Push the hook down through the fabric once more, slightly to the right of the loop made in Step 16.

18. To anchor the end of the thread, loop the thread over the hook and draw the hook back through the fabric, pulling a small loop through the loop that is already on the hook. Practice several times to develop your natural rhythm.

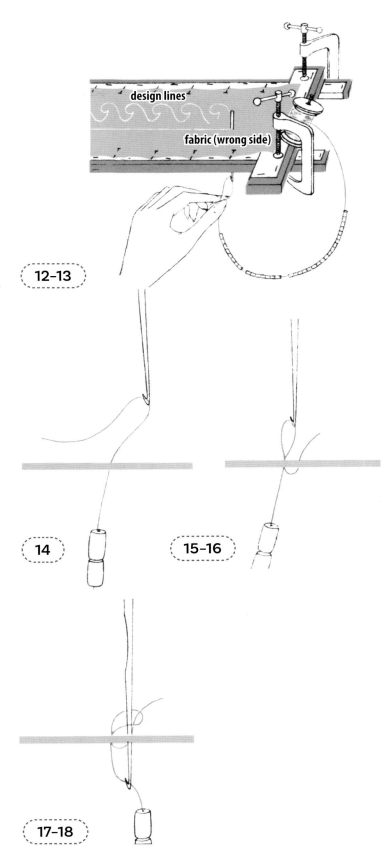

Beading the Design

19. Still holding the loop made in the preceding step on the hook, push two beads up the thread and against the fabric with your left hand.

20. Holding the beads in place, push the hook back through the fabric just in front of the second bead.

21. Loop the thread in front of the second bead over the tip of the hook.

22. Draw the hook back through the fabric, pulling a small loop through the loop that is already on the hook.

23. Repeat Steps 19–22 to attach the remaining beads to the design lines.

24. To anchor the last bead on the thread or at the end of the design line, pull the last loop back to your right and push the hook through the fabric between the last two pairs of beads.

25. Loop the thread over the tip of the hook and draw the hook back up through the fabric, pulling another loop through the loop that is already on the hook.

26. Push the hook back through the fabric just beside the point from which the thread last emerged. Then repeat Step 25.

27. Cut off the thread 6″ (15.2 cm) from the last bead, then pull the thread end through the loop at the top of the fabric.

28. Repeat Steps 12–27 to attach as many rows of beads as you need to complete the design.

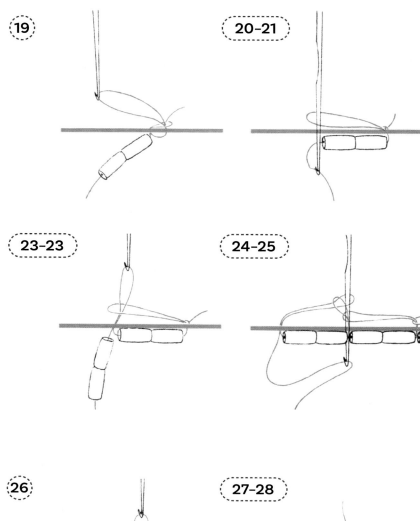

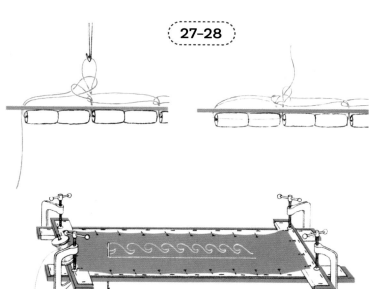

DESIGNER TIP

Hold your beading surface close to your body, high and visible, along with resting your arms next to your side. To prevent straining the eyes and hand and arm fatigue, keep the work surface close. This will also help you stitch more efficiently.

If You Are Left-Handed...
Repeat steps 12–28, working from the left-hand end of the design line. Hold the hook with your left hand and the beaded thread with your right.

Finishing the Project

Note: If the design was stitched onto a full pattern piece or partial garment, carefully remove it from the frame. For appliqués stitched onto a netting or base fabric, you will need to cut around the design and apply to the garment.

29. A. If you used a beading hook, cut out the beaded project section on the cutting lines.
   B. If you used a crochet hook, cut the net ¼″ (0.6 cm) from the beaded design.

30. Assemble the project according to pattern instructions.

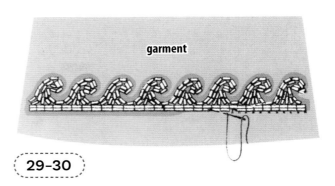

garment

29–30

Attaching the Appliqué

1. Thread a slender beading needle with beeswax-coated thread the color of the fabric. Anchor the thread with a fastening stitch on the wrong side of the project at one corner of the appliqué.

2. Bring the needle up from the wrong side of the fabric and pull it through.

3. Insert the needle through the corner bead and pull the thread through.

4. Push the needle down to the wrong side of the project again and anchor the bead with a lace knot, following the instructions on page 91, Steps 6–10.

5. Working along the appliqué edge, bring the needle up from the wrong side again beside the fourth or fifth bead. Repeat Step 4 to anchor that bead.

6. Repeat Step 5 at three- or four-bead intervals all around the appliqué. Be sure to anchor the other three corner beads.

7. To secure the loose thread ends at the beginning and end of the appliqué, thread them through the needle and insert the needle down to the wrong side of the fabric just beside the end bead. Anchor the thread with a fastening stitch on the wrong side and cut the thread next to the stitch.

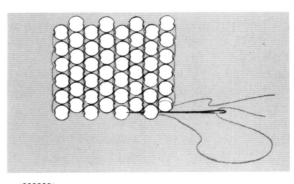

1–7

BEADS WITH THE COUCHING STITCH

Stringing the Beads

1. **A.** If your project is unlined, complete it before you attach the edging.

   B. If your project is lined or faced, complete it after you attach the edging.

2. Draw a guideline for the edging on the right side of the project. Use chalk on fabric and a soft lead pencil on leather.

3. To determine the length of edging you will need, lay a string along the design and measure it.

4. Thread a slender beading needle with a 30″ (76.2 cm) length of beeswax-coated thread that matches the color of the beads or is neutral if you plan to use two or more bead colors. Do not knot the thread.

5. String a bead onto the thread and slide the bead up to within 10″ (25.4 cm) of the end of the thread.

6. Insert the needle back into the bead again from the original end and pull the thread through.

7. Make a chain segment by stringing enough beads onto the thread to make up the length planned.

8. To make the circle at the end of a chain segment, add to the thread an even number of beads to achieve the size desired—at least eight beads are generally needed.

9. Insert the needle back into the first bead of the circle and pull the thread through.

10. To fill the center of the circle, string another bead onto the thread, and push the needle through the bead at the bottom of the circle. Pull the thread through.

11. Anchor the circle by first tying a loose knot next to the bottom bead. Weave a pin through the loops of thread and slide the knot against the bead as you tighten the loop.

12. Remove the pin and make two or three additional knots at the same point on the thread.

13. Repeat Steps 7–12 to make a series of chains and circles up to about 10″ (25.4 cm) from the end of the thread.

14. Insert the needle back into the last bead and pull the thread through. Then cut off the thread, leaving a 10″ (25.4 cm) loose end.

15. Repeat Steps 4–14 to string as many sections of the edging as you need. Be sure to continue the pattern identically on successive sections. If it is necessary to finish the thread within a chain, complete the chain at the beginning of the next section.

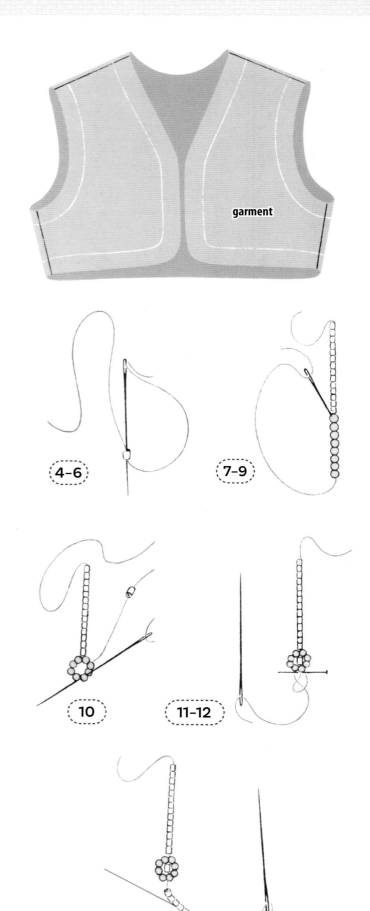

Attaching Beads on Fabric with a Couching Stitch

16. Thread the beading needle with the loose strand remaining at the starting point of the edging (Step 5). Push the needle through to the wrong side of the fabric at the beginning of the guideline that you drew in Step 2.

17. Anchor the thread with a fastening stitch. Cut off the excess thread.

18. Thread the beading needle with a new 18″ (45.7 cm) length of beeswax-coated thread.

19. Make a tiny fastening stitch on the wrong side of the project fabric just to the right of the stitch made in Step 17. Bring the needle through the fabric just to the right of the edging.

20. Holding the edging in place with your left thumb, insert the needle just to the left of the edging directly opposite the point from which the thread last emerged.

21. Slant the needle downward and push the tip out between the fourth and fifth beads just to the right of the chain. Pull the thread through.

22. Repeat Steps 20 and 21 all along the chain.

23. At the circle, anchor the outside beads on each side with separate stitches.

24. Repeat Steps 20–23 until you reach the end of the edging or edging segment.

25. Secure the end of the thread by making a fastening stitch on the wrong side of the fabric, then repeat Steps 16 and 17 to anchor the end of the edging.

26. Repeat Steps 16–25 with each remaining segment of edging.

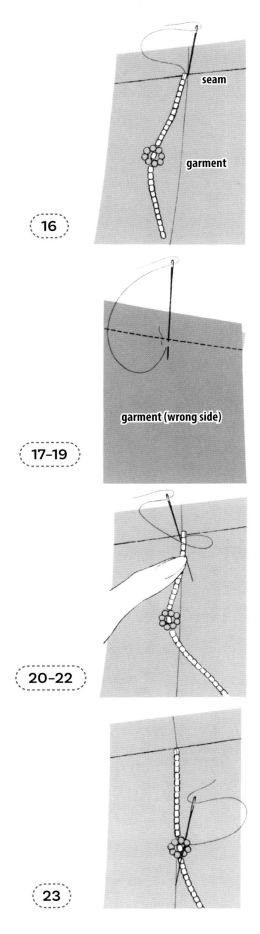

Beads Sewn to Leather

27. Thread a slender leather needle with the loose strand left in Step 5. Anchor the edging at the beginning of the design guideline with a tiny fastening stitch (page 243). Slide the needle through the leather without piercing the wrong side.
28. Cut the thread next to the stitch.
29. Thread the leather needle with a new 18″ (45.7 cm) length of beeswax-coated thread.
30. Make a tiny fastening stitch just to the right of the stitch made in Step 27.
31. Attach the edging to the leather along the design guideline by repeating Steps 20–26, Section B. Be sure to slide the needle carefully through the layers of the leather so the stitches will not show on the wrong side.

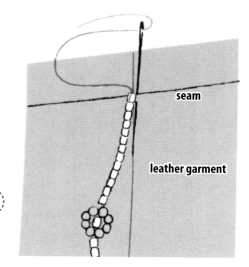

seam

leather garment

27–28

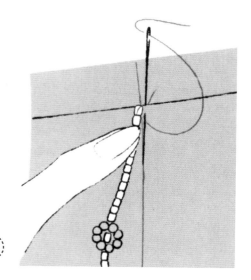

29–31

Single Beads with a Lace Knot

1. Determine the position for each bead; mark each point on the wrong side of the fabric with a tiny chalk dot.
2. Thread a beading needle with an 18″ (45.7 cm) length of nylon or beeswax-coated thread that matches the bead color. Pull the ends even for a double strand.
3. **A.** If using nylon thread, secure the ends with a fastening stitch at a chalk mark on the wrong side of the fabric.
   B. If using beeswax-coated thread, knot the ends of the threads.
4. Bring the needle up from the wrong side of the fabric at one of the chalk marks. Thread one or two beads onto the needle and pull the thread through.
5. Insert the needle back into the fabric close to the point from which the thread first emerged. Pull the thread through so that it is taut enough for the bead to lie flat against the fabric with its holes parallel to the surface, but not so taut that the fabric puckers.
6. Turn the fabric wrong side up.
7. Make a tiny fastening stitch, picking up a few threads of the fabric with the needle. Pull the thread partially through the fabric, leaving a small loop.
8. Insert the needle through the loop formed in the preceding step. Pull the thread partially through the loop, leaving a second small loop.
9. Pull the fastening stitch tight without tightening the second loop.
10. Insert the needle through the second loop and pull the thread through to tighten the knot.
11. **A.** If attaching a cluster of beads, insert the needle up through the fabric at the next chalk dot and repeat Steps 4–10 to attach the next bead.
    B. If attaching a single bead, clip the thread next to the knot.

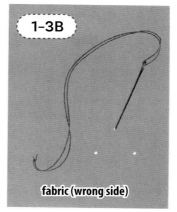

1–3B

fabric (wrong side)

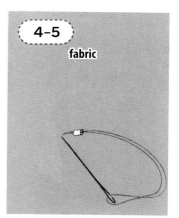

4–5

fabric

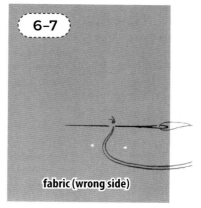

6–7

fabric (wrong side)

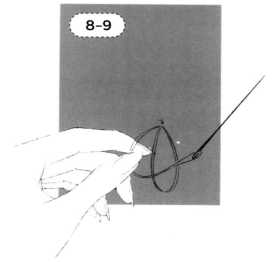

8–9

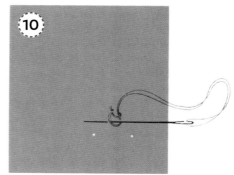

10

SEWING SEQUINS

Attaching a Single Sequin Row

1. Determine the position for the sequins, then mark the points or pattern line on the wrong side of the fabric with chalk dots or basting stitches. Use a slender needle that slips easily through the hole in the sequin and beeswax-coated thread that matches the color of the sequin. When using multicolor sequins, a clear filament thread is a better option. With your thread, make several tiny fastening stitches at your beginning chalk/basting marks.

2. Bring the needle up from the wrong side of your fabric, then insert the needle through the hole of the first sequin, which is face down (wrong side up). Take a stitch over the sequin to the right side. Flip over the sequin. Your stitch should be on the left side of the sequin.

3. Bring the needle up through the fabric on your design line to the left of the first sequin and a width of a sequin away. Insert your next sequin face down onto the needle. (If you're left-handed, insert the needle at the left-hand edge.) Bring the needle down, right next to left side of the first sequin on your design line. Flip your next sequin over to the right side.

4. Continue to add sequins by repeating Steps 2 and 3 until you reach the end of the guideline.

5. Once you apply the last sequin flip it in place, insert the needle up and back down at the left-hand edge of that last sequin. Knot the thread securely on the back side. Remove basting if necessary.

6. Finished row of sequins.

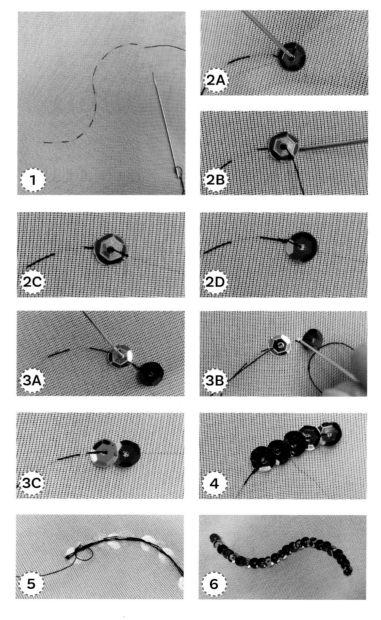

Attaching a Single Sequin with a Bead

1. Follow the instructions in Steps 1–3 for attaching single sequins (page 92). If the sequin or bead you're working with is tiny, use an extra-slender beading needle.
2. Insert the needle through the hole in the bead. Slide the bead onto the thread.
3. Hold the sequin flat against the fabric and insert the needle through the hole at the center of the sequin.
4. Pull the thread through to the wrong side of the fabric until the bead lies flat against the sequin. Secure the thread on the wrong side with fastening stitches.

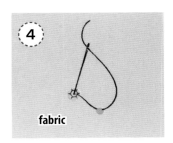

fabric

Attaching a Pre-strung Row of Sequins

1. Mark the guideline for the design with basting stitches.
2. Remove enough sequins at the beginning of the strip so that about 4″ (10.2 cm) of the foundation threads are left free.
3. Pass the foundation threads through the eye of a needle large enough to accommodate them. Insert the needle at the beginning of the guideline for your design and pull the threads through to the wrong side of the fabric. Start at the right-hand end if you're right-handed; begin at the left-hand end if you're left-handed.
4. Turn the fabric wrong side up. Knot the foundation threads in pairs. Clip off the ends close to the fabric.
5. Thread a regular sewing needle with a new strand of thread that matches the color of the sequins. Use fastening stitches to secure the thread on the wrong side of the fabric just beside the knots made in Step 4.
6. Turn the fabric wrong side down. Bring the thread up from the wrong side just below the guideline for the design and between the first two sequins.
7. Insert the needle just above the guideline at a point directly opposite the point where the thread emerged in the previous step. Without pulling the thread through, bring the needle up below the guideline, between the second and third sequins.
8. Pull the thread through, anchoring the foundation threads of the strip to the fabric.
9. Repeat Steps 7 and 8 across the row until the guideline is completely covered.
10. When you reach the end of the row, secure your last stitch on the wrong side of the fabric. Then repeat Steps 2–4 to secure the foundation threads. Remove the basting.

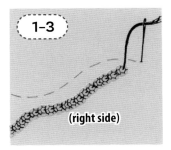

(right side)

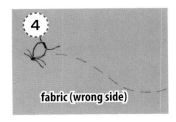

fabric (wrong side)

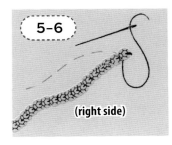

(right side)

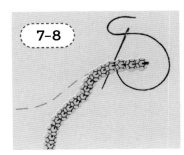

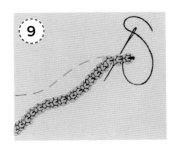

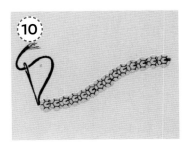

CUTTING SEQUINED OR METALLIC-SURFACED FABRIC

Modifying the Pattern (A)

1. Make duplicates of all pattern pieces designed to be cut from folded fabric.
2. Wherever possible, eliminate the center-front or the center-back seam by joining the original and duplicate pattern pieces along the seam lines. If your garment has a zipper, try to move it to the side seam.
3. To eliminate the seam on the outer edge of the collar, start by making sure that you have duplicated the collar pattern piece, as shown, if it was designed to be placed on the fold of the fabric.
4. If the collar pattern has a curved seam line on the outer edge, redraw the seam line so it's straight. The redrawn seam line should run midway between the extremes of the curve on the original.
5. Trim the collar pattern piece along the outer seam line.
6. Make a duplicate of the collar pattern piece and tape it to the original along the outer seam line, which will now be a fold line.

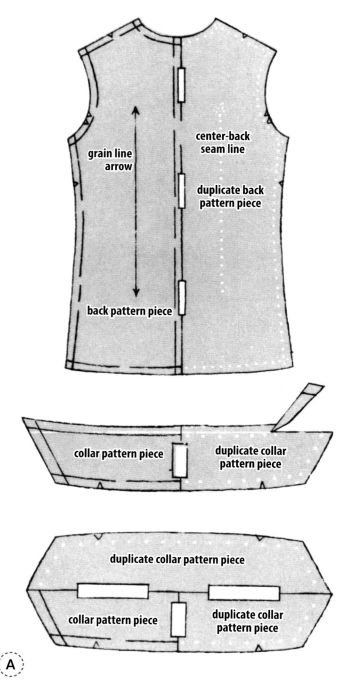

grain line arrow

center-back seam line

duplicate back pattern piece

back pattern piece

collar pattern piece

duplicate collar pattern piece

duplicate collar pattern piece

collar pattern piece

duplicate collar pattern piece

A

Laying Out the Pattern Pieces (B)

7. Spread out the sequined metallic-surfaced fabric wrong side down on a firm, flat surface.

8. Arrange the pattern pieces on the fabric with the grain line arrows parallel to the selvages. Leave at least 2″ (5.1 cm) between the pattern pieces and 1″ (2.5 cm) between the pattern pieces and the edge of the fabric. Make sure that the top-to-bottom direction on all the pieces is the same.

9. If the fabric has a design, make sure that seam lines that will be joined fall in the same position on the design. Also, make sure that each notch is at the same point on the design as its numbered counterpart.

10. Pin the patterns in place inside the seam lines. On sequined fabric, make sure to insert the pins under the sequins, not through them.

11. Cut out the garment pieces 1″ (2.5 cm) outside the seam lines. Don't trim off this excess seam allowance until after the seam is sewn.

12. Mark the garment pieces with thread tracings. Using unknotted thread, make a row of basting stitches along all seam lines. Don't sew around the corners. Instead, cut the thread and leave a 1–2″ tail (2.5–5.1 cm) and start a new line of basting. For curved edges make a row of tailor tacks along the seam line.

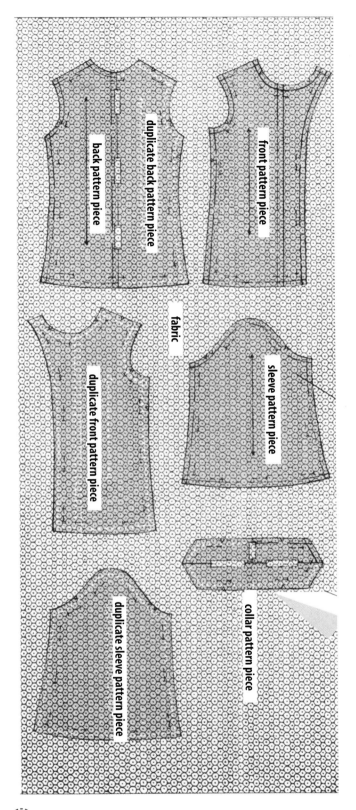

SEWING BEADS

Attaching a Single Bead

1. Mark the position for the beads as in Step 1 for attaching single sequins (page 92).

2. Thread a slender beading needle with a double strand of beeswax-coated thread that matches the color of the bead. Secure the thread on the wrong side of the fabric with fastening stitches.

3. Bring the needle up from the wrong side at the point where you wish the left-hand end of the bead—the right-hand end if you're left-handed—to be (arrow). Pull the thread through. Pass the needle through the bead holes and string the bead onto the thread.

4. Insert the needle at the point where you want the other end of the bead to be located. Bring the needle out just beside the hole from which it emerged in the previous step, as shown.

5. Pull the thread through, making sure the bead is facing wrong side down and lies securely against the fabric. Be careful not pull the thread too tight that it puckers the fabric.

6. Insert the needle just beside the hole from which it emerged in Step 4. Draw the thread through to the wrong side. Secure the thread with fastening stitches.

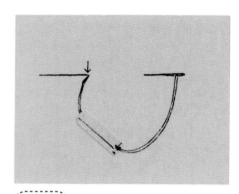

3-4

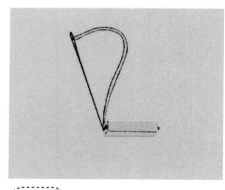

5-6

Making a Row of Beads

1. Mark the guideline for the beads with basting stitches.
2. Repeat Steps 2 and 3 for attaching single beads. Insert the needle at the point where you wish the other end of the first bead to be located. Bring the needle out exactly a bead length away from the point at which the thread first emerged.
3. Pull the thread through so the first bead faces wrong side down and lies securely against the fabric. Be careful not pull the thread too tight that it puckers the fabric.
4. String a second bead, then insert the needle at the left-hand end of the first bead (the right-hand end if you are left-handed). Bring it out a bead length away from the hole from which it emerged in Step 3.
5. Continue to add beads until you reach the end of the row. As you make the last stitch, insert the needle as in Step 4, but bring it up at the point where it last emerged (arrow). Pull the thread through.
6. When the last bead is in place, insert the needle at the end of the bead row. Pull the thread through to the wrong side and secure it with fastening stitches. Remove the basting.

Attaching a Pre-beaded Fringe

1. Measure the length of the edge of the garment to which you will attach the strip of beaded fringe and trim the strip to fit.
2. To finish the ends of the strip, start by removing about ½" (1.3 cm) of beads from one end of the strip so the backing is exposed.
3. Thread a beading needle with a double strand of thread that matches the color of the beads and is coated with beeswax. Secure the thread on the wrong side of the strip with fastening stitches.
4. Bring the needle up from the wrong side. Weave the thread in and out of the holes in the beads at the end, catching the backing fabric and any loose foundation threads.
5. Turn the strip wrong side up. Fold over the end of the strip and sew it to the backing with whipstitches. Repeat on the other end of the strip.
6. With the garment wrong side down, make a row of basting stitches along the edge at a distance from the edge where you wish the top of the strip to lie.
7. Pin the strip to the garment, aligning the top edge with the basting made in the previous step. Use small beading pins, if available.
8. Using thread that matches the color of the strip and a regular sewing needle, sew the strip to the garment with tiny, invisible slip stitches. Remove the pins and the basting stitches.
9. If you're making a continuous strip of fringe, sew the ends together with whipstitches.

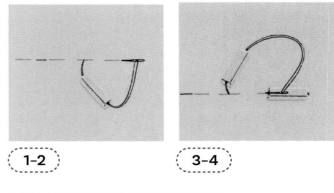

1-2   3-4

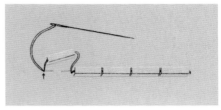

5

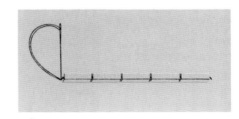

6

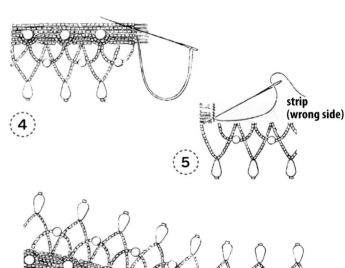

4

5

strip (wrong side)

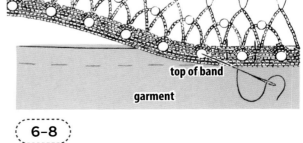

top of band

garment

6-8

Applying a Single Paillette with Bead

1. Lay the fabric wrong side up on a flat surface and mark it with tiny chalk dots to indicate where the paillettes will be applied.
2. Turn the fabric wrong side down.
3. Using a knotted strand of thread that is the same color as the paillette and coated with beeswax, bring the needle up from the wrong side of the fabric at one of the chalk dots. Insert the needle through the hole in the paillette and pull the thread through.
4. Insert the needle back into the fabric at the edge of the paillette close to the hole. Pull the thread through.
5. Bring the needle up from the wrong side of the fabric through the hole in the paillette.
6. Insert the needle back into the fabric at the edge of the paillette close to the hole. Pull the thread through.
7. Turn the fabric wrong side up.
8. To secure the paillette, insert the needle under—and at right angles to—the stitch holding the paillette to the fabric. Pick up a few threads of the fabric with the needle and pull the thread partially through, leaving a loop.
9. Insert the needle through the loop made in Step 8. Draw the thread through and pull it tight to close the loop. Cut the thread.
10. To apply the remaining paillettes, repeat Steps 2–9.

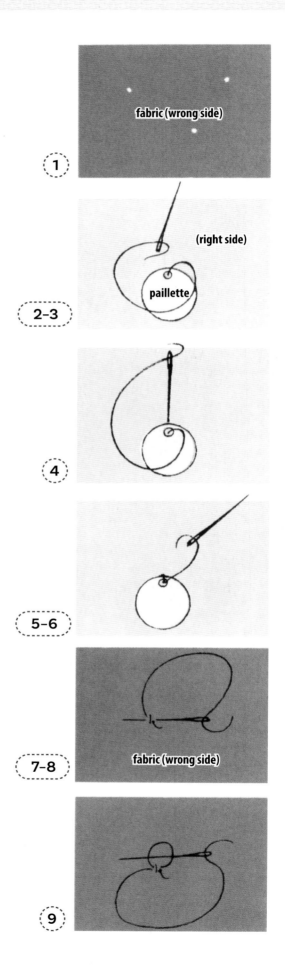

CREATING AN ELABORATE DESIGN

Preparing the Design

1. **A.** To make an elaborate design, pin over the area to be decorated a piece of organza that's the same color as the garment. Trace the outline of the garment section with chalk. Unpin the organza. Draw guidelines for the design on the organza. Stretch the organza on an embroidery hoop.

   B. To make a simple design, draw the design guidelines directly on the garment, then follow Steps 2–19 to attach the beads and sequins.

Attaching the Beads

2. Using a knotted double thread coated with beeswax and a needle that will slip easily through the hole in the bead, bring the needle up from the wrong side of the fabric. If you're right-handed, begin at the right side of the chalked design; if you're left-handed, start at the left and reverse the direction of all stitches. Pull the thread taut.

3. String four to six beads onto the needle and draw them down the thread to the fabric.

4. Insert the needle into the fabric at the end of the last bead strung. Make sure to keep the beads on the design as you work around curves.

5. To anchor the beads, bring the needle out at a point between the second and third beads strung, just below the thread on which the beads are strung. Pull the needle through.

6. Insert the needle into the fabric just above the thread. Pull the needle through.

7. If you have strung four beads, skip to Step 8. For six beads, bring the needle out between the fourth and fifth beads strung, and repeat Step 6. Catch the thread underneath the fabric in the anchoring stitch.

8. After the last anchoring stitch, bring the needle out at a point next to the last bead strung.

9. Repeat Steps 3–8 to attach the remaining beads. End off with a fastening stitch on the wrong side of the fabric.

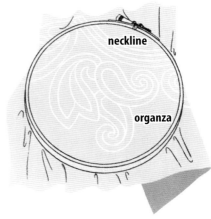

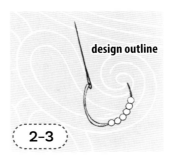

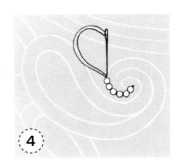

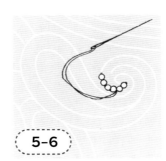

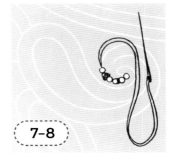

Attaching the Sequins

10. Using a single thread coated with beeswax, make several tiny fastening stitches on the wrong side of the fabric. If you're right-handed, start at a point on the right side of the chalked design. If you are left-handed, start at the left, and reverse the direction of all stitches.

11. Bring the needle up from the wrong side and pull the thread through. Insert the needle through the hole of the sequin from its wrong side. Slide the sequin onto the thread.

12. Hold the sequin flat against the fabric and insert the needle at the right-hand edge. Pull the needle through.

13. Bring the needle up through the hole in the sequin and pull it through, then insert the needle into the fabric at the left-hand edge of the sequin. Pull the needle through.

14. Bring the needle up from the wrong side on the guideline, making a stitch that equals one half the diameter of the sequin.

15. Place the second sequin wrong side up and insert the needle through the hole in the center. String the sequin onto the thread.

16. Insert the needle again at the left-hand edge of the first sequin. Pull the needle through.

17. Bring the needle up from the wrong side on the guideline, making a stitch equal to one half the diameter of the sequin.

18. Pull the thread through and, at the same time, flip the second sequin over so that it's wrong side down and overlaps the first sequin.

19. Continue to add sequins by repeating Steps 15–18. End with a fastening stitch on the wrong side of the fabric.

20. If the design is an appliqué, remove the organza from the hoop.

21. Cut out the organza ¼″ (0.6 cm) outside the outline of the design. Turn under the edges and pin the organza to the garment. Clip into the curves of the design.

22. Use slip stitches to attach the folded edge of the organza to the garment.

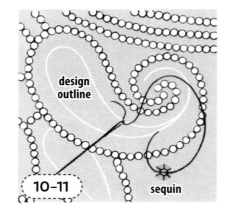

design outline

10–11

sequin

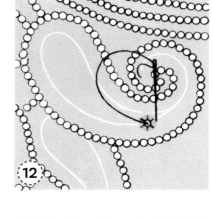

12

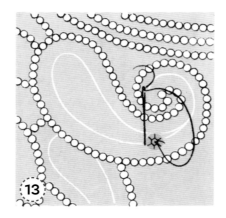

13

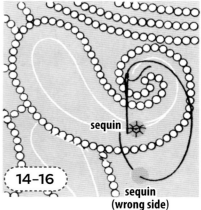

sequin

14–16

sequin (wrong side)

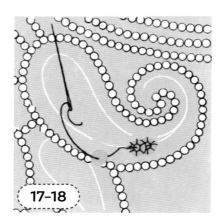

17–18

BEADING TIPS

1. Beads add weight to a garment and may cause stretch. Place beaded garments in a garment box or drawer for storage and avoid hanging.

2. For each inch you shorten a beaded garment, the fabric will bunch up more than the measured length. It's best to shorten in small increments as to not skew the desired length.

3. Beaded garments must be washed with care. Beads can snag or cause stretching of the fabric. Dry cleaning is often the suggested method in ready to wear, but most garments can be hand washed with care in the sink. Let the garment soak, hand agitate the water carefully, and rinse with cool water. Lay the garment on flat surface and soak up the water with a towel. Ideally, place it on a drying rack to finish drying.

4. Seams in beaded garments may need to be stitched flat rather than pressing with an iron to prevent melting and discoloring.

5. Avoid stitching beads into seam allowance, but if you need to remove a bead, don't cut the thread. Instead, if you have used a glass bead, take some pliers and break the thread. Turn your head away, wear protective glasses, or keep your eyes shut as you break the bead since tiny pieces may go flying. Anchor the beads on either side.

6. Finish edges of beaded garments with soft bias bindings so the beads don't irritate the skin.

7. Keep the length of your thread short when stitching. The length of your arm is a good gauge. This makes it easier to maneuver, less likely to tangle, and if some of the design comes undone, you'll only lose a small amount.

ADDING BEADS WITH A SEWING MACHINE

You have the ultimate control with hand beading and applying a single bead at a time, but you can also attach beads with your sewing machine. To apply a bead with your sewing machine, the process is fairly similar to hand sewing.

1. Mark the design on the fabric. Make sure you have a durable thread and needle that will go through the hole in the bead.

2. Set your machine speed to low if you have the option and remove the presser foot. Backstitch to anchor the thread.

3. Add the bead to your sewing machine needle and lower the needle by turning the wheel. You will need a stitch, such as a zigzag, that you have tested to make sure it's wide enough to pass over the bead. Stitch over the bead to attach it to the fabric.

4. Lift the needle and add another bead. When working with a string of beads, simply slide a bead over and onto the needle.

5. It takes a little practice to get comfortable with the method, but once you have your settings, you'll find this is a great way to add beads for simple designs.

CHAPTER 4

STITCHES AND SEAMS

Seams are used to join flat pattern pieces to create a garment that's meant to fit around the 3-dimentional figure with shape and contours. They are not only functional but transcend into decorative parts of a design. Once you learn to make a classic balanced seam in your fabric, the next step is to master variations on this core element to elevate your sewing. Additionally, varying fabrics and designs require enhanced seams for successful results.

All seam allowances should be trimmed or graded if they are to be encased inside part of the finished garment. Most factory clothing is sewn with narrower seam allowance than the standard home sewn ⅝″ (1.6 cm), thus eliminating the step of trimming. But the width to which different fabrics are trimmed varies depending on the fabric and location. A side seam may be left with a wide 1″ (2.5 cm) to allow for letting out the garment, whereas a collar or horizontal waistline on the curve requires a narrower finish so the garment will lay flat.

Wherever appropriate for the fabric and garment, the seam variations illustrated here may be substituted for the standard plain seam to further enhance your sewing.

MAKING A STITCH SAMPLE

When testing your stitch and seam sample combinations, make the sample and document the fabric type, needle, thread, stitch width, and any other variables applicable to your sample. Place the samples in a binder and use them as a handy reference in your sewing room.

CLASSIC BALANCED SEAM

Before you can modify a seam, it's important to understand what a classic balanced seam looks like.

1. With the wrong side of the fabric facing outward, pin together the pieces to be seamed by inserting the pins at a right angle to the stitching line. Make sure the edges of the fabric match so the seam is balanced.
2. Add pins at 1–2″ (2.5–5.1 cm) intervals on a straight seam and at intervals as short as ¼″ (0.6 cm) on a curved seam. These increments may be adjusted based on the fabric selection, thickness of the seam, and your skill level.

> **Optional:** To test the seam, baste just inside the seam line markings and remove the pins.

3. After trying on your garment for fit, machine stitch directly along the seam-line markings. Remove the bastings.
4. Press the seam open.

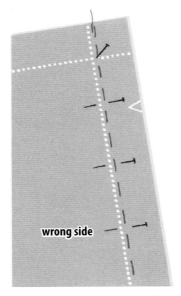
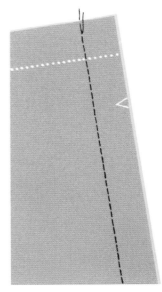

wrong side

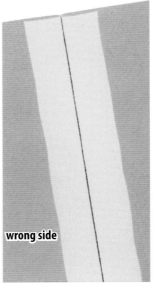

wrong side

STABILIZING A SEAM

Making the Seam (A)

1. Fabrics such as knits and bias garments, or areas that may encounter distortion or stress when sewing or wearing, should be stabilized.
2. To keep a seam from stretching, first run a line of machine stitching along the seam lines on each piece to be joined.
3. Pin and baste the pieces together, matching the lines of machine stitching. Remove pins.

Stabilizing the Seam (B)

4. Cut a piece of seam tape or twill tape the length of your seam and place it over the seam allowance so one edge of the tape extends slightly beyond the stitched seam line. Pin and baste the tape in place. Remove the pins.
5. Machine stitch the tape to the seam allowance, sewing through both pieces of fabric, as close to the original line as possible. Remove the bastings.

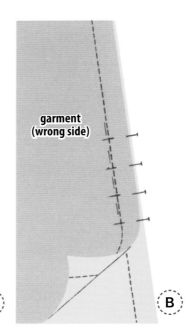

garment (wrong side)

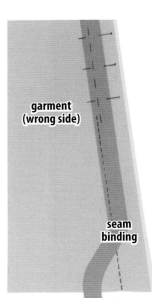

garment (wrong side)

seam binding

A   B

REVERSIBLE SEAM

Making the Seam (A)

1. Join the two pieces of fabric with a plain seam as illustrated in the Classic Balanced Seam (page 104), allowing for a ¾" (1.9 cm) seam allowance instead of the standard ⅝" (1.6 cm) seam allowance.

> **Tip:** For a double-faced or reversible fabric, each side of the seam will have two layers of fabric. Separate the two layers that make up the seam allowance of the fabric along each side of the seam, snipping the bounding threads between the fabric layers with trimming scissors as you go.

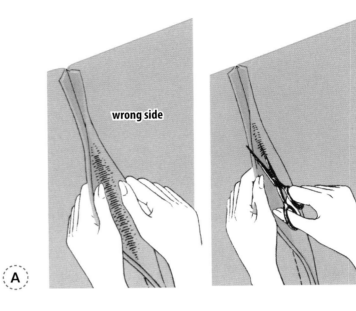

Trimming the Seam (B)

2. Spread open the seam allowance and lightly press.
3. On one side, leave the outermost layer of the seam allowance untrimmed. Trim the innermost layer to ⅜" (0.9 cm).
4. On the opposite side, trim the innermost layer of the seam allowance slightly narrower than the opposite side.
5. Trim the last layer (the outermost layer) slightly narrower than its corresponding inner layer. The layers go from the widest to the narrowest from one side to the other.

> **Tip:** Trim in the opposite direction for matching seams, such as side seams, so they're a mirror image of each other.

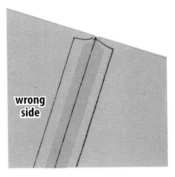

Finishing the Seam (C)

6. Fold and press the (widest) untrimmed outer layer of the seam allowance over the trimmed layer.
7. Turn under the open edge of the seam allowance approximately ¼" (0.6 cm), pin, and stitch close to the folded edge. Remove the pins. Baste first if necessary.

> **Tip:** Short appliqué pins are ideal for holding the seam allowance together on this seam. They're short and can easily catch a single thread making the seam more accurate.

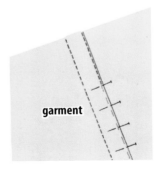

8. When completed, the seam will look equally finished on both sides of the garment and perfect for reversible garments.

LAPPED SEAM

FOR LEATHER, FELT, AND FABRICS THAT DON'T RAVEL

1. Mark a chalk seam line on each of the two pieces of the fabric to be joined. This line should be the standard ⅝″ (1.6 cm) from the edge.
2. Trim one of the pieces along the chalk line removing the seam allowance.
3. Place the edge of the trimmed piece over the seam allowance of the uncut piece, aligning the cut edge with the chalked seam line marking on the other piece. Pin the pieces together and baste. Remove the pins.
4. Machine stitch along the basted edge ¹⁄₁₆″ (1.6 mm) from the edge, sewing through both pieces. Remove basting.
5. Make a second row of machine stitching ¼″ (0.6 cm) in from the first and parallel to it.

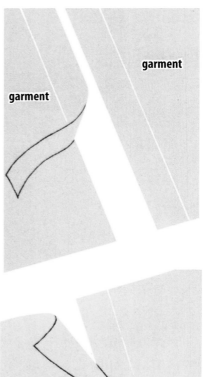

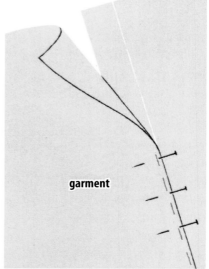

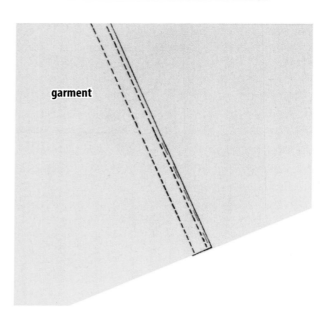

EXTRA WIDE SEAM FOR HEAVY FABRICS

Making the Seam (A)

1. Join the two pieces of fabric with the plain seam featured in the Classic Balanced Seam (page 104) using a 1″ (2.5 cm) seam allowance instead of the standard ⅝″ (1.6 cm) seam allowance.

> **Tip:** To give the wider seam allowance support, tape the seam. Unfold a strip of ½″ (1.3 cm) wide bias tape and pin one edge of the tape to the raw outside edge of one side of the seam allowance. Pin and baste close to the edge. Remove the pins.

2. Machine stitch the tape to the seam allowance along the outer fold line of the tape. Remove the basting.

Binding the Edge (B)

3. Keeping the free edge of the tape unfolded, wrap the tape around the raw edge of the seam allowance.
4. Pin and baste the tape in place. Remove the pins.

Finishing the Binding (C)

5. Let the seam allowance lie open and make a row of machine stitching along the fold of the tape.
6. Bind the other half of the seam allowance the same way.

Alternate Seam Finish for Heavy Fabrics (D)

7. Finish both raw edges of the seam allowance with a zigzag stitch, overlock machine stitch, or pinked edge instead of binding them with tape.

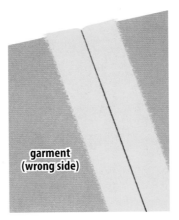
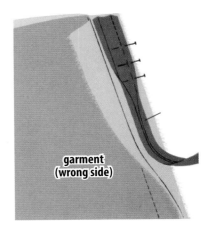

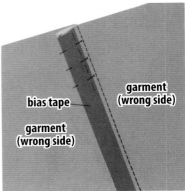

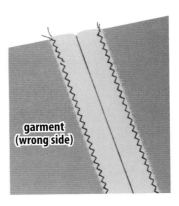

BONING CHANNEL FOR STRUCTURE

Preparing the Fabric (A)

1. Boning on the inside of the garment is sandwiched between the outer layer of fashion fabric and the inner layer of fabric or bias tape. First, make sure that the fashion layer is durable enough so the boning will not show or poke through to the outside of the garment if the fabric is lightweight.

Optional: Add interfacing to the wrong side of the fashion fabric. This will provide another barrier between the boning and outside of the garment. Options for interfacing include sew in, fusible, muslin, broadcloth, tailoring canvas, and garment flannel to name a few.

Tip: Preshrink any inner layers in very hot water prior to sewing into the body of the garment to prevent shrinkage during sewing.

Boning Channel in between Layers (B)

2. When backing your fashion fabric with a layer of muslin, canvas, or similar stable fabric, it's possible to sew the boning channels directly onto the layers of fabric.

3. Using a ruler, determine how wide your boning is. Standard plastic and steel boning is ¼″ (0.6 cm) wide.

4. The boning channel should measure approximately 1⁄16″ (1.6 mm) bigger on each side of the boning. It should be large enough for the boning to easily channel through without stressing the stitching, but not loose enough that the boning twists and moves around.

5. On the inside of the garment, carefully mark and measure the boning channel locations using chalk and a ruler. Stitch from top to bottom of the seam or from edge to edge if placed in partial seams. Test the width and adjust slightly if necessary.

6. Plot out where the boning will be located on the garment and create consecutive boning channels.

7. Cut the boning so it's ¾–1″ (1.9–2.5 cm) shorter than each end of the seam so it will not be sewn into any seam allowance on either side. If using plastic boning, round off each end of the plastic with sharp scissors. For steel boning, cap each end with tool dip, a boning cap, or cover with a small piece of twill tape to soften the edge. If using wider boning, adjust the stitching to accommodate the larger size.

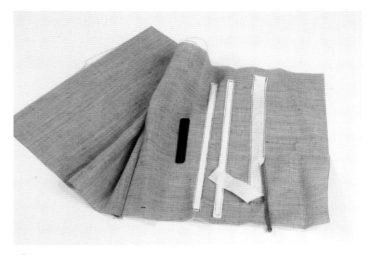

Selecting a Tape Boning Channel

1. Creating a boning channel from a tape eliminates additional bulk across the entire piece of fabric. Additionally, the channel can be placed on the fashion side of the fabric for interest and as a design detail made from an array of fabrics and colors.

2. Cotton twill tapes are ideal for a boning channel because they're sturdy. They come in a variety of colors and can be dyed if necessary; however, matching fashion fabrics make nice visible channels if they're not too delicate. Apply interfacing to the fabric if necessary.

3. Select a tape that's slightly wider than your boning. There should be enough room to stitch it to the fabric and allow for inserting the boning.

4. On the inside or outside of the garment, carefully mark and measure the boning channel locations using chalk and a ruler. Place the tape down and pin in place with appliqué pins.

5. Basting is optional. Stitch next to the edge of the tape from top to bottom of the seam or from edge to edge if placed in partial seams. Test the width and adjust slightly if necessary. Remove pins and insert boning.

FRENCH SEAM

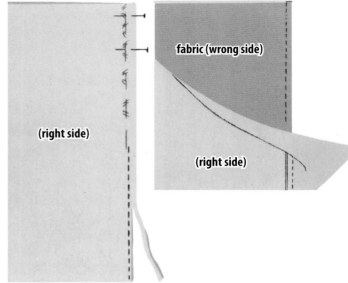

1. With the wrong sides together, align the seam lines of the two pieces of fabric to be seamed and pin.
2. Baste on the seam line. Remove the pins and any tailor tacks.
3. Machine stitch ¼″ (0.6 cm) outside the seam line. Remove the basting.
4. Trim the seam allowances to within ¼″ (0.6 cm) of the stitching.
5. Fold the seamed fabric over so the wrong sides are out.
6. Roll the seamed edge between your fingers to bring the stitching to the edge. Press.
7. With the fabric still folded wrong sides out, machine stitch along the seam line, making sure to enclose the raw edges.
8. Open the fabric wrong side up and press the seam flat to one side.

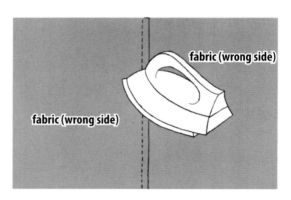

SELF-BOUND FRENCH SEAM

1. To make a French seam on an outside edge between two layers of sheer fabric that aren't interfaced, start by following Steps 1–7 for making a French seam.
2. Refold the seamed fabric so the wrong sides are together and the French seam is between two layers of fabric.
3. Roll the seamed edge between your fingers to bring the stitching to the edge.
4. Using a pressing cloth, press the seam.
5. Finish the garment by following your pattern instructions.

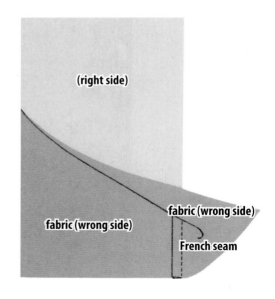

QUILTED SEAMS

Quilting has been around for as long as anyone can remember, so making a quilted garment seems like a natural combination of the quilting technique with fashion. Quilted garment styles span from the crafty aesthetic seen in a whimsical vest or colorful accessory, or very fashion forward styles, like the Quilted Reversible Coat (page 209). The quilted garment is meant to feature the layering and pattern of the cut fabric pieces. Patterns and silhouettes with simple shapes and lines work best, but quilting can also be applied to targeted areas like the lining of a wedding gown bodice, it can be applied to strategic areas of a garment such as the pockets and sleeves, or all over.

Quilting traditionally features cotton fabrics, but you're not limited to a single fabric type in a quilted fashion garment. Silks, wool, and suiting fabrics make beautiful garments when combined with quilted seams and panels. Additionally, pre-quilted fabrics and panels are available to simplify the process. The charm of using an actual quilt top that may be a family heirloom adds the sentimental and historical element, making your garment even more special. When using antique or heirloom quit tops, make sure the material is void of stains, wear, or worn areas, and that the sentimental value isn't so high that you would want to select something different.

A PATCHWORK OF STRIPS

Cutting the Strips of Fabric (A)

1. Press the fabric you plan to use.
2. If both selvages are intact, straighten the cut edges of the fabric in the following fashion: place the fabric on a flat surface and lay an L-shaped square on one corner with the short edge of the square aligned with the selvage. Draw a line with a chalk pencil or lead pencil along the long edge of the square—at right angles to the selvage and as close to the original cut edge as possible. Moving the square as you go, continue the line across the fabric to the opposite selvage. Trim the fabric along this line.
3. If only one selvage is intact, straighten the two cut edges that adjoin it as described in Step 2. The remaining edge may be left as is, unless you plan to use it as a marking guide for patches. In that case, draw a line between the two straightened edges at right angles to both of them and as close to the outside of the fabric as possible. Trim along this line.
4. If both selvages have been removed, draw a pencil square on the fabric close to the outside edges and parallel to the grain of the fabric. Be sure that the lines meet at right angles. Trim along the lines.
5. Decide what size you want the finished strips to be and add ½″ (1.3 cm) to both the length and width to provide for ¼″ (0.6 cm) seam allowances all around.
6. With the fabric wrong side up, mark off the length or width for each strip you will need along the edges on opposite sides of the fabric.
7. Draw a line between each pair of marks and cut out the strips along the lines.
8. Repeat Steps 1–7 for each piece of fabric you're using.

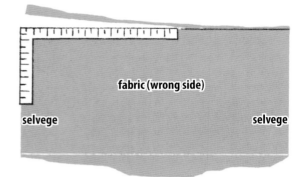

fabric (wrong side)

selvege selvege

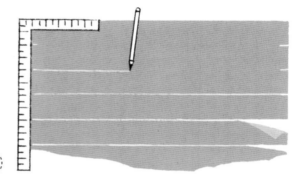

(A)

Add a creative twist and some quilting skills by cutting designs in various popular quilting styles. Sew them together prior to cutting and sewing the basic patchwork strip. In this example, an additional triangular shape was cut before sewing into rows.

Joining the Strips of Fabric (B)

9. With the fabric wrong side down, arrange the strips attractively side by side into a row of the size you want.
10. Starting at one end of the row, turn the second strip wrong side up over the first strip.
11. Align the strips and insert pins, first at the corners and then at 4″ (10.2 cm) intervals along the top edges.
12. If the strips are long or the fabric is slippery, baste ³⁄₁₆″ (0.5 cm) inch in from the edge and remove the pins.
13. Stitch the strips together by machine or by hand, leaving a ¼″ (0.6 cm) seam allowance. To sew them by hand, use a small running stitch, ending with a few backstitches, and cut off the thread. Remove the pins or basting. Spread the strips flat, wrong side up, and press the seam allowances toward the first strip.
14. Turn the third strip in the row wrong side up on top of the second strip. Align the edge of the third strip with the unsewn edge of the second one. Pin, baste, and stitch the strips together, following the directions in Steps 11–13. Press the seam allowances toward the first strip.
15. Continue joining the strips in the same manner, pressing all the seam allowances in the same direction, until your patchwork is complete.

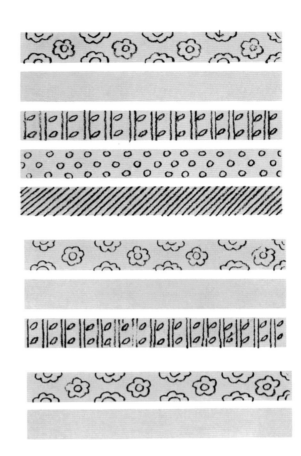

PIECING BY A GRID

Cutting Out the Patches (A)

1. Preshrink any new fabrics and clean any remnants to be used. Press. Determine the size of the patches, adding ½″ (1.3 cm) to the length and width for a ¼″ (0.6 cm) seam allowance.
2. Place one piece of fabric wrong side up. Follow a lengthwise and crosswise grain to draw lines the length and width of the scrap. The lines should be at right angles to each other, intersecting near one corner.
3. Draw a grid on the fabric, making its rectangles the length and width determined in Step 1.
4. Place two other fabrics, wrong side up, under the marked fabric. Align the grains.
5. Pin the fabrics together, being careful not to pin on the grid lines.
6. Cut through all fabric thicknesses along the lines in one direction, making strips. Cut the strips into patches. Remove the pins.
7. If using more than three fabrics for piecing, mark and cut the remaining fabrics by repeating Steps 2–6.

fabric (wrong side)

B

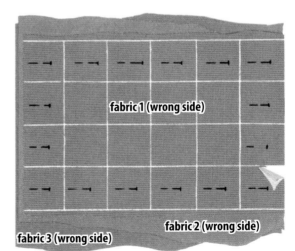

fabric 1 (wrong side)

fabric 3 (wrong side)   fabric 2 (wrong side)

A

Arranging the Patches on the Pattern (B)

8. On the pattern piece, such as the jacket front pattern shown here, position the patches in a row across the widest part of the pattern. Arrange the patches in the order you prefer, overlapping each piece ½″ (1.3 cm) to determine the number of patches required for the row.
9. Repeat Step 8 until the pattern piece is covered. Overlap each adjacent row ½″ (1.3 cm).
10. Check the total effect of your arrangement, rearranging or interchanging patches as desired.
11. Write numbers with chalk on an end patch of each row.

Joining the Patches into a Strip (C)

12. Starting at one end of row 1, pin together the first two patches, wrong sides out, aligning the edges to be joined.
13. Machine stitch ¼″ (0.6 cm) from the edge. Remove the pins.
14. Continue to piece together all the patches of row 1 in the same manner.
15. Press open the seams.
16. Make the second strip from the patches in row 2 repeating Steps 12–15.

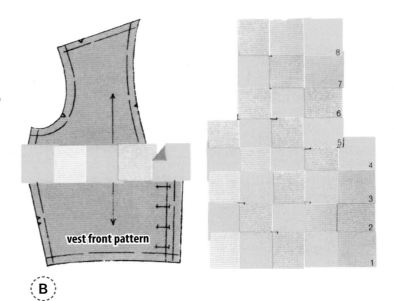

vest front pattern

B

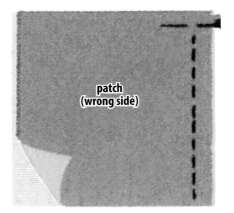

patch (wrong side)

C

Joining the Strips into Patchwork Fabric (D)

17. Place strips 1 and 2 together, wrong sides out, aligning the edges to be joined and matching the seams carefully. Pin at each seam and at the corners.
18. Baste ³⁄₁₆″ (0.5 cm) from the edge. Remove the pins.
19. Machine stitch ¼″ (0.6 cm) from the edge. Remove the basting.
20. Press open the seam, then turn the piece over and press on the other side.
21. Join row 3 of the patches into a strip by repeating Steps 12–15. Then, attach strip 3 to strip 2, following Steps 17–20. Repeat these steps to complete the patchwork fabric.
22. Check the pattern against the patchwork fabric to be sure the fabric is large enough to accommodate the pattern.
23. Repeat Steps 8–22 to make patchwork fabric for any remaining pattern pieces. If you need two patchwork fabric pieces to cut out a pattern, such as the vest front pattern here, flop the pattern before you make the second piece.

Cutting Out the Pattern (E)

24. If the pattern piece is designed to be cut from a single thickness of fabric, cut as you would any fabric. For pattern pieces designed to be cut from a double thickness, place the two patchwork pieces together, wrong sides out. Match the seams. Pin the fabrics together near the edges.
25. Place the pinned-together fabrics on a flat surface. Position the pattern over it, aligning the grain line arrow with the nearest parallel seaming. If the pattern has buttonhole markings, shift the pattern up or down to avoid placing the markings on thick seam allowances. Pin. Cut along the pattern.
26. Finish the garment according to the pattern instructions.

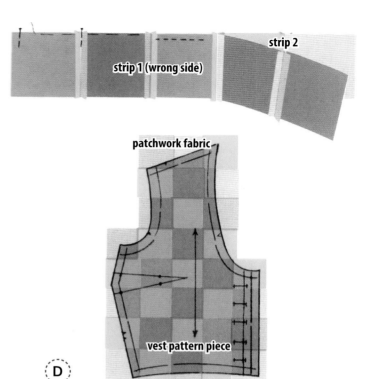

strip 1 (wrong side)   strip 2

patchwork fabric

vest pattern piece

(D)

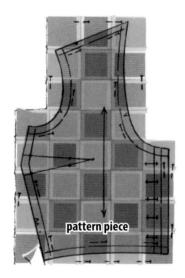

pattern piece

(E)

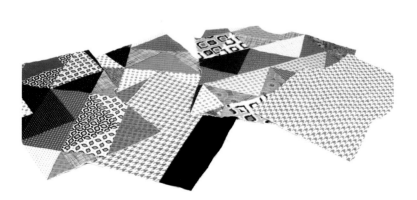

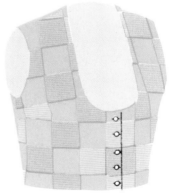

ASSEMBLING A QUILTED GARMENT

Dividing the Pattern (A)

1. Draw the design you want for the patchwork on the appropriate patterns, avoiding buttonholes and dart markings. The straighter the lines, the easier it will be to sew the fabrics together.
2. Number each pattern segment.
3. Draw grain line arrows on all segments.
4. Cut the pattern segments apart along the lines drawn in Step 1.
5. Pin the pattern segments to paper along the cut edges.
6. Add ⅝" (1.6 cm) seam allowances to the edges.
7. Trim away the excess paper along the newly drawn seam allowances.

Cutting and Marking the Fabrics (B)

8. Pin each pattern segment to the fabric selected for it, making sure to align the grain line arrows with the grain of selvage edges. Cut out the segments.
9. Using a tracing wheel and dressmaker's carbon paper, transfer the pattern markings onto the fabrics. Do not remove the patterns.
10. Cut and mark any patterns that have not been divided into segments.

Assembling the Pattern Parts into the Original Pattern Piece (C)

11. Arrange the pattern segments—still pinned to the fabrics, in the order of the original pattern—following the identifying numbers you wrote in Step 2. Remove the pattern segments.
12. Pin together two fabric segments, wrong sides out, aligning the edges to be joined.
13. Baste ½" (1.3 cm) from the edge. Remove the pins.
14. Machine stitch on the seam line. Remove the basting.
15. Trim the seam allowances to ½" (1.3 cm).
16. When the fabric segments have been sewn together, press the seams open.
17. Repeat Steps 12–16 to sew the remaining fabric segments together.
18. Finish making the garment, following the pattern instructions.

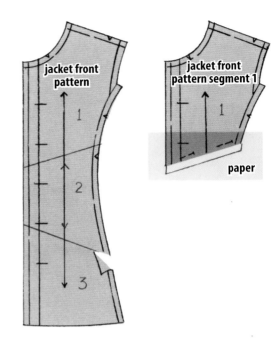

jacket front pattern

jacket front pattern segment 1

paper

A

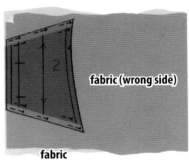

fabric (wrong side)

fabric

B

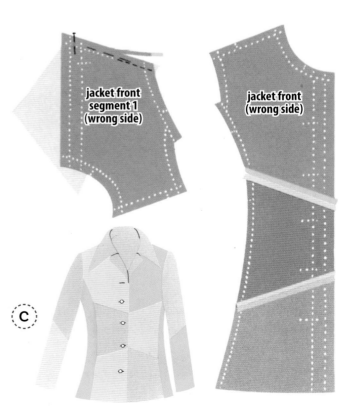

jacket front segment 1 (wrong side)

jacket front (wrong side)

C

QUILTING A GARMENT

Preparing to Quilt (A)

1. Use your pattern pieces to cut the batting interlining and muslin backing pieces you will need to quilt the garment. Leave a 1″ (2.5 cm) seam allowance to allow for the contraction that will occur as you quilt.

> **Alternate:** Cut a rectangle larger than the pattern design and trim away the excess after quilting.

2. Cut out the garment pieces as usual, but don't transfer the pattern markings.
3. Place one garment section on a flat surface, wrong side down.
4. Using a ruler and pencil, draw quilting lines to create the design you desire. If the garment section has been pieced—such as the jacket front shown here—you can use the piecing seams as quilting lines, and space other lines parallel to them.
5. Plan quilting lines to avoid buttonholes. Check against the pattern and correct lines as necessary.

Assembling the Garment, Interlining, and Backing Pieces (B)

6. Place the backing piece right side down on a flat surface.
7. Center the interlining on top of the backing, smoothing out any bumps or wrinkles.
8. Position the garment section wrong side down on the interlining, aligning the edges.
9. Pin the three layers together, placing some pins within the body of the garment, as well as around the edges.
10. Baste the layers together, starting from an edge near the middle of the section and stitching to the opposite edge. Sew parallel to, but not on, a quilting line.
11. Make many lines of basting across different parts of the section to prevent the layers from shifting.
12. Baste ½″ (1.3 cm) from all edges. Remove the pins. If quilting by hand, skip to Section D.

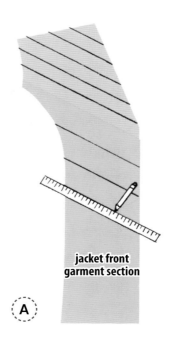

jacket front garment section

(A)

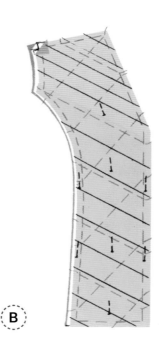

(B)

Quilting by Machine (C)

13. Thread your sewing machine with mercerized cotton or polyester-coated cotton thread and set the gauge at eight to ten stitches to the inch. Test the tension on scraps of materials.

14. Starting at the center quilting line, or the piecing seam near the center, machine stitch along the line from one edge of the garment section to the other. As you stitch, press down the layers on each side of the needle, pulling the garment fabric somewhat to the sides to keep the fabric from slipping.

15. Stitch the rest of the quilting lines, working progressively on adjacent lines. If the quilting lines are on the bias, sew in alternating directions (arrows) to prevent the piece from stretching.

16. Remove the basting made in Steps 10 and 11. Leave the basting along the edges until the garment is assembled. Skip to marking and trimming the quilted garment section.

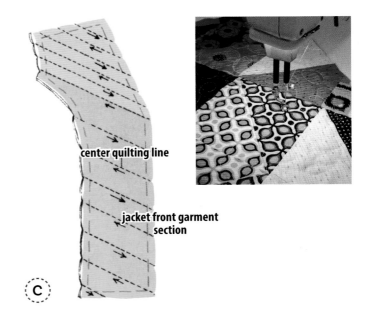

center quilting line

jacket front garment section

C

Quilting by Hand (D)

17. Center the quilting piece inside an embroidery hoop that has an adjustable screw. Tighten the hoop.

18. Thread your needle with quilting thread, or mercerized cotton thread coated with beeswax. Knot the thread.

19. Insert the needle ½″ (1.3 cm) from one end of the center quilting line; make two or three small running stitches (page 195) through all layers, then pull the needle through. As you sew, flatten the fabric just ahead of the stitches with your thumb.

20. Repeat along the quilting line, making five to eight stitches to the inch.

21. If the hoop is wider than the fabric so that the ends of a line of quilting are inside it, unclamped, go over the stitching with your fingers on a flat surface to keep the thread from puckering the fabric.

22. End the stitches with a fastening stitch (page 243), ½″ (1.3 cm) from the edge.

23. Working progressively on adjacent lines, stitch all lines in the same way. Remove the hoop and bastings made in Steps 10 and 11.

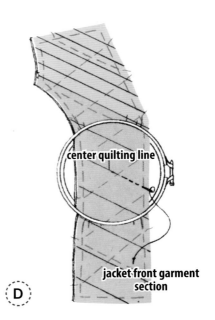

center quilting line

jacket front garment section

D

Marking and Trimming the Quilted Garment Section (E)

24. Place the quilted garment section backing side up.

25. Position the pattern piece on it, matching the edges. Pin.

26. Trim the excess seam allowances along the pattern cutting lines.

27. Transfer the seam lines to the backing, using dressmaker's carbon paper and a tracing wheel. Remove the pattern.

28. To quilt other garment sections, repeat Steps 1–27.

Assembling the Quilted Garment Sections (F)

29. Pin, baste, and machine stitch the seams. Finish the seams by following the instructions for joining unlined garment sections with a decorative enclosed seam with this addition: after the seam is trimmed, remove the interlining in the seam with small scissors to make the seam less puffy. Remove all the basting.

30. Finish the edges of the garment with single bias binding (pages 68–69).

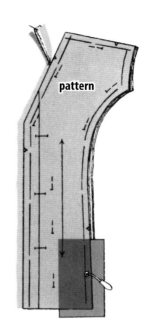

E

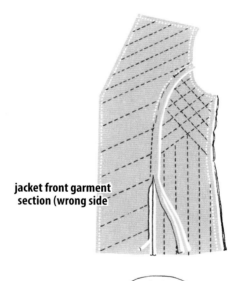

jacket front garment section (wrong side

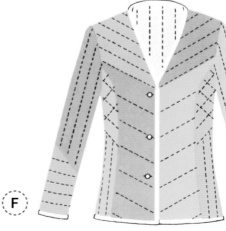

F

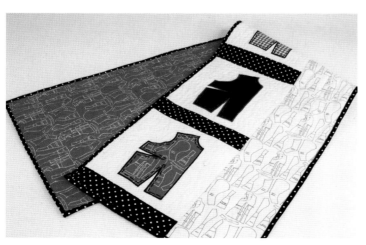

Take your scraps or coordinating fabric and make a fun fashion bodice table runner for your sewing room. Pattern available on www.designerjoi.com.

CHAPTER 5

FABRIC MASTERY

Choosing the correct fabric for your project is just as important as using the right tools. When choosing your fabric, consider the pattern you're using, how it should fit, how you want your garment to look, and select a fabric that will match those three elements. Hold your fabric against the dress form to see how it drapes. Is it bulky? Is it drapey? Is it structured? Will it be flattering? Is the weight appropriate for your project?

A discreet hem on a fine fabric will elevate the look and quality of your clothing with professional-looking results. A hand rolled hem, for example, is barely visible on the edge of a skirt or sleeve of a chiffon jacket. This technique may take more time than a machine stitch but is well worth the effort. A more decorative version is the hand overcast shell stitch (page 128), and more elegant still is finishing off the edges with a lace border. Once you have a fabric selected, the joy of sewing is when you can pair a flattering sewing technique with a beautiful fabric and enjoy the mastery of sewing.

SEWING DELICATE FABRICS

Sheer, delicate-surfaced, and soft knit fabrics require more care when handling due to their fabric characteristics. A slippery surface, or one that may snag easily, can skew the shape of the pattern when cutting if not careful. Delicate fabrics should not be folded to cut; instead, make a duplicate pattern piece so that it's possible to cut out garment sections from a single layer. Another tip is to thread baste around the pattern and then cut the pieces out to prevent shifting. For see-through fabrics that must be underlined or fabrics that you don't want to mark, the underlining layer can hold all the markings and serve as a cutting guide. Finally, save the scraps from your delicate fabrics. They serve as wonderful self-bias fabric strips to bind and finish off necklines, zipper tapes, and seam allowances. Don't forget to select a delicate needle size and stitch length and width to prevent snagging when hand or machine sewing for the best sewing results. It's easy to prevent any issues and protect the integrity of the fabric with a few simple techniques that ensure successful results.

DELICATE FABRICS

FABRIC TYPE	SHOPPING SUGGESTIONS	CUTTING, MARKING, BASTING	SEWING	CLEANING AND PRESSING
SHEERS AND EMBROIDERED SHEERS Batiste, chiffon, gauze, georgette, handkerchief linen, marquisette, organdy, organza, voile	These lightweight, transparent fabrics come in natural fibers, such as cotton, silk, or linen, as well as in synthetics, like nylon, rayon, or polyester. Chiffon or georgette prove especially slippery to handle, so buy a little extra yardage to provide for wider seam allowances and possible cutting errors. Select China or synthetic silk for smooth linings and underlinings; substitute a binding of garment fabric for conventional facings.	Prepare duplicates of pattern pieces designed to be cut from folded fabric, then lay out and cut the sheer in a single layer. When attaching pattern pieces to the fabric, insert silk pins in the seam allowances at frequent intervals. Provide extra-wide 1" (2.5 cm) seam allowances. Indicate stitching lines and other pattern markings with tailor tacks. Use silk thread for the tailor tacks and bastings and remove both as quickly as possible to avoid marking the fabric permanently.	Machine stitch at 12 to 15 stitches to the inch, using a size 9 or 11 needle and choosing silk thread for silk, and dual duty or cotton thread for other fibers. Place tissue paper beneath the fabric to prevent it from shifting or snagging in the machine; gently tear away the paper after finishing each seam. Allow chiffon, which stretches, to hang into its final shape for 24 hours before hemming the garment.	Check the fabric label to determine the recommended pressing and cleaning methods. Most sheers must be dry cleaned, but some cottons and synthetics may be hand washed. All can be pressed safely; before pressing, test a fabric swatch. Set embroidered sheers face down on a terry towel for pressing to protect them from flattening.
DELICATE SURFACES Charmeuse, China silk, silk broadcloth, crepe de Chine, moiré, paduasoy, pongee, satin, satin crepe, taffeta	These lightweight, translucent, or opaque fabrics come in silk, cotton, and a wide range of synthetics. With slippery China silk, crepe de Chine, and satin crepe, provide for wider seam allowances and possible cutting errors by buying a little extra yardage. With satins, moirés, taffetas, and other shiny fabrics, check to see if the sheen follows a distinct direction; if so, buy the yardage recommended for fabrics with nap.	For fabrics with sheen direction, follow the layout recommended for napped fabrics. Insert silk pins in the seam allowances to attach pattern pieces to the fabric. Provide extra-wide 1" (2.5 cm) seam allowances on slippery China silk, crepe de Chine, and satin crepe. Indicate stitching lines and other pattern markings with tailor tacks. Use silk thread for marking and basting. If the garment is underlined, make all markings on the underlining fabric.	Machine stitch at 12 to 15 stitches to the inch, using a size 9 or 11 needle and choosing silk thread for silk, and dual duty or cotton thread for other fibers. Use an even feed foot attachment to prevent puckering or stretch the fabric taut while stitching it.	Check the fabric label to determine the recommended pressing and cleaning methods. Most delicately surfaced materials must be dry cleaned. Nearly all of them can be pressed safely with a cool, dry iron and light pressure; before pressing, test a fabric swatch. Place a pressing cloth over the fabric and use brown paper under seams to avoid marking the garment.
FINE KNITS Jersey, lightweight double knits, lightweight matte jersey, tricot	These lightweight, translucent, or opaque fabrics come in cotton, silk, and wool as well as in such synthetics as rayon, polyester, or nylon. When a knit has a napped surface, buy the yardage recommended for fabrics with nap. For washable finished garments, cotton knits must be preshrunk by being immersed in cool water and then thoroughly dried.	For knits with napped surfaces, follow the layout recommended for nap fabrics. Insert ballpoint pins in the seam allowances to attach pattern pieces to the fabric. Transfer pattern markings with a smooth-edged tracing wheel and dressmaker's carbon paper. Cut with sharp knit scissors, leaving extra-wide 1" (2.5 cm) seam allowances wherever possible.	Machine stitch at 12 to 15 stitches to the inch, using a size 11 or 14 ballpoint needle, dual duty thread, and a very fine zigzag stitch. Stretch the fabric taut while stitching. Sew straight seam binding across the shoulders and around the waistline of the garment to prevent stretching in these areas.	Check the fabric label to determine the recommended pressing and cleaning methods. Most fine knit fabrics must be dry cleaned, but can be pressed safely. Before pressing, test a swatch of fabric.
METALLICS AND SEQUINED SURFACES	Metal or metalized plastic threads and metal or plastic sequins may be woven through or applied to all kinds of natural and synthetic sheers, delicately surfaced fabric, fine knits, and laces. On both metallic and sequined surfaces, the sheen of the threads and sequins follows a distinct direction; purchase the extra amount of yardage recommended for fabrics with nap in order to be able to lay out all the garment pieces in the sheen direction. Choose a matching plain fabric for lining. Satin cording can be substituted for facings to finish of edges at the neckline and armholes.	Make duplicates of all pattern pieces designed to be cut from folded fabric, then lay out and put the metallic or sequined fabric in a single layer. Follow the layout recommended for nap fabrics. Insert ballpoint or silk pins—depending on the basic fabric—to attach pattern pieces to the fabric. Pin under the sequins, not through them. Mark straight seam lines with thread tracing, indicate other pattern markings with tailor tacks. Cut with a sharpened pair of old shears—metallic threads and sequins will dull blades and may eventually ruin shears.	Use the pins, needles, and thread that are recommended for sewing the base fabric under the chart entries for sheers, delicate surfaces, and fine knits (above). Metallic threads and sequins may dull needles; change them as they become dull. If sequins break in the seams, pull them off and attach new sequins.	Check the fabric label to determine the recommended pressing and cleaning methods. Most metallic or sequin surfaced fabrics must be dry cleaned, but can be pressed safely wrong side up with a cool, dry iron and pressing cloth. Before pressing, test a fabric swatch. Steam may discolor and even melt some metallics.

Straightening the Edges of Fabric (A)

1. Spread the fabric wrong side up on a flat surface.
2. To straighten the crosswise edges of the fabric, start by placing an L-shaped square near one crosswise edge. Align one side of the square with a selvage edge.
3. Draw a chalk line along the other side of the square so the line is at a right angle to the salvage.
4. Cut along the chalk line from one selvage to the other.
5. Repeat at the opposite end of the fabric.

Making a Duplicate Pattern Piece (B)

6. Lay a piece of tracing paper that's large enough to accommodate the pattern piece to be copied on a firm, flat surface. If necessary, tape together sheets of tracing paper.
7. Lay a sheet of dressmaker's carbon paper, carbon side down, over the tracing paper. If the carbon is smaller than the pattern piece, place it at one end.
8. Lay the pattern piece, marked side up over the carbon paper, and pin the three together or use pattern weights to secure.
9. Using a smooth-edged tracing wheel, outline the entire pattern piece and trace over all the notches, seam line, and other markings. Re-pin the carbon paper to the other end and trace any remaining markings.
10. Remove the original pattern piece and carbon paper. Cut out the duplicate pattern piece and add any other pattern markings.
11. If the original pattern was designed to be placed on the fold of the fabric, tape the duplicate to the original along the fold and cut your fabric in a single layer.

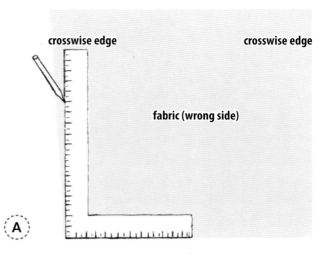

crosswise edge   crosswise edge

fabric (wrong side)

(A)

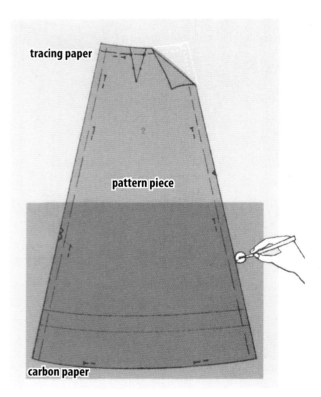

tracing paper

pattern piece

carbon paper

(B)

USE UNDERLINING AS THE PATTERN FOR CUTTING SLIPPERY FABRICS

Cutting the Fabric (A)

1. Before cutting and marking your fashion fabric pieces, cut out the underlining pieces from a fabric suitable for an inner underlining layer. Silk organza, fine broadcloth, cotton voile, and ultra-fine interfacing are ideal choices. Use all pattern pieces except those for facings.

2. Place all markings on the underlining pieces.

3. Lay a single layer of garment fabric wrong side up on a flat surface. If the fabric is longer than your work surface, fold up the extra fabric so it won't hang over the edge and prevent it from slipping while you work.

4. Arrange as many pieces of the underlining—marked side up—as can fit on the fabric. Leave approximately 2″ (5.1 cm) between each piece. Match the grain directions of the underlining and the fabric; refer to the grainline arrows on the pattern pieces as necessary. Pin at 2″ (5.1 cm) intervals within the seam allowance.

5. Cut out the garment pieces 1″ (2.5 cm) beyond the edge of the underlining pieces.

6. Repeat Steps 3–5 to cut any remaining pieces.

Basting the Underlining to the Garment Pieces (B)

7. Working on one garment piece at a time, remove the pins. Smooth the fabric and re-pin.

8. Starting at the center of the piece, run parallel rows of long, hand basting stitches down the length of the piece. To eliminate puckers and wrinkles, smooth the fabric toward the outside edges as you sew.

9. Baste around the edges of the underlining, just outside any seam lines. As you baste, smooth the layers of fabric outward from the basting made in the previous step. Don't stitch around the corners; instead, begin each line at a right angle to the last one basted. Remove the pins.

10. Check to be sure both the underlining and the garment fabric are smooth. If either layer wrinkles, clip nearby basting and re-baste.

11. Trim the garment fabric even with the edge of the underlining.

12. Treat the basted layers as one when you stitch the garment together. Don't remove the bastings until the garment is complete.

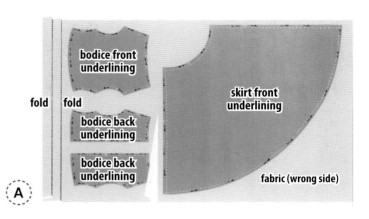

A — bodice front underlining, fold, fold, bodice back underlining, bodice back underlining, skirt front underlining, fabric (wrong side)

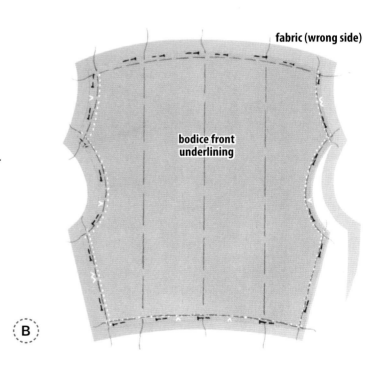

B — fabric (wrong side), bodice front underlining

DESIGNER TIP

If using a fusible interfacing—when you don't need an underlining—mark the interfacing with the pattern markings, such as dart placement and other details, thus avoiding having to mark your delicate fabric.

DESIGN APPLICATION:

When sewing layered garments, you can baste the layers in the same way to create precise placement and to smooth the edges as you sew smaller sections.

HAND-ROLLED NARROW HEM

Marking the Hemline (A)

1. Mark the hemline by placing pins or chalk mark at desired finished length.

> **Tip:** Measure from the floor up for accuracy. Avoid measuring from the waist down, otherwise the hem may hang uneven. Unevenness may occur due to the contour of the body, whereas from the floor up provides correct even length all the way around.

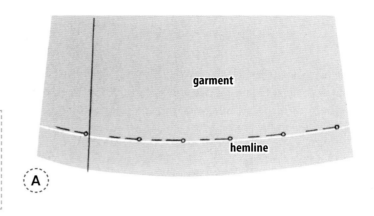

2. Connect the markings with a chalk line all around the edge of the garment. Remove any pins.

Preparing the Hem (B)

3. **A.** If working with a fabric that ravels, make a row of machine stitching ¼″ (0.6 cm) below the hemline marked in the previous step. Trim off the garment edge close to the machine stitching.
B. On a non-raveling fabric, do not stitch; simply trim off the garment edge ¼″ (0.6 cm) below the hemline marking.

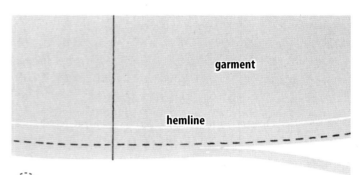

Sewing the Hem (C)

4. To sew the hem with a rolled-hem stitch, start by turning the garment wrong side out. Turn up the hem edge of the garment ⅛″ (3.2 mm).

5. Using a knotted thread, make a horizontal stitch ¼″ (0.6 cm) long in the hem just inside the top of the fold. Be careful not to catch the front of the garment.

6. Pick up one or two threads of the garment fabric directly below the raw edge of the hem and on a line with the stitch made in the previous step.

7. Take another horizontal stitch in the hem just below the top of the fold, ¹⁄₁₆″ (1.6 mm) from the stitch made in Step 5.

8. After repeating Steps 6 and 7 for about 1″ (2.5 cm) hold the sewn section of the hem securely, and gently but firmly pull the thread taut with your other hand. The hem will roll over on itself, and the stitches will disappear.

9. Continue the rolled-hem stitches, pulling the thread taut every inch. End with a fastening stitch (page 243) hidden in the fold.

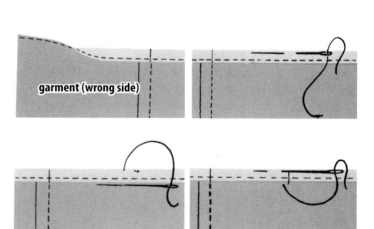
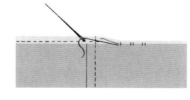

MACHINE-STITCHED NARROW HEM

Preparing the Hem (A)

1. Mark the hemline by placing pins or chalk mark at desired finished length.

> **Tip:** Measure from the floor up for accuracy. Avoid measuring from the waist down, otherwise the hem may hang uneven. Unevenness may occur due to the contour of the body, whereas from the floor up provides correct even length all the way around.

2. Setting your machine at a stitch length of 20 stitches to the inch or finer, make a row of machine stitches just below the hemline markings.

Sewing the Hem (B)

3. Turn the garment wrong side out. Turn up the hem along the machine-stitched hemline.
4. Trim the raw hem edge as close to the machine stitching as possible.
5. Next, turn the hem edge up on the row of stitching. Using the same fine stitch length used in Step 2, run a line of machine stitching, or narrow zigzag stitches, as close as possible to the folded hem edge.

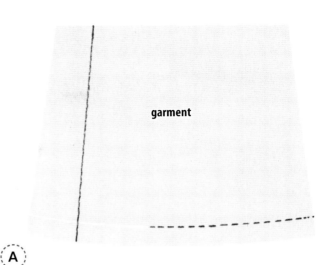

A

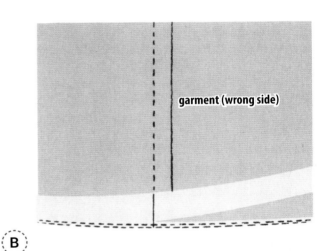

B

OVERCAST SHELL HEM

Turning up the Hem (A)

1. Mark the hemline, following the instructions for the hand-rolled hem.
2. Turn the garment wrong side out. Turn up the hem edge ⅛″ (3.2 mm) and press it flat.
3. Turn up the hem again along the hemline; press.

Sewing the Hem (B)

4. Using a knotted double thread, insert the needle in the garment fabric from the wrong side. Make sure to insert it just below the hem so the knot will be concealed inside the hem. Pull the needle through.
5. Bring the needle over the hem to the wrong side and insert it at the inside folded hem edge ¼″ (0.6 cm) from the point that it was inserted in Step 4. Go through all thicknesses of fabric, but don't pull the needle through.
6. Angle the needle and bring the tip over the top of the hem. Insert it—again at the inside folded hem edge— ¼″(0.6 cm) from the previous stitch. It will pull the fabric down, creating a scalloped effect. Don't pull the needle all the way through the fabric.
7. Repeat Step 6 one or two times, weaving the needle over and then back into the hem.
8. Pull the needle through the fabric to complete the first series of stitches. You're now ready to begin the next series of stitches.
9. Continue to repeat Steps 5–8, pulling the stitches tight after each series of stitches, until you have formed a shell-shaped scallop around the hem edge. End with a fastening stitch (page 243) hidden in the fold.

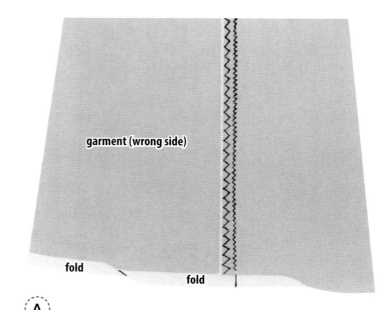

garment (wrong side)

fold   fold

A

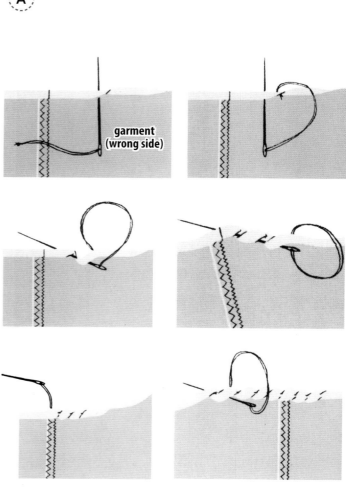

garment (wrong side)

B

SEWING LACE

ALL ABOUT LACE

The filigrees and florals that give lace its charm also add some challenges to layout and cutting. Laces feature some of the most ingenious seams of all. The pieces are overlapped and sewed along the lace design so that, when excess fabric has been trimmed away, not even the sharpest eye can detect the stitching. This does take some careful planning and positioning, so the patterns match precisely. Lace patterns and embroidered fabrics both lend themselves to pattern layouts arranged lengthwise and crosswise. The choice depends on the width of material, the direction of design and the selvage edges which may feature scallops and additional decorative elements. Whatever direction the pattern arrangement takes, all pattern pieces should be laid out on a single thickness of fabric. To do this, duplicates

(page 94) should be made of those pieces normally placed on a double thickness of fabric. These duplicates make it possible to position each pattern piece so that the design of the fabric will fall attractively on the garment as it is sewn together.

Some general tips to follow when sewing lace include eliminating the center front or back seam whenever possible, joining pieces with an invisible seam, and cutting outside of the seam allowance leaving excess for matching and overlapping any motifs. When marking lace pieces, mark straight hemlines and other straight pattern pieces with thread tracing and all other markings with tailor tacks.

FABRIC TYPE	SHOPPING SUGGESTIONS	CUTTING, MARKING, BASTING	SEWING	CLEANING AND PRESSING
LACE YARDAGE AND TRIMMING	Lightweight laces may be made from cotton, linen, fine wool, silk, or synthetics, such as rayon, nylon, or acetate. Lace trimmings are sometimes also embellished with beads, sequins, metallic threads, or ribbons. Lace yardage usually comes in conventional 36–45" (1–1.25 yd) fabric widths, lace trimmings in widths ranging from ¼" (0.6 cm) to several inches. Purchase at least an extra half yard of lace to allow for matching the designs. To determine yardage requirements for lace trimming, pin seam tape around the area to be trimmed and measure its length. Select China or synthetic silk for underlinings.	On richly ornamented lace, pattern pipes can be laid out lengthwise or crosswise; on other laces, follow the conventional lengthwise layout recommended in the pattern. Use silk pins with colored heads—which will stand out against the lace designs— to attach pattern pieces to the fabric or to fasten the trimming in place. Mark straight seam lines with basting stitches; use tailor tacks for other pattern markings. Make tacks and bastings with dual duty or cotton thread.	Fragile laces require hand sewing with a fine needle and silk thread. Others may be machine stitched. Set the machine at 15 to 20 stitches to the inch and use a size 11 or 14 needle with silk, dual duty, or cotton thread, depending on the weight of the lace. For invisible seaming, use a fine zigzag stitch.	Check the label to determine the recommended pressing and cleaning methods. Most lace and lace trimmed garments must be dry cleaned, but can be pressed with a cool iron and light pressure. Before pressing, test a swatch. Place laces with raised designs face down on a terry towel for pressing to protect them from flattening.

CUTTING LACE GARMENTS ON THE CROSSWISE GRAIN

Laying Out the Garment Pieces (A)

1. For each garment piece that will have the scalloped or finished edge of the lace along the hem, determine the desired finished hem length. Mark a new hemline on the pattern piece parallel to the original hemline.
2. Make duplicates (page 94) of all pattern pieces designed to be cut from folded fabric.
3. Wherever possible, eliminate the center-front or the center-back seam by joining the original and duplicate pattern pieces along the seam lines.
4. Spread out the lace fabric wrong side down on a firm flat surface.
5. Loosely arrange the pattern pieces on the fabric so there is at least one repeat of the lace motif plus 1″ (2.5 cm) between the edges of the pattern pieces that are side by side.
6. On the main garment section, make sure the center line is in the middle of a lace motif.
7. If the hemline of the pattern piece is straight, align the hemline with a scalloped or finished edge. If the hem curves less than ¾″ (1.9 cm), the pattern can be laid out the same way.
8. If the hemline curves more than ¾ inch (1.9 cm), align only the center part of the hemline with a scalloped or finished edge.
9. Match the seam lines and the notches. Pin the pattern pieces in place and cut them out, following the directions in Section A (left; Steps 6–9).

> **Tip:** When cutting pieces on the lengthwise grain, loosely cut the pattern pieces leaving at least one design motif and 1″ (2.5 cm) between pattern pieces and the cut edge. Make sure the center line falls in the middle of a motif and the edges are at least 2″ (5.1 cm) inside the edge so the border can be used in the hem and openings.

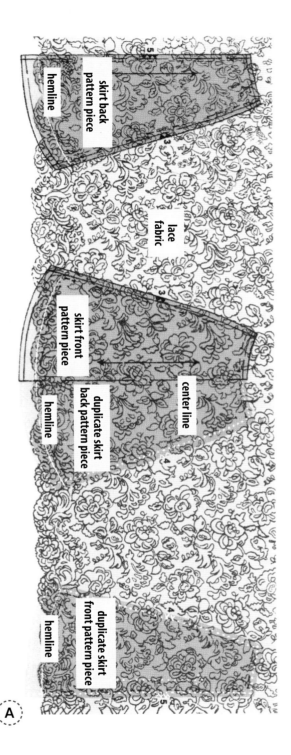

Finishing the Lace Pieces (B)

10. On each pattern piece with a curved hemline, remove the pins from the bottom part of the pattern piece so you can use it as a guide while you're adjusting the hem edge.

11. Cutting along the design motif nearest the scalloped edge of the lace, cut from the side seams across to the point where the hemline on the pattern piece curves away from the scalloped edge.

12. Raise the cut edge so it overlaps the garment section and is aligned with the hemline on the pattern piece. If necessary, make ⅛″ (3.2 mm) clips along the cut edge so the section will lie flat. Pin.

13. Baste the hem in place and remove the pins on the scalloped edge.

14. Re-pin the bottom of the pattern piece to the fabric.

15. Mark the straight seam lines on the garment pieces with hand basting. Mark all other pattern markings with tailor tacks (page 244). Remove the pattern pieces.

16. On each garment piece with a curved basted hem, sew the hem to the garment by making an invisible lace seam (page 133, Steps 4–6). The lace design will not match perfectly.

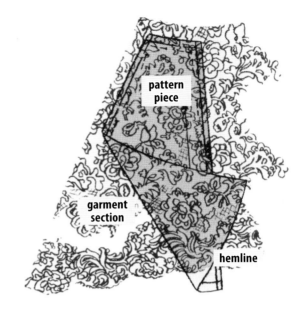

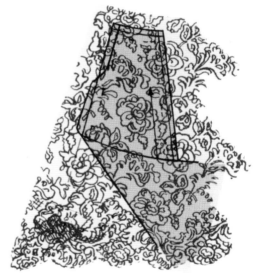

B

INVISIBLE LACE SEAM

1. To cut and mark the lace pieces, follow the instructions on page 131.
2. With the wrong sides down, overlap the edges of the lace pieces to be joined so the thread-traced seam lines and the designs closest to them are perfectly aligned. Pin along the thread-traced seam lines.
3. Baste the pieces together along the seam line and remove the pins.
4. Baste the pieces of lace together again. This time, sew just to one side of the pattern in the design that is closest to the seam line. The basting may cross the seam line.
5. Following the basted edge of the pattern in the design, sew the lace pieces together. To hand sew, use a whipstitch (page 244). To sew by machine, use narrow zigzag stitches and set the machine at 15 to 20 stitches to the inch, depending on the fineness of the lace. The finer the lace, the fewer stitches are needed. Remove the bastings.
6. Cut away both the top and bottom layers of lace close to the stitching, making sure you do not snip the stitches.

ADDING A LACE HEM WITH A CURVED EDGE

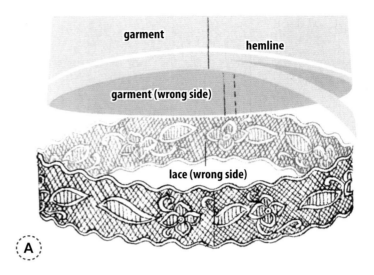

Preparing the Hem and Lace (A)

1. Mark the hemline by making a hand-rolled hem.
2. Trim off the hem ¼″ (0.6 cm) below the hemline.
3. Measure the circumference of the hem along the trimmed edge.
4. Following the instructions for lace seams on page 133, cut a strip of lace and join the ends so you have one continuous circular strip equal to the circumference of the hem measured in Step 3.

Attaching the Lace (B)

5. Turn up the hem along the hemline so the hem is against the outside of the garment. Press the hem flat.
6. Pin the lace over the hem so the upper edge of the lace just conceals the raw hem edge. Pin at 1″ (2.5 cm) intervals and match the lace seam with a garment seam.
7. Sew along the upper edge of the lace, going through all fabric thicknesses. To machine stitch, use a setting of 15 to 20 stitches to the inch. To hand sew, use a prick stitch (page 243). Remove the pins as you sew.

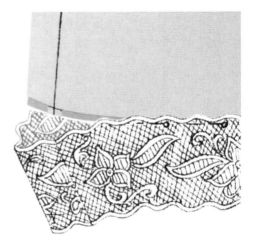

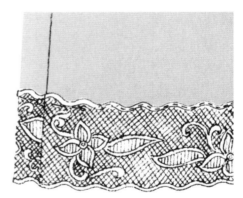

ADDING A LACE HEM WITH A STRAIGHT UPPER EDGE

Attaching the Lace (A)

1. Prepare the hem and the lace strip, following the instructions for the lace hem with a curved upper edge (Steps 1–4).
2. Turn the garment wrong side out. Turn the lace strip right side out and slip it over the hem edge of the garment, wrong sides together.
3. Align the straight edge of the lace with the raw edge of the hem. Pin at 1″ (2.5 cm) intervals. Match the lace seam with a garment seam.
4. Setting your machine at 15 to 20 stitches to the inch, machine stitch along the hemline. Remove the pins as you stitch.
5. Trim the garment seam allowances as close to the stitching as possible.

Finishing the Hem (B)

6. Turn the garment right side out and fold down the lace so that it's away from the garment.
7. Sew along the straight edge of the lace, going through all fabric thicknesses. To machine stitch, use the same fine setting used in Step 4. To hand sew, use a prick stitch.

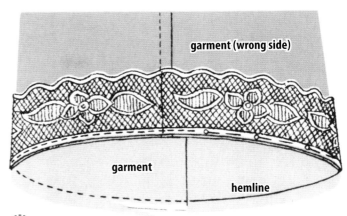

A

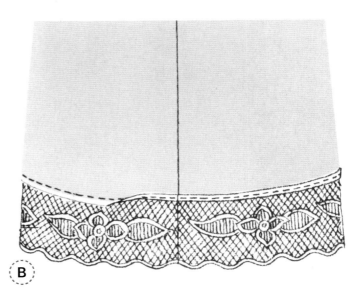

B

HEMMING A LACE GARMENT WITH A LACE BORDER

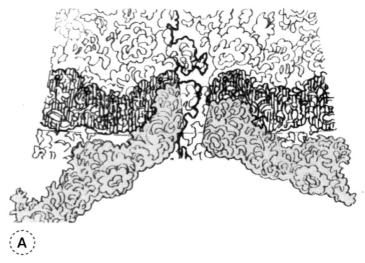

Basting the Border in Position (A)

1. With the garment right side out, align the bottom, scalloped edge of the lace border that was set aside when you cut out the garment with the basted hemline. Pin at 1″ (2.5 cm) intervals, leaving the end of the border free.
2. Baste along the raw upper edge of the border. Remove the pins.

Stitching the Border (B)

3. Join and trim the overlapping ends of the lace, following the instructions for the invisible lace seam on page 133.
4. Finish basting the border to the garment.
5. Stitch the lace border to the garment with a hand stitch or machine zigzag stitch, following the instructions for the invisible seam (page 133, Step 5).

SEWING WOOL AND HEAVY FABRICS

CHOOSING WOOL FABRICS

Wool fabrics fall into the category of natural fibers, and more specifically, natural protein fibers because they have an animal origin. Wool is made up of hair fibers and the breed, type of hair, and hair location affect the fabric characteristics and quality. Any form of animal hair is considered wool, although the most recognized include sheep, goat, camel, and rabbit.

Wool from sheep is the most obvious. The Merino breed is one of the best quality wools used in fine to coarse fabrics including fabric with the same name, Merino Wool, which is often used in coats.

Goat hair provides fibers that are fine in texture and are coveted for their superior luster. The specialty mohair fabric and yarn comes from the Angora goat (different from the Angora rabbit), and the utmost in luxury, cashmere comes from the goat as well.

Angora fibers and wool come from the Angora rabbit. This soft and silky wool is more costly and is often made into luxurious sweaters.

Camel's hair, a soft, tightly woven, lightweight fabric produced from the hair of the Asiatic Bactrian camel, provides a soft and warm coarse hair and is the best of the camel hair fibers. Top qualities—used for fine coats, pants, and skirts—have extremely short, fine naps and are light tan; poor grades have coarser naps and are brownish black.

The properties of a fiber directly affect the characteristics of the fabric it is woven into. Natural protein fibers resist wrinkling due to their microscopic structure that will stretch and spring back naturally. They're hygroscopic, absorbing moisture and comfortable in a cool damp climate but are weaker when wet because they shrink. Natural protein fibers are harmed by dry heat. They are flame resistant and dye well.

Wool fabrics may take on the name of the animal or breed it's derived from, such as Angora, Merino, and cashmere. Other fabrics that are popular in wool or wool blends include:

- **Blanket Cloth:** A thick, tightly woven, medium-to-heavy weight fabric with a deep soft surface nap; best used for a warm, simple garment, such as coats, blankets, and bags. Blanket cloth often comes in large stripes and plaid patterns.
- **Flannel:** A soft, tightly woven fabric with a fine nap, available in light shirt cloth, as well as heavyweight coating. Flannels are also made of cotton and fiber blends: all wool flannel comes chiefly in solid colors, plaids, and stripes. Flannels are a great inner layer to add warmth in garments that require additional heat retention.
- **Gabardine:** A firm, tightly woven twill fabric characterized by closely set diagonal ribs. Very popular for suiting, gabardine comes in light and medium weights in a wide range of colors and may also contain a fiber blend.

- **Melton:** A smooth, heavyweight fabric with a fine, short nap, usually made up in coats and jackets. Melton comes in a wide array of colors.
- **Tweed:** A durable fabric of medium weight that is often twilled or diagonally ribbed, suitable for sportswear only if it is the tightly woven variety. Tweeds often require interfacing or a layer of silk organza to stabilize the weave. Quilting is common in higher end apparel and assembly to stabilize the threads. Tweeds come in many colors and textures, some soft and finely napped like herringbone tweed, others nubby like Harris tweed.

Whatever your wool fabric, consider the characteristics such as drape, weight, texture, feel, and quality, and pair the right wool with your pattern for the best results.

PREPARING AND CUTTING WOOL

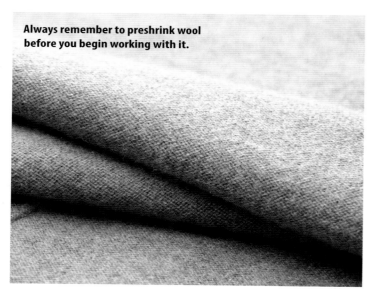

Always remember to preshrink wool before you begin working with it.

Almost all wool has a directional nap, meaning that the fibers flow in a specific direction. Make sure you purchased the amount of fabric recommended for a "with nap" pattern and lay out the pattern on the fabric accordingly. It's a good idea to lay all your pattern pieces out on the fabric prior to cutting. Before starting to cut and sew, pre-shrink all wool by dry cleaning or steam shrinking with your iron. To do this, slowly hover the iron over the fabric while steaming, allowing the fibers a chance to shrink up. If the basic fabric is heavy, use a lightweight fabric for facings and cut out pattern pieces from a single layer of cloth. Transfer pattern markings with a needlepoint tracing wheel and dressmaker's carbon paper, tailor's chalk, or use thread tacks to avoid marking the fabric. Select the correct weight of pin for holding pieces together, such as fine point pins for Angora or medium weight for wool coating.

SEWING WOOL

Mercerized cotton or polyester thread are the best choices for wool. Baste seams either by hand or machine as needed based on the characteristics of your fabric. If you're matching a stripe or a plaid on a coat, then basting will ensure precise placement. A solid color medium weight coat fabric may not require basting. The best needle size for wool is a size 14 to 16, with the machine set for 10 to 12 stitches to the inch. With heavy fabrics, cut away the material inside darts and trim down seams to avoid bulk. Under stitching will help hold facings and edges to the inside. The extra wide seam page 107 is ideal for sewing wool.

CARING FOR WOOL

Most wool fabrics require dry clean only care. This is especially true for complex garments, such as coats and structured trousers. However, with care, most may be cleaned at home. Never place wool in a dryer. Detergents and soaps created specifically for wool fabrics can be used by hand in a sink, bathtub, or delicate cycle in the washing machine. Lay the wet garment to dry on a towel to absorb the moisture. Once the excess moisture has been absorbed by the towel, place the garment flat on a drying rack, and once dry, flip it over to dry the other side. Touch up with an iron if necessary to soften the fabric and remove stiffness. The coil structure of the wool hair fiber is prone to shrinkage especially when wet. Therefore, when wet, wool should never be placed in a dryer. We know dry heat is bad for wool but resist the urge to even tumble dry low—it will shrink. Fabrics, such as twill and other nap fabrics, should be pressed from the wrong side or on the right side with a pressing cloth. Make sure your iron is set to the wool and steam settings. Follow the cleaning instructions on the bolts and on the fabric for the best results with your selected fabric, and always, test the cleaning method on a large fabric swatch.

There are ways to carefully clean wool at home without a trip to the dry cleaners.

Make sure to first test your pattern on sample knit fabric.

SEWING WOOL AND HEAVY FABRICS

Knits are made by locking loops of yarns together rather than weaving them. As a result, they are more flexible than other materials. The degree of stretchability and recovery of a knit varies with the fiber content and the way the loops are joined. Structurally, there are two types of knits, single and double knits. Single knits are constructed by creating a single layer of closely looped yarns, and double knits are made by joining two layers of fabric together. Knits are often created with synthetic fibers or blends, and spandex reinforced knits provide more flexibility and are commonly used in sportswear.

Stitches or the loops run vertically on the front or face of the fabric with smaller horizontal configurations identifying the back. Knits that roll toward the front, such as jersey, have a distinctive front and back. Double knits may look the same front to back, as they don't roll so they may be reversible and are often easier to sew for a beginner.

It's important to note that knits require patterns specifically designed for stretch fabrics, unless the knit is very stable and mimics the characteristics of woven fabrics.

Even then, you should test your pattern in a sample before cutting your fashion fabric. The direction of stretch for a one- or two-way stretch knit has stretch going back and forth or up and down, but not both. Fabrics that are one-way require the stretch to go around the body. A four-way or multidirectional stretch knit has stretch going back and forth, along with up and down. This type of fabric has the ultimate stretch, such as a spandex.

Knits, when made from or blended with natural fibers, should be prewashed to prevent shrinking in the final garment, and a ballpoint or stretch needle should be used when sewing. If your knit has a nap, such as in French terry cloth, use a press cloth when pressing and stabilize seams that may stretch with a stay tape. Flexible stitches are necessary for stretching the garment over the body.

SWEATER KNITS

General Description	Pattern Selection	Fabric Handling
GENERAL DESCRIPTION	Because knits fit more closely than woven fabrics, patterns for them require less ease; the amount of ease needed depends on the stretchiness of the knit to gauge whether it is relatively stable, moderately stretchy, or very stretchy. To judge a pattern's suitability for each knit type, see below. The ease needed at the bustline is generally 1–2" (2.5–5.1 cm) (or as much as 3" or 7.6 cm for firm knits and loose-fitting styles); for the sleeve, 1" (2.5 cm); for the sleeve cap, ¾–1" (1.9–2.5 cm); for the hip, 1–2" (2.5–5.1 cm).	Preshrink fabric by washing or dry cleaning, as specified on the label. Preshrink notions that are not polyester or nylon, except ribbing trims. Nonwoven interfacing needs no preshrinking, but woven interfacing does; the fusible kind should be dried flat, fusible side up. Use a pattern layout for napped fabrics, since knits are directional. Pull the edges of a knitted fabric; if it runs, place the pattern pieces so the runs are hidden in the hem. If the edges curl in cutting, flatten with spray starch.
RELATIVELY STABLE KNITS These fabrics closely resemble woven fabrics in feel. Lengthwise stretch is negligible; crosswise stretch is about 15 to 20 percent. Most double knits fall into this category.	Use patterns suitable for woven fabrics of similar weight, but fit the garment closer to the body. Use standard zipper or button openings, as these fabrics will not stretch enough to slip over hips or head. Pattern styles shaped by darts, as well as by eased seams, are suitable.	Use an L-shaped square to establish a straight crosswise edge. Stay stitch necklines and waistlines with a straight stitch, setting the machine at 10 to 12 stitches to the inch.
MODERATELY STRETCHY KNITS Somewhat less firm than relatively stable knits, these fabrics cling slightly. The crosswise stretch is about 20 to 30 percent; the lengthwise stretch is the same or slightly less.	Patterns suggested for knits are recommended. If standard patterns are used, choose simple styles with a minimum of darts and fitting and purchase patterns a size smaller than usual; eliminate any excess ease when the garment is fitted on the body. These fabrics are sufficiently stretchy for pullover necklines and pull-on waistlines.	Lay out preshrunk fabric and establish both lengthwise and crosswise straight edges with an L-shaped square.
VERY STRETCHY KNITS These fabrics behave like hand knits; they stretch in both directions, usually between 40 to 60 percent, though sometimes a great deal more. They cling closely to the body. They should always be stored flat (they may stretch out of shape on hangers).	Look for patterns designed especially for stretchy knits. Otherwise, choose a pattern labeled "suitable for knits" one size smaller. Pull-on and similar sweater styles are especially suitable.	Allow preshrunk fabric to lie flat for several hours or overnight to relax to its natural shape. Mark lengthwise and crosswise straight edges with an L-shaped square. To keep fabric from stretching during cutting, do not let any part of it hang over the cutting surface edge. If the fabric slips in cutting, pin to a backing of tissue paper.
LIGHTWEIGHT KNITS Thin, supple, and sometimes diaphanous, these fabrics are not only stretchy, but also drape and cling to the body and have practically no bulk.	Choose styles that are either clinging and close-fitting, or are soft, with draped effects or flowing gathers. Avoid styles that are rigidly structured.	Handle delicate knits with care, to avoid snagging; if laundering to preshrink them, place them in a mesh bag. To cut a slippery fabric, pin it to tissue paper to hold it in place, or lay it on a soft surface, such as toweling or carpet so the scissor blade will not stretch it out of shape.
BULKY KNITS Whether fluffy or flat, stretchy, or moderately stretchy, these fabrics have a thick, resilient feel and are often loosely constructed.	Choose patterns that do not require facings, or eliminate extra bulk at edges by either of two alternatives; make facings of thin lining fabric, or substitute ribbon binding or knitted edging for facings.	Use ribs and an L-shaped square to establish a straight edge. Make tailor tacks extra-long to accommodate the extra thickness of the fabric.

Accessories	Sewing Tips
Use ballpoint needles in the finest size suitable for the fabric weight and density. In fine needles (sizes 9-11), use size A silk or nylon thread, or fine polyester; in medium needles (size 14), regular polyester or cotton-polyester thread. Sharp scissors are essential; dull scissors will drag flexible knits out of alignment. For very slithery knits, use scissors with a serrated lower blade. Other aids that simplify working with knits are special presser feet and ballpoint or fine steel pins.	Since knitted fabrics use more yarn per inch than woven fabrics, lint builds up faster and machines must be cleaned often. Synthetic knits and threads leave residues on needles, blunting or roughening them; change needles often. If seams pucker or the machine skips: clean the machine; clean or change the needle; shorten the stitch; try a finer needle and thread; loosen tension. To keep shoulder seams from stretching, stabilize with tape.
Shrink proof or preshrunk standard zippers, underlinings and interfacings can be used with firm knitted fabrics; knits conform to dimensions of the materials used with them. Attach fusible interfacings to facings or surfaces that do not show on the finished garment. Mark with dressmaker's carbon and a smooth-edged tracing wheel.	Sew with basic stretch seams. On double knits which do not curl, seam allowances can be left unfinished and trimmed to ⅜" (0.9 cm) to lessen bulk.
Zippers with knitted tapes are recommended; elastic waistbands can be substituted for waistline zippers. Use interfacings designed especially for knits, and then only in such areas as necklines, collars, and cuffs; underlinings are not recommended. An overedge presser foot eliminates curling and bunching in narrow seams.	Make seams by either stretch seam method. Use tape to prevent stretching in seams bearing weight (shoulders, waistlines, and armholes). When finishing hems by hand, use two rows of catch stitches, one in the middle of the hem and the other just below the top edge. Eliminate facings where possible; use bound edges.
Underlinings and interfacings are not recommended. Zippers, if used, should have knitted tapes. Use an overcast presser foot to keep narrow seam allowances from curling. In straight or fine zigzag stitching, use a special small hole throat plate to keep the fabric from poking through the hole, or use tissue paper under the fabric.	Make seams by the stretch methods. Use tape to prevent stretching in seams that bear weight. Finish hems by hand using two rows of catch stitches; one in the middle of the hem and the other just below the top edge, or use rib-knit edging.
Use a size 9 or 11 ballpoint machine needle and fine silk pins or ballpoint pins to avoid snagging. To finish narrow seams, use an overcast presser foot and a zigzag stitch. For straight or fine zigzag stitching, use a narrow hole throat plate to keep the fabric from poking through the hole. Use narrow coil zippers.	Support the fabric with both hands as it feeds through the machine. If stitches skip, check the stitch length; make sure the thread is the right size for the needle. Make sure the needle is not clogged and the point is clean. Use tissue paper under the fabric to keep it from getting caught by the machine when making buttonholes and zigzag stitches.
Use pins with large colored heads or T-shaped heads to keep them from slipping through the loops of the fabric.	To prevent loops from catching on the machine, wrap the presser foot prongs with transparent tape and place tissue paper under fabric. Press seams over toweling to avoid ridges.

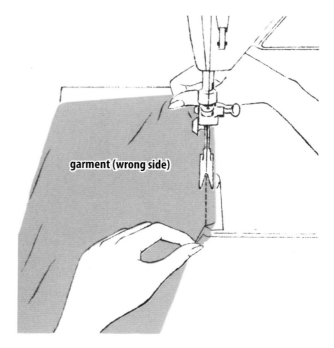

garment (wrong side)

Making the Seam (A)

1. The traditional technique for sewing a knit seam begins by joining two pieces of fabric with a plain seam, as illustrated on page 104. When machine stitching the seam, set your machine at nine to ten stitches to the inch, and stretch the fabric taut from behind the needle, as well as in the front to keep it taut.

2. When you fold open the seam allowance, the edges might curl under rather than lie flat.

Finishing the Seam Edges (B)

3. Run a line of machine stitching through both halves of the seam allowance ¼″ (0.6 cm) from the stitching line made in step 1. Again, stretch the fabric taut as you stitch.

4. Trim the seam allowances as close to the second line of stitching as possible.

Ⓐ

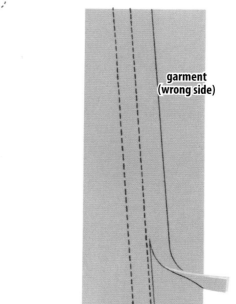

garment
(wrong side)

DESIGNER TIP

If you do not want to stretch the fabric, use a lightening stitch built into your sewing machine to create a seam with stretch. Another option is stretch thread, such as Mettler Seraflex, that's highly elastic with seams that stretch up to 65% more than conventional sewing threads when used in the bobbin and needle.

Ⓑ

THE OVERLOCK STITCH

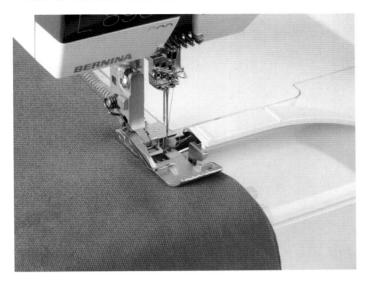

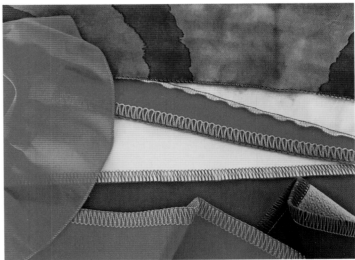

Overlock stitches are strong, secure, and will prevent your fabric from unraveling.

The overlock stitch is a flexible stitch that finishes off the edge of a fabric. When using an overlock machine or serger, a knife blade will also cut off any excess and the stitch may be created with two or more needles. Most conventional sewing machines feature a variety of mock overlock stitches that look and perform like a serger. A hand overedge finish is also an option for specialty fabrics or creative effects.

Testing Knit Fabric for Degree of Stretch (A)

1. In an area of fabric that's at least 6″ (15.3 cm) in from any of the edges, measure a 6″ (15.3 cm) section along the crosswise grain, marking each end of the section with a safety pin.
2. Grasp the fabric between your thumb and forefinger near each safety pin and stretch the section as far as you can without twisting the fabric out of shape. Measure the stretched section by holding it against the ruler.
3. If the 6″ (15.3 cm) section stretches to 7″ (17.8 cm) or less, the fabric is a relatively stable knit. If it stretches to between 7–8½″ (17.8–21.6 cm), it has moderate stretch. If the fabric stretches to more than 8½″ (21.6 cm), it is very stretchy.
4. If your fabric has minimal stretch, then you can treat it like nonstretch fabrics. If your fabric has a moderate to high degree of stretch, then you will want to use a knit pattern, or reduce the pattern size to work with the stretch of the fabric.

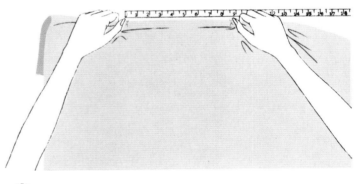

(A)

Preparing Knit Fabric to Sew (B)

5. Preshrink the fabric if necessary (see chart, pages 140–141).

6. For a very stretchy knit, spread the fabric out on a large flat surface and let it "relax" and flatten for at least a few hours before cutting and marking it.

7. If the fabric is tubular, cut it open along a lengthwise crease, following a rib or a stripe in the fabric so the lengthwise cut edges will be straight. Skip to Step 10.

8. If the fabric has straight selvage-like edges, skip to Step 10.

9. If the fabric is not tubular and does not have straight selvage-like edges, straighten the lengthwise edges by trimming them along a rib, chain of stitches, or stripe.

10. To straighten the remaining edges, use an L-shaped square to draw a chalk line at a right angle to the straight edges. If the knit is too soft to mark with chalk, use pin markers.

11. Trim the edges along the marking.

12. If the fabric does not have a lengthwise rib or stripe that can be seen easily when laying out the pattern, find a narrow rib or chain of stitches just inside each lengthwise edge and baste along it. These bastings will serve as a guide for positioning the pattern pieces.

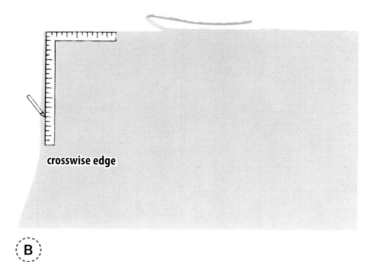

crosswise edge

B

Laying Out Knit Fabric with a Center Crease (C)

13. To avoid the permanent center crease caused by folding the fabric onto the bolt, fold up both lengthwise edges, wrong sides out, so they meet near the crease. Keep the folds parallel to the bastings made in preparing knit fabric (above). Fold up excess fabric so it will not hang over the edge of your work surface.

14. Lay the pattern pieces on the fabric. Be sure the top-to-bottom directions of all pieces are the same, grain line arrows are parallel to the bastings, and pieces marked "place on fold" are along a fold. Pin the pattern pieces.

15. Cut out the garment pieces along the cutting lines.

16. **A.** If the knit fabric is firm, mark each garment piece using dressmaker's carbon and a smooth-edged tracing wheel.

    B. If the fabric is too soft to mark with carbon, mark all circles, dots, and critical junctures of seam lines with single tailor tacks (page 244). When you sew, use the seam guide on your sewing machine to assure straight seams.

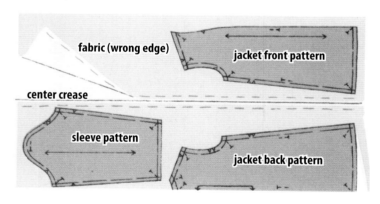

fabric (wrong edge)

jacket front pattern

center crease

sleeve pattern

jacket back pattern

C

Laying Out Knit Fabric with a Prominent Lengthwise Rib (D)

17. Spread the fabric wrong side down in a single layer. Fold up excess fabric so it will not hang over the edge of your work surface.
18. Lay the pattern pieces on the fabric, avoiding creases; make sure all top-to-bottom directions are the same.
19. On pattern pieces marked "place on fold," align the fold line with a rib and leave space so each piece can be flipped, as shown by the dotted lines. Pin.
20. On all other pieces, align the grain line arrow with a rib; leave space so pieces can be used a second time (dotted lines). Pin.
21. For a pattern piece with a fold line, cut first along the cutting lines to each end of the rib at the fold line.
22. Unpin the pattern. Turn the piece over with the fold line at the same rib. Re-pin and finish cutting.
23. For a pattern piece with a grain-line arrow, cut it out marked side up. Unpin and turn the piece over.
24. Re-pin the piece to the fabric with the same top-to-bottom directions previously used. Then, cut the piece.
25. On each piece, mark dots, circles, and critical junctures of seam lines with single tailor tacks (page 244).

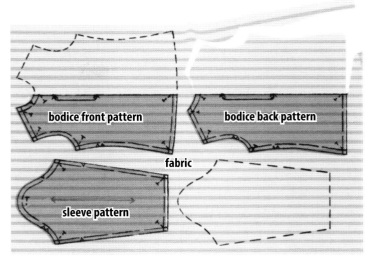

bodice front pattern

bodice back pattern

fabric

sleeve pattern

Laying Out Knit Fabric with a Crosswise Stripe (E)

26. Make a duplicate for all pattern pieces.
27. Spread the fabric wrong side down in a single layer. Fold up excess fabric so it will not hang over the edge of your work surface.
28. Arrange the pattern pieces on the fabric, avoiding any creases present in the fabric, and make sure top-to-bottom directions on all pieces are the same, and grain line arrows and fold lines are at right angles to the stripes. Pin the pattern pieces in place.
29. On adjacent garment pieces, be sure notches with the same numbers fall at the same points on the striped design so you can match stripes at seams.
30. Cut out the pieces along the cutting lines.
31. If the knit fabric is firm, transfer all pattern markings—including seam lines—to each garment piece with dressmaker's carbon and a smooth-edged tracing wheel.
32. If the fabric is too soft to mark with carbon, mark dots, circles, and critical junctures of seam lines with single tailor tacks (page 244).

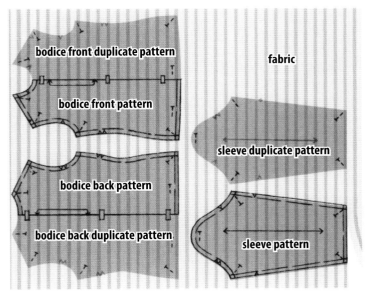

bodice front duplicate pattern

fabric

bodice front pattern

sleeve duplicate pattern

bodice back pattern

bodice back duplicate pattern

sleeve pattern

CHAPTER 6

CREATIVE HAND STITCHES

The bright, contemporary look of the monogrammed "J" shown here comes partly from its design and partly from the needlework techniques used to make it. The design and its ingenious mixing of techniques is taken from the Monogram Alphabet (pages 244–245) and has been worked with multiple strands of embroidery thread and set off against a wool background.

Of course, to accent lingerie and other delicate fabrics, nothing less than a finer weight of yarn and stitch will do. Delicate stitches, such as the knot stitch edging and sheaf, beautifully embellish the border of a sleeve or neckline, while the shadow stitch is meant for sheers and finishes off the front and back of the fabric for a polished look. For edges, cotton and silk embroidery thread of a weight and color compatible with the fabric to be decorated will enhance any design.

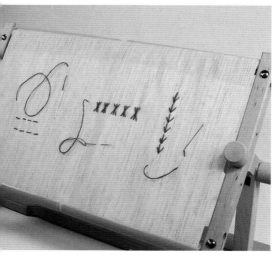

When adding creative hand stitches to your designs, the designer has a variety of choices for customizing the look. Threads range from matte finish to shiny. Designs stitched with fewer strands create an open and dainty look that better represent the stitches in smaller scale designs, whereas multiple strands of heavier threads create a dense finish that better fills designs in larger scale and size.

Regardless of your fabric or design, there's a creative hand stitch or monogram available to be sewn in any color or thread combination for a look exclusive to your style.

KNOT EDGING

1. Hold the fabric so the hemmed (or folded) edge is closest to you. Using knotted thread, slide the needle inside the hem at the left-hand edge of the fabric and bring it out on the fold, close to the edge. Pull the thread through.
2. Insert the needle ¹⁄₁₆″ (1.6 mm) above the folded edge and ¼″ (0.6 cm) to the right of the hole from which the thread emerged in Step 1. Bring the needle out on the folded edge and slide the thread emerging from the previous stitch under it, as shown. Pull the thread through loosely, leaving a loop.
3. Without inserting it into the fabric, slip the needle from left to right under the middle and right-hand threads of the loop. Slide the thread extending from the loop under the needle, as shown. Pull the thread through tightly to form a knot.
4. Working from left to right, repeat Steps 2 and 3 every ¼″ (0.6 cm) along the length of the hemmed edge. Secure the last stitch by making a small fastening stitch (page 243) on the wrong side of the hem. Clip the excess thread.

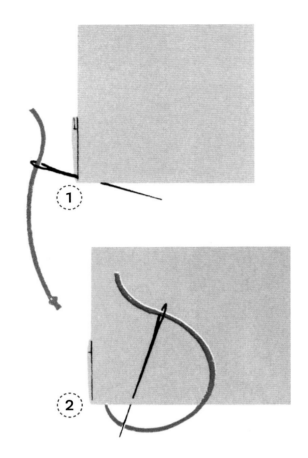

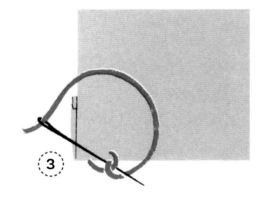

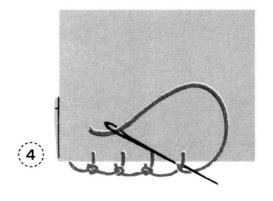

KNOTTED CLOSED BUTTONHOLE

1. Mark a guideline on the fabric by making a row of basting stitches ¼″ (0.6 cm) from, and parallel to, the hemmed (or folded) edge. Hold the fabric so the hemmed edge is closest to you. Using knotted thread, slide the needle inside the hem at the left-hand edge and bring it out on the fold, close to the edge.
2. Insert the needle on the guideline ⅛″ (3.2 mm) to the right of the hole made in Step 1. Bring the needle out close to the folded edge, just to the right of the hole made in Step 1. Pull the thread through to form a diagonal stitch.
3. Without inserting it into the fabric, slip the needle from left to right under the diagonal stitch. Slide the thread extending from the completed stitch under the needle, as shown. Pull the thread through, pulling it toward you tightly to form a looped knot along the folded edge of the fabric.
4. Insert the needle on the guideline just to the right of the top of the previous diagonal stitch. Bring the needle out close to the folded edge, ¼″ (0.6 cm) to the right of the bottom of the previous diagonal stitch. Slide the thread extending from the completed stitch under the needle, as shown, and pull the thread through.
5. Insert the needle on the guideline ¼″ (0.6 cm) to the right of the top of the previous stitch. Bring the needle out close to the folded edge, just to the right of the bottom of the previous stitch. Slide the thread extending from the completed stitch under the needle and pull the thread through.
6. Without inserting it into the fabric, slip the needle from left to right under the last two completed diagonal stitches. Slide the thread extending from the previous stitch under the needle, as shown. Pull the thread through, pulling it toward you tightly to form a looped knot along the folded edge of the fabric.
7. Make similar stitches along the length of the hemmed edge by repeating Steps 4–6. Secure the last stitch by making a small fastening stitch (page 243) on the wrong side of the hem. Clip the excess thread and remove the basted guideline.

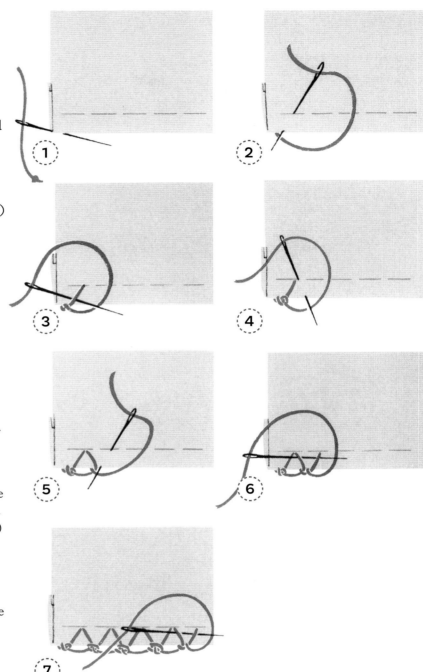

SHEAF STITCH

1. Mark guidelines on the fabric by making two parallel rows of basting stitches separated by a distance equal to the desired length of the stitches. Then, using knotted thread, bring the needle up from the wrong side of the fabric at the right-hand end of the upper guideline. Pull the thread through.

2. Insert the needle at the right-hand end of the lower guideline. Bring it out on the lower guideline about $\frac{1}{16}''$ (1.6 mm) to the left of the point at which it was inserted, as shown. Pull the thread through to form the first vertical stitch.

3. Insert the needle on the upper guideline about $\frac{1}{16}''$ (1.6 mm) to the left of the previous stitch. Bring the needle out on the upper guideline about $\frac{1}{16}''$ (1.6 mm) to the left of the point at which it was inserted. Pull the thread through to form the second vertical stitch.

4. Insert the needle on the lower guideline about $\frac{1}{16}''$ (1.6 mm) to the left of the previous stitch. Bring the needle out midway between the guidelines, just to the left of the last completed stitch, as shown. Pull the thread through to form the third vertical stitch.

5. Slide the needle from right to left under the three vertical stitches, as shown, without inserting it into the fabric. Pull the thread through tightly, gathering the three vertical stitches into a bunch.

6. Repeat Step 5. Then, reinsert the needle into the fabric in the hole from which the thread emerged in Step 4. Pull the thread through to the wrong side of the fabric.

7. Working from right to left, repeat Steps 1–6 to make similar stitches at the desired intervals until the guidelines are covered. End off on the wrong side of the fabric by slipping the needle underneath the nearest stitch and pulling the thread to the back. Tie off with a small knot.

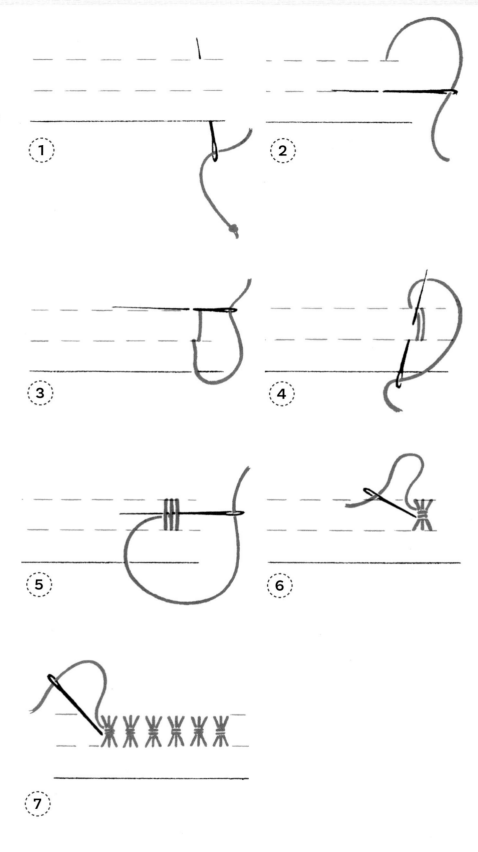

SHADOW STITCH

1. Mark guidelines on the fabric by making two parallel rows of basting stitches separated by a distance equal to the desired length of the stitches. Then, using knotted thread, bring the needle up from the wrong side of the fabric ⅛″ (3.2 mm) from the right-hand end of the lower guideline. Pull the thread through.

2. Insert the needle on the lower guideline ⅛″ (3.2 mm) to the right of the hole from which the thread emerged in Step 1. Slant the needle upward and bring it out on the upper guideline 1/16″ (1.6 mm) to the left of the hole from which the yarn emerged in Step 1. Pull the thread through.

3. Insert the needle on the upper guideline ⅛″ (3.2 mm) to the right of the hole from which the thread last emerged. Slant the needle downward and bring it out on the lower guideline ⅛″ (3.2 mm) to left of the previous stitch made on the lower guideline. Pull the thread through, creating an X-shaped stitch on the wrong side of the fabric.

4. Repeat Steps 2 and 3 to make similar stitches from right to left until the guidelines are covered. On the last stitch, insert the needle on the upper guideline ⅛″ (3.2 mm) to the right of the hole from which the thread last emerged, and pull the thread through to the wrong side of the fabric. End off on the wrong side of the fabric by slipping the needle underneath the nearest stitch and pulling the thread to the back. Tie off with a small knot.

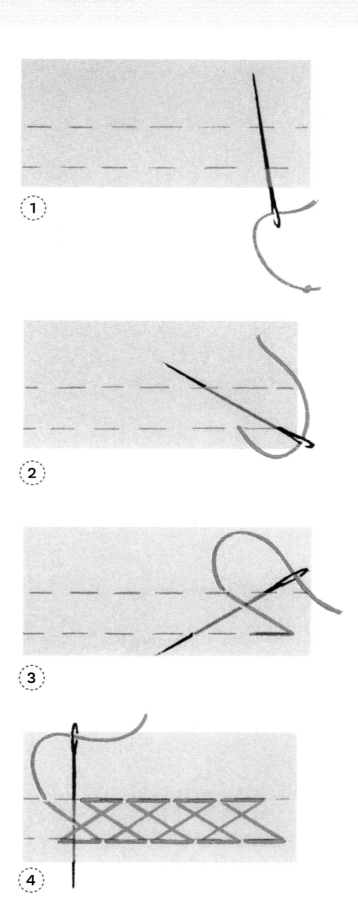

FEATHER STITCH

1. Mark a guideline on the fabric by making a single row of basting stitches. Then, using knotted thread, bring the needle up from the wrong side of the fabric at the top and about ⅛″ (3.2 mm) to the left of the guideline. Pull the thread through.

2. Make a counterclockwise loop and hold down the thread loop with your thumb, as shown. Insert the needle about ⅛″ (3.2 mm) to the right of the guideline and about ⅛″ (3.2 mm) lower than the hole made in Step 1. Bring the needle out on the guideline ⅛″ (3.2 mm) above the point at which it entered the fabric. Pass the needle over the thread held down with your thumb and pull the thread through.

3. Make a clockwise loop and hold down the thread loop with your thumb, as shown. Insert the needle about ⅛″ (3.2 mm) to the left of the guideline and about ⅛″ (3.2 mm) higher than the hole from which the thread last emerged. Bring the needle out on the guideline ⅛″ (3.2 mm) below the point at which it entered the fabric. Pass the needle over the thread loop held down with your thumb and pull the thread through.

4. Make similar stitches by repeating Steps 2 and 3 until the guideline is covered. After making the last stitch, push the needle through to the wrong side of the fabric just below the last loop. End off on the wrong side of the fabric by slipping the needle underneath the nearest stitch and pulling the thread to the back. Tie off with a small knot.

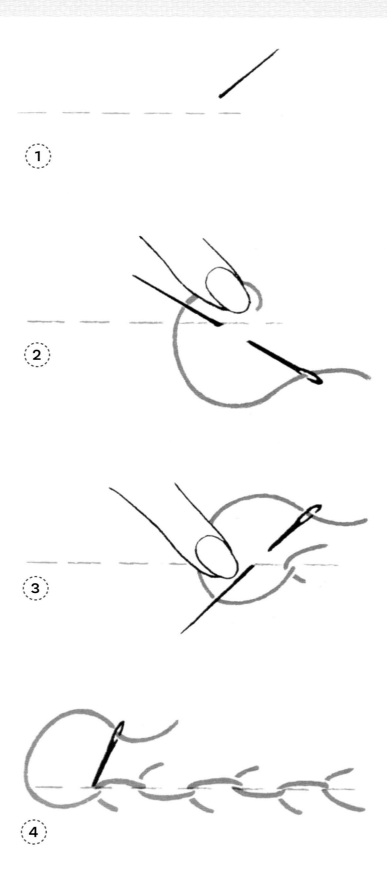

FERN STITCH

1. Mark a guideline on the fabric by making a single row of basting stitches. Then, using knotted thread, bring the needle up from the wrong side of the fabric ¼″ (0.6 cm) below the top of the guideline. Pull the thread through.

2. Insert the needle ⅛″ (3.2 mm) above and ⅛″ (3.2 mm) to the right of the hole from which the thread emerged in Step 1. Bring the needle out at the top of the guideline and pull the thread through.

3. Insert the needle in the hole from which the thread emerged in Step 1 and bring it up ⅛″ (3.2 mm) above and ⅛″ (3.2 mm) to the left of this point. Pull the thread through.

4. Complete the first fern stitch by reinserting the needle in the hole from which the thread emerged in Step 1 and pulling the thread through to the wrong side of the fabric.

5. Begin the next stitch by bringing the needle up from the wrong side of the fabric on the guideline, ¼″ (0.6 cm) below the bottom of the previous fern stitch. Pull the thread through. Repeat Steps 2–4.

6. Working vertically, make similar stitches until the guideline is covered. Complete the last stitch as shown in Step 4 and pull the thread through to the wrong side of the fabric. End off on the wrong side of the fabric by slipping the needle underneath the nearest stitch and pulling the thread to the back. Tie off with a small knot.

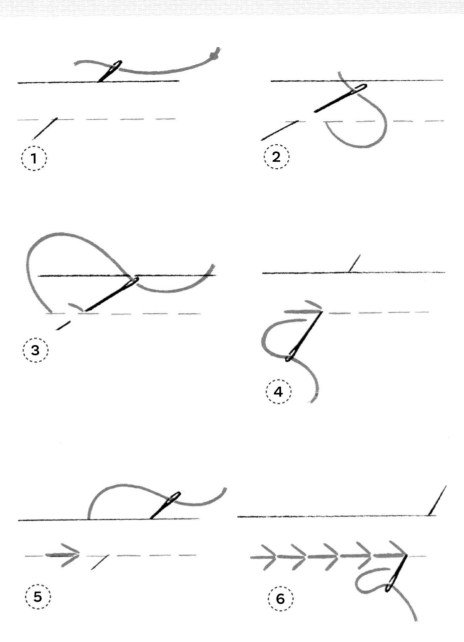

CROSS STITCH COUCHING

1. To start the stitches, thread a separate large-eyed tapestry needle with one or more strands of knotted thread or yarn. Bring the needle up from the wrong side of the fabric with the knot resting on the back of the fabric. Lay the thread along your stitching guide or pattern and run the tapestry needle into the fabric going to the back.

2. For this stitch, you will be using two needles. To tie the horizontal thread in place, make evenly spaced cross stitches until you finish the first row. If you're making more than one row, follow Steps 6 and 7 for making Chinese couching. Make either half or full cross stitches, as desired, but if you choose full cross stitches, secure the last stitch of each row on the wrong side of the fabric.

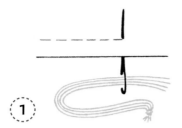

If You Are Left-Handed...
Begin at the upper left-hand end of the guideline and hold the horizontal thread down with your right thumb. Make the tying stitches from left to right across the horizontal thread.

MONOGRAM STITCHES

An Arsenal of Embroidery Stitches

The embroidery stitches demonstrated on the following pages range in difficulty, from the simple running stitch to the more complex padded satin stitch. Beneath the visible surface of the plain satin stitch (page 244) lies a layer of foundation stitching, which gives the finished work a padded effect. For light padding, as shown, a foundation of running stitch is suggested; for medium padding, an outline, chain, or split stitch; for heavy padding, the satin stitch itself. Another versatile stitch is called couching, a technique in which lengths of thread are tied to the fabric with small auxiliary stitches. In the anchored couching stitch (page 158), the main thread is stitched into the fabric, or anchored, at periodic intervals. It is then couched, or tied down, between the anchored ends with a second thread. In the unanchored version of this stitch (page 159), the embroiderer anchors the main thread just at the beginning of the stitch, then holds it on the surface of the fabric while couching it with a second thread; at the end, both threads are anchored. In making any of these stitches, use an embroidery hoop, taking care not to distort the fabric by pulling the thread too taut.

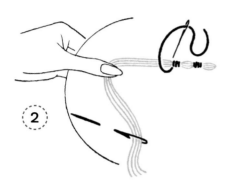

Get creative in your monogram design by combining different kinds of stitches.

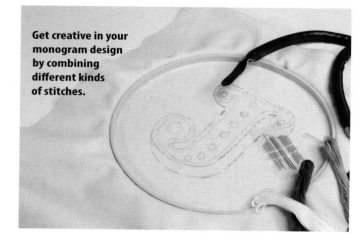

THE RUNNING STITCH

For Outlining and Light Padding

1. Using knotted thread, bring the needle up from the wrong side of the fabric. Pull the thread through.

2. Insert the needle down to the wrong side of the fabric, then bring it up and weave it in and out of the fabric several times at ⅛″ (3.2 mm) intervals. Pull the thread through.

3. Insert the needle again and continue making several stitches at a time until you complete the design. Secure the last stitch on the wrong side of the fabric (Ending Off, page 243).

If You Are Left-Handed...
Follow the instructions in Steps 1–3, but proceed as shown from left to right instead.

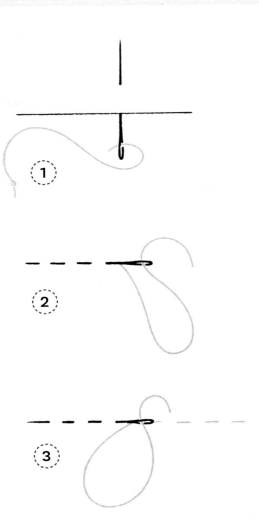

THE PADDED SATIN STITCH

For Filling Small Areas with a Puffed, Cushiony Effect

1. To make the padding for this stitch, select a heavyweight thread or use more strands of your regular thread, and knot the end. Bring the needle up from the wrong side of the fabric just inside the guideline for the design; if the design is pointed, as in this example, start near the point at the lower right-hand end. Pull the thread through.

2. Make a row of running stitches (page 155) just inside the guideline until you reach the other end of the design.

3. Rotate the fabric 180° and make another line of running stitches about ⅛" (3.2 mm) away from the first line. Continue to make similar lines of running stitches until the design is filled. Secure the last stitch on the wrong side of the fabric (Ending Off, page 243).

4. To make the covering for this stitch, knot a strand of regular thread and bring the needle up from the wrong side of the fabric below and slightly to the left of the hole made in Step 1.

5. Cover the lines of running stitches with the satin stitch (page 244), working at right angles to the running stitches. Secure the last stitch on the wrong side of the fabric (Ending Off, page 243).

> **If You Are Left-Handed...**
> Follow Steps 1–5 as shown, but start the running stitches at the top point instead.

Embroidery techniques, patterns, and themes have been passed down from generation to generation all across the globe. This vintage pocket was purchased by the author at an antique store. She was told it was part of a traditional dress from the owner's homeland. It was too beautiful and inspirational to pass up.

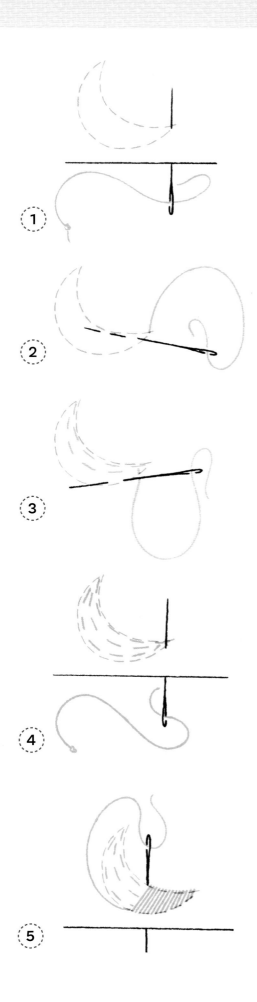

THE OUTLINE STITCH

For Outlining Designs

1. Using knotted thread, bring the needle up from the wrong side of the fabric on the guideline for the design.
2. With your left thumb, hold the thread away from the needle as shown. Point the needle to the left and insert it ¼″ (0.6 cm) to the right of the hole from which the thread emerged in the previous step. Then, bring the needle up midway between the beginning of this stitch and the hole from which the thread last emerged. Pull the thread through.
3. Repeat Step 2, bringing the needle up a fraction to the right of the previous stitch. Continue making similar stitches along the guideline until the design is completed.
4. Secure the last stitch on the wrong side of the fabric (Ending Off, page 243).

> **If You Are Left-Handed...**
> Follow Steps 1 and 2, but hold the thread with your right thumb and point the needle to the right. Follow Steps 3 and 4, but work from right to left, bringing the needle up a fraction to the left of each previous stitch.

THE SPLIT STITCH

For Outlining Designs

1. Work Step 1 of the outline stitch (above).
2. Work Step 2 of the outline stitch.
3. Repeat Step 2 of the outline stitch with two exceptions: let the thread fall toward you and bring the needle up near the end of the previous stitch so that the needle splits the thread of the stitch. Pull the thread through.
4. Repeat Step 3 until the design is completed. Then, secure the last stitch on the wrong side of the fabric (Ending Off, page 243).

> **If You Are Left-Handed...**
> Follow Steps 1 and 2, but hold the thread with your right thumb and point the needle to the right. Follow Steps 3 and 4, but work from right to left.

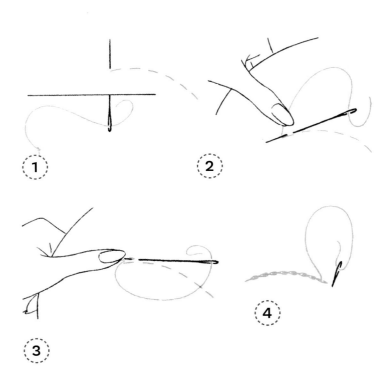

THE ANCHORED COUCHING STITCH

For Filling Large Areas

1. Using knotted thread, bring the needle up from the wrong side of the fabric and make a group of straight stitches in whatever arrangement your design requires. Secure the last stitch on the wrong side of the fabric (Ending Off, page 243).

2. Using knotted thread of the same or a contrasting color, bring the needle up just to the right and close to the top of the first straight stitch.

3. Insert the needle down to the wrong side of the fabric just to the left of the straight stitch and directly opposite the hole from which the thread emerged in the previous step. Slant the needle downward and to the right and bring it up just to the right of the straight stitch.

4. Insert the needle down to the wrong side of the fabric just to the left of the straight stitch and directly opposite the hole from which the thread emerged in the previous step. Slant the needle upward and bring it up just to the left of the next straight stitch.

5. Continue in this manner, repeating Steps 3 and 4, and staggering the stitches at random. Secure the last stitch on the wrong side of the fabric (Ending Off, page 243).

> **If You Are Left-Handed...**
> Follow Steps 1–5 as shown, but cross over the straight stitches from left to right and insert the needle downward from right to left instead. In Step 4, bring the needle up just to the right of the next stitch.

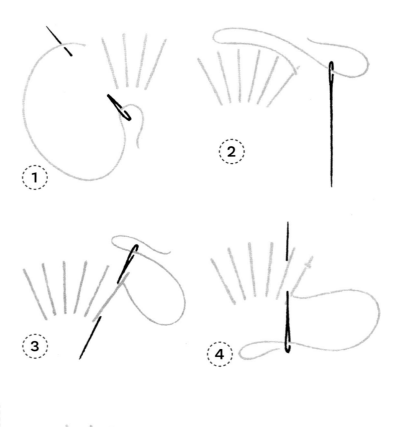

THE COUCHING VARIANT STITCH

For Filling Large Areas

1. Using knotted thread, bring the needle up from the wrong side of the fabric at one end of the guideline of your design. Pull the thread through, then hold the thread down on the design with your left thumb.

2. Thread another needle with the same or a contrasting color and knot the end. Bring the needle up from the wrong side of the fabric just to the right and about ¼″ (0.6 cm) from the end of the thread you're holding down. Pull the thread through.

3. Insert the needle down to the wrong side of the fabric just to the left of the thread being held down and directly opposite the hole from which the thread emerged in the previous step. Slant the needle downward and bring it up just to the right of the thread being held down. Pull the thread through.

4. Continue making similar stitches along the entire length of the thread being held down. The distance between stitches is arbitrary but should remain constant throughout the design.

5. Approximately ¼″ (0.6 cm) from the end, secure the last stitch on the wrong side of the fabric (Ending Off, page 243). Then, secure the end of the thread being held down in the same way.

> **If You Are Left-Handed…**
> Follow Steps 1–5, but hold the thread with your right thumb and bring the needle up just to the left of the thread being held down. Then, insert the needle just to the right of the thread being held down.

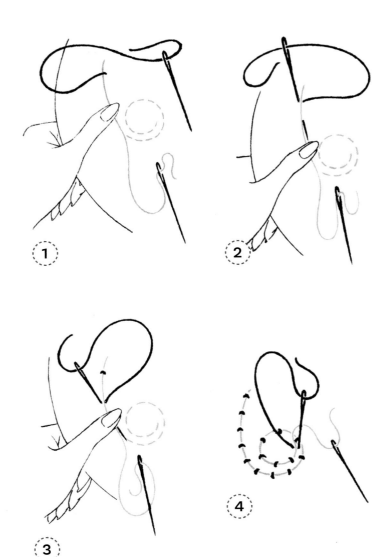

THE BULLION STITCH

For Filling Areas

1. Using knotted thread, bring the needle up from the wrong side of the fabric. Pull the thread through.
2. Point the needle away from you and insert it down to the wrong side of the fabric at the desired distance from the hole from which the thread emerged in the previous step. Then, bring the needle partially up in the same hole from which the thread last emerged; do not pull the needle or the thread all the way through.
3. Hold the bottom of the needle firmly with your left thumb and wind the thread around the needle counterclockwise, as shown.
4. Continue to wind the thread around the needle until the length of the coil equals the distance between the two holes.
5. Hold the coiled thread with your left thumb and pull the needle out of the coil with your right thumb and forefinger.
6. Pull the thread gently toward you until the coil lies flat on the fabric.
7. Insert the needle down to the wrong side of the fabric just to the right of the hole into which it was inserted in Step 2; bring it partially up the desired distance away and repeat Steps 3–6.
8. Continue to make as many similar stitches as your design requires. Secure the last stitch on the wrong side of the fabric (Ending Off, page 243).

If You Are Left-Handed...

Follow Steps 1–3 as shown, but hold the bottom of the needle firmly with your right thumb and wind the thread clockwise around the needle instead.
Follow Steps 4–9, but hold the coil with your right thumb and pull the needle with your left thumb and forefinger. Make the second stitch to the left of the first stitch and continue from right to left.

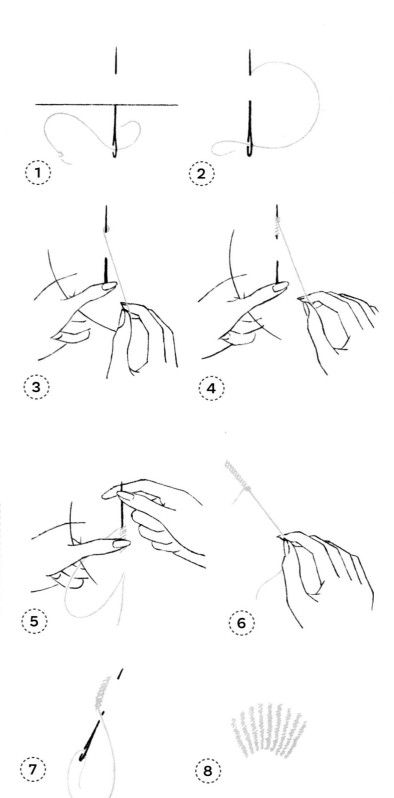

THE TURKEY STITCH

For a Tufted, Fuzzy Texture

1. Using unknotted thread, insert the needle down to the wrong side of the fabric, then bring it up ⅛″ (3.2 mm) to the left of the first hole.
2. Pull the thread only partially through, leaving about an inch of the unknotted end on top of the fabric.
3. Let the thread loop toward you, as shown. Point the needle to the left and insert it ¼″ (0.6 cm) to the right of the hole from which the thread emerged in the previous step. Bring the needle up in the same hole occupied by the unknotted end; this will lock the stitch.
4. Pull the thread through. Then, with your left thumb holding the thread away from you, point the needle to the left and insert it ¼″ (0.6 cm) to the right of the hole from which the thread emerged in the previous step. Bring it up at the end of the previous stitch.
5. Pull the thread only partially through, leaving a loop about ½″ (1.3 cm) high.
6. Repeat Step 3, bringing the needle up in the same hole occupied by the end of the just-completed loop.
7. Repeat Steps 4 and 5.
8. Repeat Step 6, then continue repeating Steps 4–6, making as many little loops as your design requires. End the row with Step 6 to lock the last stitch. Cut the thread that emerges from the last stitch about 1″ (2.5 cm) from the top of the fabric.
9. Work a new row, starting as close as possible to the first stitch made in Step 1.
10. Continue to make as many rows as your design requires.
11. When all the rows are completed, snip each loop at the top with a scissors and trim to the height desired.
12. For a more sheared look, cut across the massed top of loops.

> **If You Are Left-Handed…**
> Follow Steps 1–12, but point the needle to the right and insert it ¼″ (0.6 cm) to the left of the hole from which the thread last emerged. In Step 4, hold the thread away from you with your right thumb, as shown.

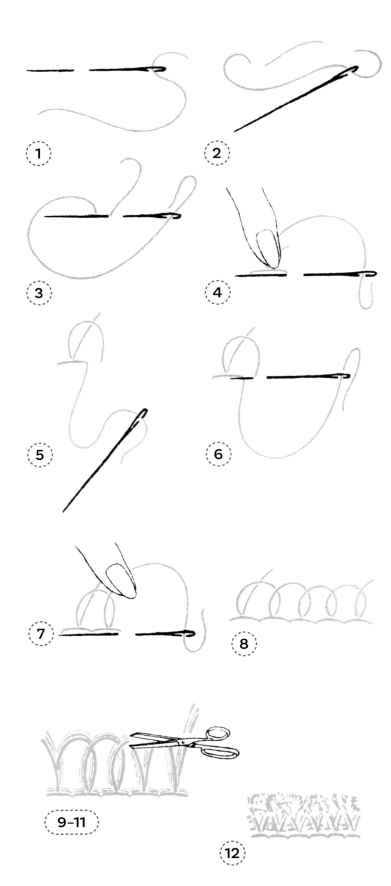

CHAPTER 7

ENHANCING THE PATTERN

Pattern enhancements done with excellence can dramatically alter and add creative effects to a garment while retaining all core design elements and fitting contours. Working first on the pattern and then creating a sample muslin garment, these elements need not be overly complex, but rather well thought out and placed for the most flattering fit and best use of your selected fabric. Take basic dart rotation, for example. This foundation skill is more than a core flat pattern trick. Darts can be moved for better fit and visual appeal. It's always acceptable to move fitting elements on any pattern to best utilize them on your figure. Converting a dart to a princess line, piecing a detail on the bias, adding embellishments to the edges, or changing the contours of a neckline are only the beginning. Many times, a simple garment with clean lines and impeccable fit will outshine the most complex ill-fitting garment.

Top off your sewing with classic understitching of a facing to retain the shape and prevent it from slipping into view on a finished garment. Clipping seam allowances is equally important to release fabric tension that provides unsightly wrinkles in necklines and contours. As our sewing skills improve, never forget to circle back to classic pattern skills that will enhance the end results. Experiment, make a test garment, and use them to your advantage.

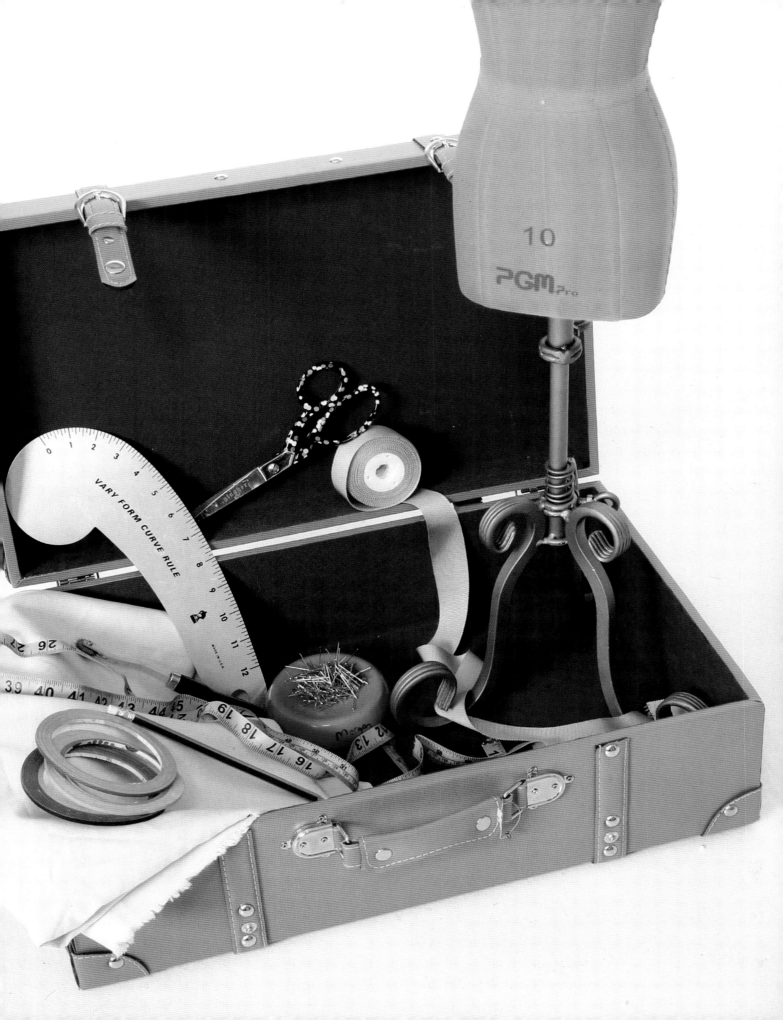

DARTS AND PRINCESS SEAMS

Darts are among the most subtly creative of pattern shaping elements. No more than a triangle of folded cloth, the core, bust, and waist darts serve as the foundation for an unlimited selection of styles when transferred from one location to another, or transformed into fitting elements, such as seams, tucks, pleats, and gathers.

The steps for converting a bust dart to a princess seam is a foundational skill in flat pattern design. There are a few methods for these modifications with subtle differences, and when carefully planned, dart transformations result in dramatic differences in the classic pattern sloper shape.

Modifying the Bodice Front Pattern (A)

1. On the basic bodice front pattern, determine the location for your princess seam. A princess seam only need pass through the bust point so it may originate from the armhole, shoulder, or elsewhere. Use a ruler to connect the point where the princess line will start to the bust point. If the dart begins in the armhole, use a curved ruler to connect the points.

2. Make a cross mark on the new line about 1″ (2.5 cm) above the bust point.

> **Optional:** Make an additional cross mark about 1″ (2.5 cm) below the bust point as an additional reference. This mark will indicate notches on the new seam line for sewing the pattern pieces back together.

3. Before cutting the pieces apart, draw a grainline arrow on the center front pattern and the side front pattern both parallel to the center front.

4. Cut along the line drawn in Step 1. Cut out and remove the waistline dart. You now have two pieces.

5. Tape the bust dart closed, leaving a ⅛″ (3.2 mm) separation at the tip.

6. Tape a piece of paper under the separation and trim the edge.

7. If needed, take a curved ruler to each side of the seam line and trace a smooth line. Be careful not to remove too much pattern, but simply skim off a slight amount to create the new line.

Modifying the Bodice Back Pattern (B)

8. On the pattern for the bodice back, mark a placement for the dart following the example in Step 1.

9. Make a cross mark on the new line about 1″ (2.5 cm) above the dart tip.

10. Before cutting the pieces apart, draw a grainline arrow on the center back pattern and the side back pattern both parallel to the center back.

11. Cut the pattern along the new line, eliminating the waistline dart of the pattern. Smooth out the seam line if needed according to Step 7.

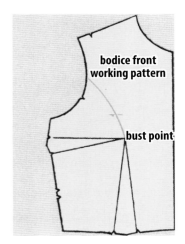
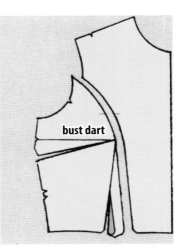

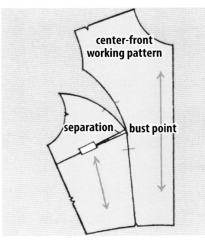

A

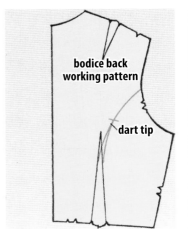
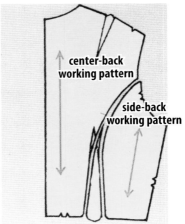

B

DESIGNING WITH A DART ROTATION

Once you master the dart to princess seam modification, you can further enhance this skill by applying darts to various locations, which result in better fit of your garments or better application with your selected fabric. Dart rotation is more than the foundation of flat pattern design. On the surface, it seems simple, but learning to place the dart strategically and intentionally in targeted locations in the shoulder, combining with the waist dart, creating a French dart, or any other shape takes moments to apply and adds depth to your sewing and fitting abilities with the results you achieve.

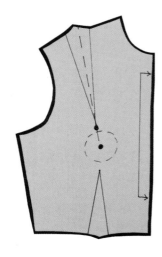

TRANSFORMING THE BUST DART INTO A SHOULDER DART

Moving the Dart (A)

1. On the bodice front pattern, draw a line from the bust point to the center of the shoulder edge. Cut along the line.
2. Cut along the lower line of the bust dart.
3. Tape the bust dart closed, matching the cut lower edge of the dart with the upper line.

Drawing the New Dart (B)

4. Tape a piece of paper under the new dart opening; the paper should extend at least 1″ (2.5 cm) beyond the edge of the pattern.
5. Measure from the bust point into the center of the new dart opening and make a mark to indicate the tip of the dart. For a shoulder dart, the tip should be 1½–2″ (3.8–5.1 cm) above the bust point on the technical pattern. When you fit the pattern in muslin, this may change slightly due to the differences in individual figures.
6. Draw the new dart by connecting the mark made in the preceding step with both ends of the dart opening at the outer edge of the pattern.

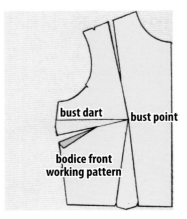
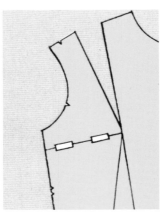

A

bust dart · bust point · bodice front working pattern

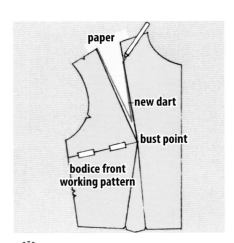

B

paper · new dart · bust point · bodice front working pattern

Finishing the Outer Edge of the Dart (C)

7. Close the newly drawn dart as you would when sewing by folding it in half and matching the side lines, then turn the dart toward the center of the garment.

8. To mark the outer edge of the dart, make a perforated line in the excess paper by running a tracing wheel along the edge of the pattern. This will create the triangular shape of the dart base in scale and proportion to the pattern.

9. Open the dart and trim the paper on the outer edge along the perforated line.

10. Draw a grainline arrow parallel to the center-front edge.

11. Shorten the waistline dart so it stops approximately 1½″ (3.8 cm) from the bust point. This is the technical placement for the dart tip; however, the length of the darts may be customized and refined in the muslin fitting for the best fit and most flattering placement.

Experiment with rotating the dart to various locations all around the pattern for a variety of styles. As you rotate the dart the length and shape of the dart will change. This is normal. For example, if the bust dart is rotated to the center-front, it will shorten significantly. Make a variety of samples to test this and then determine what placement will make your clothing more flattering and a better fit.

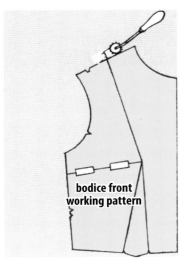

bodice front working pattern

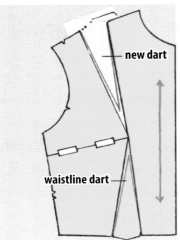

new dart

waistline dart

C

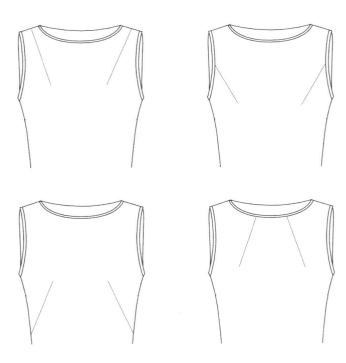

CHANGING THE NECKLINE

The elegance of simple necklines like these derives from the smooth perfection with which the facing is attached. The simplicity is often more striking than a complex collar when executed with certain precision that ensures the facing lies hidden without puckering or buckling. Staystitching the neckline along the bodice neckline prevents the fabric from stretching out of shape as the garment is formed and is the final step for polishing off the pattern. Faced necklines come in variety of shapes, including the square, V-neck, bateau, sweetheart, scalloped, and asymmetrical.

THE FACED SQUARE NECKLINE

Preparing the Bodice (A)

1. To keep the inner edge of the neckline square, before assembling the bodice, machine stitch around the bodice front and back necklines, just outside the seam lines.
2. Baste the bodice pieces together and adjust for fit. Stitch and press any darts indicated by the pattern. Stitch and press the shoulder and side seams. Insert the zipper.

Preparing the Facing (B)

3. Pin the two small back sections of the facing to the larger front section along the shoulder seam lines, keeping the wrong sides out. Baste and remove the pins.
4. Machine stitch and remove the bastings.
5. Press the seams open.
6. To finish off and keep the outer edge of the facing from raveling, machine stitch ¼" (0.6 cm) from the edge, serge (overlock stitch), or attach a lining if the pattern requires it.
7. For machine stitched edges without an overlock finish, use pinking shears to trim ⅛" (3.2 mm) off the raw edges outside the stitching made in Step 6.

Square necklines are quite flattering, as they make the neck look longer and emphasize collarbones.

bodice front (wrong side)

A

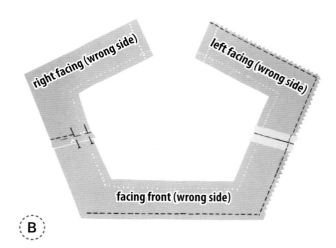

right facing (wrong side)

left facing (wrong side)

facing front (wrong side)

B

Attaching the Facing to the Bodice (C)

8. Turn the bodice right side out.
9. Place the facing wrong side up over the bodice neckline, matching it to the bodice first at the shoulder seams and then at the corners.
10. Pin the facing to the bodice at 1″ (2.5 cm) intervals around the neckline. Baste and remove the pins.
11. Machine stitch the facing to the bodice along the seam line. Stop about 1″ (2.5 cm) from each corner and reset the machine to 15 stitches to the inch. Continue stitching to the corner. To make the corners square, stop the machine where the direction of the seam line changes with the needle down and raise the presser foot: pivot the fabric. Lower the presser foot: stitch for 1″ (2.5 cm). Stop, reset the machine to 12 stitches to the inch, and continue to stitch. Remove the bastings.
12. To ensure a right angle at each corner, clip diagonally into the neckline seam allowances at each corner, cutting up to but not into the stitching.
13. Trim the seam allowance of the facing to ⅛″ (3.2 mm). Trim the seam allowance of the bodice to ¼″ (0.6 cm).
14. To reduce the bulk at the double seams, trim the facing shoulder seam allowances diagonally, above the machine stitching.
15. Repeat Step 14 on the garment shoulder seam allowances.

Finishing the Facing (D)

16. Turn the bodice wrong side out and pull the facing up above the neckline.
17. Press the neckline seam allowances toward the facing.
18. Turn the bodice right side out, keeping the facing pulled up above the neckline.
19. To prevent the facing from rolling out and showing on the finished garment, run a line of machine stitching—called understitching—around the facing and through the seam allowances beneath, as close to the neckline seam as possible.

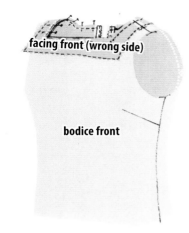

facing front (wrong side)

bodice front

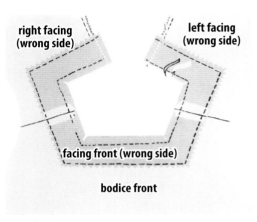

right facing (wrong side)

left facing (wrong side)

facing front (wrong side)

bodice front

C

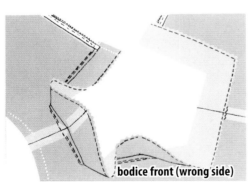

bodice front (wrong side)

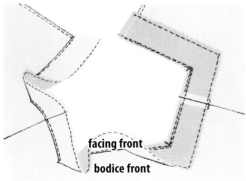

facing front

bodice front

D

Finishing the Neckline (E)

20. Turn the bodice wrong side out and fold the facing toward the inside of the bodice, making sure the seam line joining the facing to the bodice falls just inside the edge. Press from the facing side.

21. Attach the outer edge of the facing to the seam allowances at the shoulder seams with a hemming stitch, making sure not to catch the bodice fabric underneath.

22. Fold under the loose edges of the facing so that the folds are ⅛″ (3.2 mm) from the zipper teeth. Slip stitch (page 244) the fold to the zipper tape. Press the folded edges.

23. Fold under the loose edges of the facing so that the folds are ⅛″ (3.2 mm) from the zipper teeth. Slip stitch (page 244) the fold to the zipper tape. Press the folded edges.

24. Finish the closure by attaching a hook and eye on the facing above the zipper.

25. Turn the bodice right side out.

> **Note:** The process is the same for all faced necklines of different shapes.

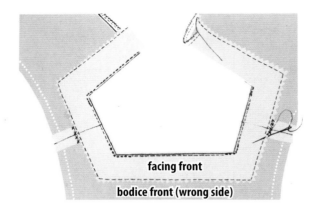

facing front

bodice front (wrong side)

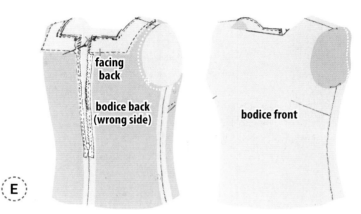

facing back

bodice back (wrong side)

bodice front

E

PIECING ON THE BIAS

Bias of a fabric or a pattern is any direction that is not parallel to the straight of grain. (The straight of grain runs parallel to the selvage of the fabric and on patterns, is usually parallel to the center front or center back). Whether you're working on a new pattern or modifying one of your favorites, fabric must be checked to make sure it's on grain and hasn't been pulled out of shape by handling. This will ensure that the finished garment hangs correctly. Once your fabric has been checked and straightened (if needed) it's ready for the pattern to be cut. To further enhance your sewing, it's possible to fold a pattern and convert it to a bias design. Utilizing the bias in the pattern opens endless possibilities for manipulating the fit and aesthetic of any design. Bias can soften how a stiff fabric hangs on the body, may better feature a particular pattern, or allow for contouring over the body. True bias is placed at a 45° angle to the grain, but any degree of grain is considered bias. You're not required to use the full true bias, which features optimum stretch, since a small amount can enhance a pattern. Test your design in a sample fabric to see the results.

Finding the True Crosswise Grain (A)

1. Make a small cut into one finished, or selvage, edge of the fabric and snag a crosswise thread with a pin. Gently pull on the thread so it shows up as a puckered line along the width of the fabric.
2. Cut along the puckered line from one selvage to the other; this is the true crosswise grain.
3. Repeat at the opposite end of the fabric so the ends can be matched for straightening the grain.

Finding the True Bias (B)

4. After straightening the fabric (left), place it on a flat surface and fold it diagonally so one selvage is parallel to the crosswise edge and perpendicular to the other selvage. The diagonally folded edge is the true bias.

Converting a Pattern to True Bias (C)

5. Draw a line at a 45° angle to the straight grainline or fold the pattern at a right angle to the center front. The diagonal line created is the true bias and a 45° angle. Mark the true bias line and use this to line the pattern up with the grain on the fabric.

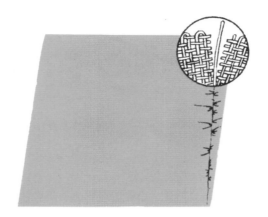

A

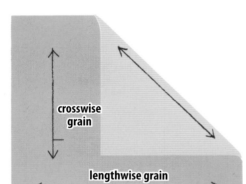

crosswise grain

lengthwise grain

B

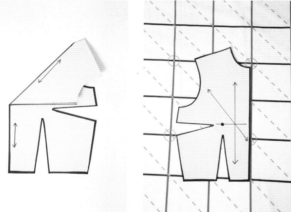

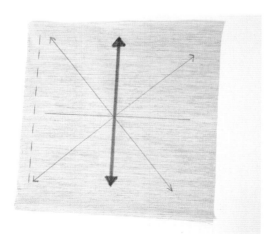

C

Laying Out Bias Cut Patterns (D)

Bias patterns should never be cut on the fold. They should always be cut as the full pattern piece, paying close attention to the direction of the bias against the fabric and that each piece is a mirror image of its counterpart.

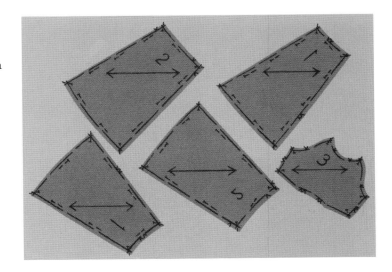

1. Trace a duplicate pattern for each pattern piece that will be used more than once. For example, a bodice that is cut on the fold would have a copy of the pattern taped together at the center front to create a single pattern. The direction of the bias grain is the same on the whole pattern. If you want the drape to hang opposite of each side, such as in skirts with a chevron effect, cut a mirror image of the pattern, but test the drape to determine your desired effect. Trace the grain line arrow in each duplicate piece.
2. Spread open the straightened fabric and loosely arrange the pattern pieces according to the accompanying pattern cutting guide, making certain the grain line arrows are parallel to the selvage edges.
3. Pin each pattern piece diagonally at the corners; then pin parallel to, and just inside, the cutting line. Arrange and pin all pattern pieces before cutting any.

BIAS SEWING TIPS

- Press all pieces before you sew.
- Thread trace the stitching lines before sewing.
- Baste all seams and let hang before final fitting and hemming.
- Garments may grow often, so repeat hanging as necessary.
- If adding a zipper on the bias, use stay tape and extend past the zipper opening to weigh down.
- Use stay tape on shoulder seams or anywhere you want to stabilize the stretch.

- Use knit interfacings for bias garments.
- Use weights on bias cowl necklines to hold the drape.
- Use directional sewing by starting at the center and sew outward.
- Bias takes more yardage, so plan generously (1 yard for each major piece).
- Add extra seam allowance (½–1" or 1.3–2.5 cm more) to allow for growth.
- Mark pieces before you remove the pattern.

ADDING FLAIR

By inserting godets into the side seams or any seam, you can achieve a striking new flair to your garment. A contrast of a different color, print, or texture can elevate any design, or by adding a complementary fabric, you can change up a basic design into something more interesting. This is a great technique that can be applied to a custom garment or used to restyle ready-to-wear pieces. Before you begin, be sure the original dress and the contrasting fabric are compatible in weight and care needs.

Preparing the Side Seams (A)

1. Determine how long you want the flared godet panel to be.

> **Note:** If shortening the garment, measure and cut off the bottom prior to adding the godet.

2. Turn the garment wrong side out. Measure up from the hem the length/height of the flair. Mark the seam with several running stitches. Open the side seams up to the running stitches.

3. To reinforce the seam above the opening, machine stitch over the existing line of stitching for 1″ (2.5 cm) above the running stitches.

4. Lightly press the opened seams, taking care not to press out the seam lines completely, as they will be used later as stitching lines.

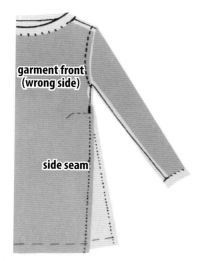

garment front (wrong side)

side seam

A

Cutting Out the Godets (B)

5. For the side godets, you will need enough fabric to create a godet for each side, unless you're adding a single flair at the center back or center front. For garments with multiple flairs, measure out your patterns to determine if you have enough for all inserts.

6. Straighten the grain of the fabric and place it wrong side up on a flat surface. Draw a vertical line parallel to the selvage and equal to the length of the opened side seam from the running stitches to the basted hemline.

7. Determine how wide you want your gore at the bottom and place two dots as shown. (If working with a finished lace, your gore pattern will end at the finished bottom seamline and you will only add a seam allowance to the sides of the pattern piece. If you have a raw hem, refer to the illustration to add a seam allowance at the sides and the bottom of your gore pattern, as described in the next step.)

8. Draw two lines equal in length to the vertical line, running diagonally from the top of the vertical line toward the dots. These new lines will become the stitching lines.

9. Connect the bottom of the triangle with a curved line.

10. Draw two cutting lines ½″ (1.3 cm) outside the lines drawn in Step 8. Where the lines intersect, square off the tip to ½″ (1.3 cm) above the point where the stitching lines meet. Then, draw a line 1½″ (3.8 cm) below and parallel to the bottom curved line. Cut out the godet along these lines.

11. Repeat Steps 5–10 to cut out the second/multiple godets. Mark the hemlines with lines of basting stitches.

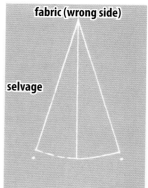
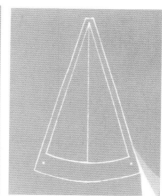

fabric (wrong side)

selvage

B

> **Tip:** Utilizing fabric bias or adding flair to the pattern will add further options to your designs.

Attaching the Godets (C)

12. Place the garment on a flat surface, wrong side up.
13. Spread apart one of the opened side seams and pin the pointed end of one of the godets, wrong side up, to the garment.
14. Pin the garment to one side of the godet. Baste and remove the pins.
15. Machine stitch along the seam lines and remove the basting.
16. Attach the godet to the other seam in the same way.
17. Press the seam allowances toward the garment. Sew them together using an overcast stitch. Serge with an overlock as another option.
18. Repeat Steps 12–17 to attach the second godet.
19. If not working with a lace edge that is finished, hem the garment and/or the godet flair according to the fabric and original hem of the garment.

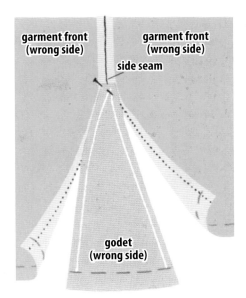

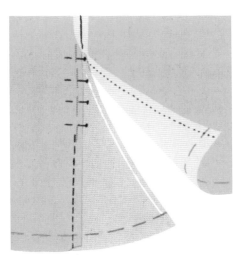

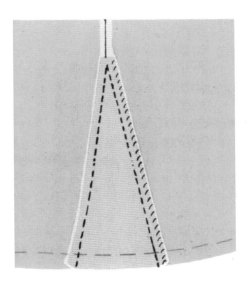

FRONT CLOSURE WITH BUTTON

Button closures, whose basic function is convenience, can be transformed into beautifully decorative focal points of any plain or simple garment. A closure can be edged with scallops or lace, or trimmed with ribbon, braid, or embroidery. Its buttons can be anything from delightful antiques to discreet pearls spaced close together. Whatever your style, think beyond basic function when adding your next button closure.

Making the Overlap for the Buttons (A)

1. Tape a large piece of paper along the center front edge of the working pattern for the bodice front. The paper should be big enough so you can draw a facing on it.

2. To determine the width of the overlap, measure the radius of the button you intend to use and add ½″ (1.3 cm).

3. To mark the front fold line, measure out from the center front edge the overlap width you determined and draw a line parallel to the center front.

4. Extend the neckline and waistline to the front fold line.

5. To mark the position of the top buttonhole, measure down from the neckline along the center front line an amount equal to the overlap width, and draw a short line.

6. Mark another buttonhole by drawing a short line at or near the bustline.

7. Mark one or more buttonholes equally spaced between the top and the bustline buttonholes.

8. Finally, mark the buttonholes below the bustline, spacing them at the same interval as the other buttonholes.

9. To finish each buttonhole marking, measure out ⅛″ (3.2 mm) into the overlap from the center front line and make a vertical mark. This is the outer placement line.

10. To mark the inner placement line, measure in a distance equal to the diameter and thickness of the button you plan to use.

Make a statement with just a few oversized buttons.

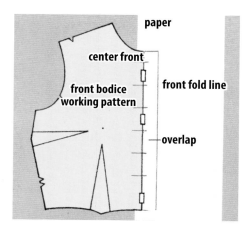

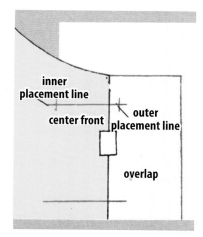

Making the Facing (B)

11. To mark the edge of the facing, start by measuring 2″ (5.1 cm) in from the neckline along the shoulder line of the front pattern and making a mark.

12. At the waistline, measure 3″ (7.6 cm) in from the adjusted center front line and make another mark.

13. Starting at the waistline mark, draw a line parallel to the center front up to a point about 2″ (5.1 cm) above the bustline. Connect the line to the shoulder mark with a gentle curve, as shown.

14. Fold the paper under the pattern along the front fold line.

15. Mark the outline of the facing on the paper with perforations by running a tracing wheel along the line for the edge of the facing and along the neck, shoulder, and waist edges of the pattern.

16. Unfold the paper and trace over the perforated lines.

17. Trim the paper along the facing outline.

18. To make a facing for the back neckline trace around the back of the pattern measuring 2″ (5.1 cm) from the neckline edge.

Apply this pattern enhancement to any garment that does not have a front closure, or further embellish a pattern that does feature a front opening.

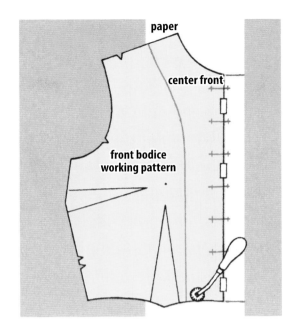

B

SLEEVE SLASH AND SPREAD

Even the most dramatic sleeves are created from simple tubular shapes of fabric. Adding fullness to the top, bottom, or both ends of a sleeve—combined with just the right fabric selection—pays off with spectacular results in the fashion garment. This sleeve is also ideal for those still learning to fit more set-in sleeve styles. The gathers provide a stress-free fit and the focus can be placed on stunning fabric combinations. To further master this technique, it's important to thoughtfully place the fullness so that it falls gracefully on the front and back of the sleeve, which illustrates excellence in sewing.

Adding Fullness to the Pattern (A)

1. Make a copy of a basic sleeve pattern. Adjust the length if desired and, ideally, start with a sleeve that has been fitted to your body.
2. Divide the cap line into six equal segments.
3. Using the marks made in the preceding step as a guide, draw six lines from the top of the sleeve cap to the bottom edge. Make sure all the lines are parallel to the front and back edges of the pattern.
4. Cut along the lines up to, but not through, the cap edge of the pattern.
5. On a large sheet of paper, draw a line as a guide for centering the sleeve pattern. Lay the pattern on the paper.
6. Fan out the pattern to the desired fullness, spacing the segments equally at the bottom and centering the line in the middle. Tape the pattern in place. For advance application, adjust the fullness to further accentuate your figure.

Accented sleeves instantly elevate the entire outfit.

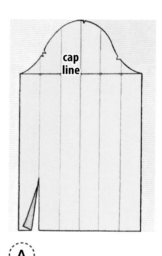

cap line

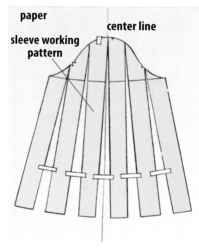

paper

center line

sleeve working pattern

(A)

Drawing the Bottom Edge (B)

7. Use a curved ruler to draw a new bottom line, connecting the front and back bottom corners of the pattern.
8. Convert the center line to a grain line arrow.
9. Cut out the pattern along the new bottom line, and then around the remaining edges of the working pattern.

Making the Facing Pattern (C)

10. Pin a piece of paper under the bottom edge of the bell sleeve pattern.
11. With a pencil, trace the bottom edge and the lower 2″ (5.1 cm) of the front and back edges.
12. Run a tracing wheel over the bottom of the center line, marking the paper with perforations.
13. Remove the pattern.
14. Connect the ends of the 2″ (5.1 cm) lines with a curved line that parallels the bottom line.
15. Draw a grain line arrow using the perforations made by the tracing wheel in Step 13 as a guide.
16. Cut out the facing pattern along the outline.
17. Finish off the facing to your desired look. With right sides together, attach to the hem of the sleeve. The fullness will be gathered up to fit into the facing or edge finish.

For a classic Bishop Sleeve, halfway between the center line and the back edge of the pattern, make a mark ¾″ (1.9 cm) below the bottom edge. Halfway between the center line and the front edge, make a mark ½″ (1.3 cm) above the bottom edge. When using the curved ruler, draw a new S-shaped curve. Mark a placket opening by drawing a vertical line 2½–3″ (6.4–7.6 cm) long, starting at the new back mark. Sew a placket and cuff according to your basic shirt pattern.

> For more creativity and options, make an elastic cuff and gather the excess at the wrist. Create a puffed cap by slashing through the top of the pattern and adding ½–1″ (1.3–2.5 cm) height, create a short sleeve with fullness, and add fullness evenly in the top and bottom and gather both—the top into the armscye and the bottom into the hem. Experiment with different fabrics, drape, and combinations.

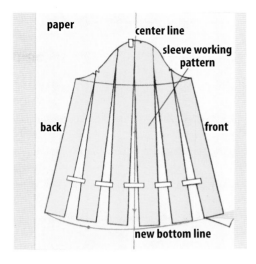

B

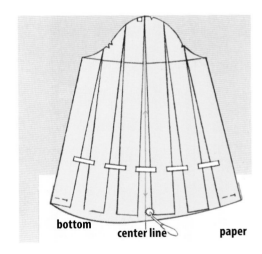

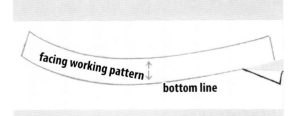

C

MAKING A SCALLOPED FACED HEM

A wide hem, scalloped hem, or a garment that has been underlined requires a different technique than the basic turn under and stitch version. These hems require a hem with a bias interfacing. This is a hem that has been slightly stiffened to reinforce the shape at the hemline, just as the underlining reinforces the shape of the garment. All these variations will be further enhanced if you add a bias edge finish around the inside edge of the hem of the same material as the garment or its underlining—another custom touch.

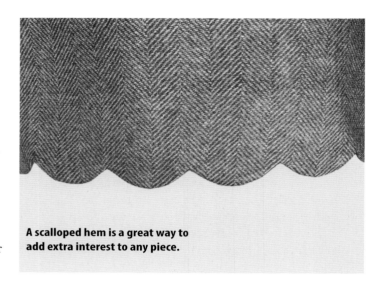

A scalloped hem is a great way to add extra interest to any piece.

Preparing to Make the Hem (A)

1. Mark the hem; use chalk or pins measuring from the floor up to determine the finished length. Run a line of basting stitches so the hemline will be visible on both sides of the garment.
2. Trim the raw edge at the garment evenly 1″ (2.5 cm) below the hemline marking.
3. Measure the circumference of the garment along the bottom raw edge.
4. Make a facing from 2½″ (6.4 cm) wide strips of the garment fabric cut on the lengthwise grain and join the pieces to make a continuous circular strip 1″ (2.5 cm) longer than the circumference of the garment at the raw edge.

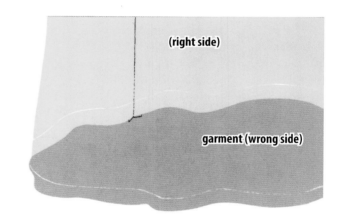

(right side)

garment (wrong side)

Attaching the Facing (B)

5. Pin and baste the facing wrong side up to the right side of the garment along the hemline marking. Stitch through all layers of fabric, matching the seams facing the side seams and other vertical seam intersections wherever possible. Baste the top edge of the facing to the garment ¼″ (0.6 cm) from the facing's raw edge. Remove the pins.

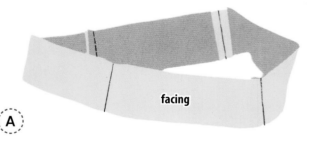

facing

A

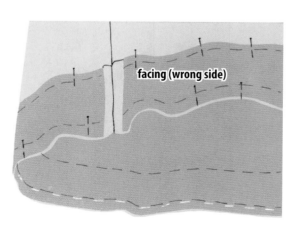

facing (wrong side)

B

Making the Scallops (C)

6. Make a tissue pattern template for the scallops. Pin and baste the actual tissue pattern for the scallops onto the facing, placing the curved bottom edges of the scallops on the hemline marking, and centering the garment's side seams and other vertical seam intersections over the scallop curves wherever possible.

7. Using a very small machine stitch—15 to 20 stitches an inch—stitch around the curved edges of the scallops using the edge of the tissue pattern as your guide. Pivot the needle at each point between scallops by leaving the needle in the fabric, raising the presser foot, and turning the fabric underneath it. Then, lower the foot again and proceed down the next scallop. Tear off the tissue pattern.

8. Trim the scallop edges to ⅜″ (0.9 cm) and cut notches around the scallop curves and clip into the points, being careful to cut up to but not into the machine stitching.

Finishing the Scallops (D)

9. Turn the facing to the right side, rolling the edges of the scallop between your fingers to bring the edges out.

10. Press first on the facing side and then on the garment side.

11. On the wrong side of each scallop, make a line of small running stitches near the curved edge, catching the facing and the seam but not the outer fabric of the garment.

12. Finish the raw edge of the facing with bias binding and stitch the finished hem edge to the garment with a blind hemming stitch or tack to the seam allowance or underlining of the garment. Remove bastings and press.

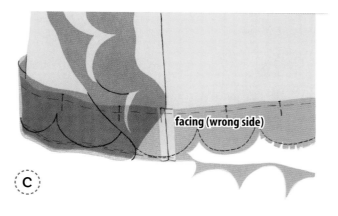

facing (wrong side)

 C

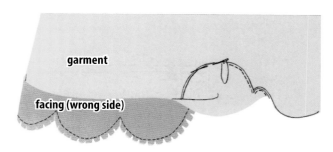

garment

facing (wrong side)

D

MAKING THE RUFFLE

Ruffles can change how a garment feels and looks, from traditionally feminine to eccentrically whimsical. These elements form part of a garment's design and are frequently made from the same fabric as a garment, or for more whimsy, from contrasting or complementary fabrics, colors, and textures. Fabric strips cut on the crosswise grain become crisp and perky, and strips cut on the bias produce soft ruffles that drape gracefully. If the ruffle is more than a few yards long, then gathering in sections helps with consistency in the spacing and helps to avoid breaking of the basting threads. Ruffles can be attached into a seam on one edge or attached to the outside of a garment with both edges visible. Even the edge of the ruffle can feature a decorative hem or embellishment.

Ruffles are perfect for making any dress or skirt more fun and playful.

Determining the Size of the Ruffle

1. To determine the width of the ruffle, add hemming and seam allowances to the desired width of the finished ruffle as follows: 1″ (2.5 cm) for inseam ruffles, ⅝″ (1.6 cm) for headed ruffles, and ½″ (1.3 cm) for double ruffles.
2. To determine the length of the ruffle, double the measurement of the garment edge to which it will be attached. If the ruffle is over 4″ (10.2 cm) wide, triple the measurement.

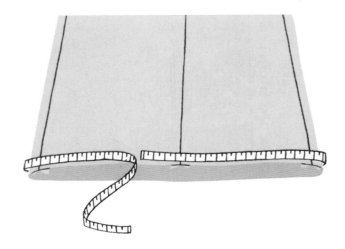

MAKING A RUFFLE STRIP CUT ON THE GRAIN

Straightening the Fabric (A)

1. To make sure one crosswise edge of the fabric is straight, make a small cut into one of the finished or selvage edges near one end. Then, snag a crosswise thread with a pin. Gently pull the thread so it shows up as a puckered line along the width of the fabric.
2. Cut along the puckered line from one selvage edge to the other, thereby following one thread in a straight line.

Marking and Cutting the Strips (B)

3. To determine the number of strips of fabric you will need for the ruffle, divide the width of the fabric into the total length of the ruffle measured in Determining the Size of the Ruffle, Step 2. Make sure to add 1″ (2.5 cm) for every strip to provide ½″ (1.3 cm) seam allowances at each end.
4. Fold the fabric in half wrong sides out and pin the selvages together.
5. Using the width you found in determining the size of the ruffle in Step 1, mark off as many strips as you will need along the selvage and then along the fold.
6. Draw parallel chalk lines to join the marks made in Step 5.
7. Trim off both selvages.
8. Cut the strips along the chalk lines through both layers of fabric. Remove the pins and unfold the fabric.

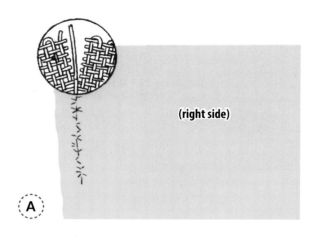

(right side)

A

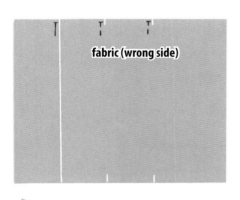

fabric (wrong side)

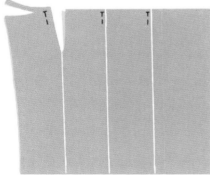

B

Joining the Fabric Strips (C)

9. If the ruffle is to be made from one strip of fabric, skip to Step 16.

10. If the ruffle requires more than one strip of fabric, mark ½″ (1.3 cm) seam allowances with chalk on the wrong side of the fabric at both ends of each of the strips.

11. Place two strips together wrong sides out, aligning the seam lines, and pin.

12. Baste just outside the seam line and remove the pins.

13. Machine stitch and remove the basting.

14. Repeat Steps 10–13 until you have one long ruffle strip.

15. Press open the seams.

16. Measure the strip and cut it to the length found in Determining the Size of the Ruffle, Step 2, making sure to add 1″ (2.5 cm) for ½″ (1.3 cm) hems at each end.

17. If the ruffle is to be attached to a garment edge that has no opening (on the hems of many skirts, for example), join the ends of the strip to make a continuous circular strip by repeating Steps 10–13. Press open the seam.

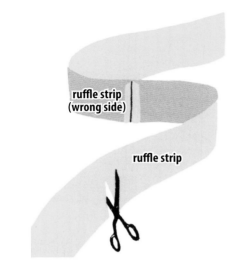

ruffle strip (wrong side)

ruffle strip

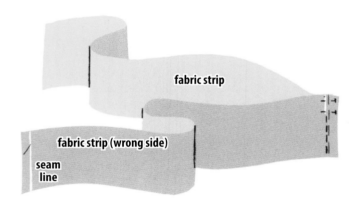

fabric strip

fabric strip (wrong side)

seam line

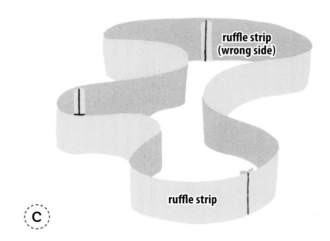

ruffle strip (wrong side)

ruffle strip

C

MAKING A RUFFLE STRIP CUT ON THE BIAS

Marking and Cutting on the Bias (A)

1. Straighten the fabric as described in Making a Ruffle Strip Cut on the Straight of the Grain, Section A.
2. Fold the fabric diagonally so a crosswise edge is aligned with a selvage edge and the wrong sides are together. Pin the edges.
3. Cut along the folded edge. Remove the pins and the top piece of fabric.
4. To determine the number of strips of fabric you will need to make the ruffle, measure the diagonal edge, and divide the measurement into the total length of the ruffle found in Determining the Size of the Ruffle, Step 2. Make sure to add ½″ (1.3 cm) for every strip to provide ¼″ (0.6 cm) seam allowances at each end.
5. With a ruler at a right angle to the diagonal edge of the fabric, measure the ruffle width you found in Determining the Size of the Ruffle, Step 1, marking off as many strips as you need.
6. Draw parallel chalk lines to join the marks made in Step 5.
7. Trim off both selvages.
8. Cut the strips along the chalk lines.

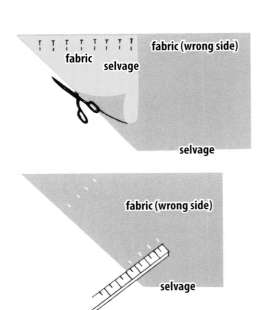

A

Joining the Fabric Strips (B)

9. If the ruffle is to be made from one strip of fabric, skip to Step 16.

10. If the ruffle requires more than one strip of fabric, mark ¼″ (0.6 cm) seam allowances with chalk on both ends of each strip.

11. Place two strips together, wrong sides out, so the strips form a V-shape. Align the seam lines and pin.

12. Baste just outside the seam line and remove the pins.

13. Machine stitch and remove the basting.

14. Repeat Steps 10–13 until you have one long ruffle strip.

15. Press open the seams.

16. **A.** If the ruffle is to be attached to a garment edge that has an opening (on the hem of an apron, for example), cut off one end of the strip at a right angle to the long edges. Measure the strip to the length you found in Determining the Size of the Ruffle, Step 2, making sure to add 1″ (2.5 cm) for ½″ (1.3 cm) hems at each end and cut at a right angle to the long edges.

    B. If the ruffle is to be attached to a garment edge that has no opening (on the hems of many skirts, for example), measure the strip to the length you found in Determining the Size of the Ruffle, Step 2, adding ½″ (1.3 cm) for ¼″ (0.6 cm) seam allowances at each end. Cut away the excess material, making sure the cut is parallel to the end of the strip. Join the two ends to make a continuous circular strip by repeating Steps 11–13. Press open the seam.

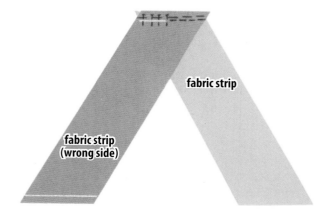

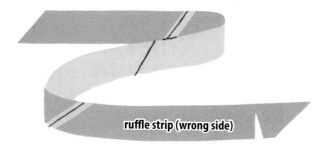

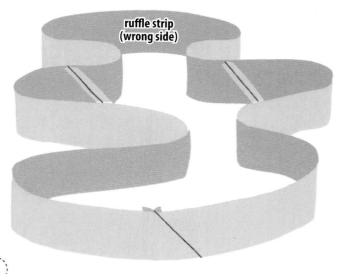

B

Hemming the Ruffle Strip (C)

1. For ruffles with one edge sewn into the garment, only one edge needs hemmed. With the ruffle strip wrong side up, turn up one of the long edges ⅛″ (3.2 mm) and press flat, turn again, and press.

2. Machine stitch ³⁄₁₆″ (0.5 cm) from the fold. Remove the basting and press. Alternate hems include overlock serging, adding trims or a raw edge if the fabric allows.

3. For ruffles with two exposed edges hem both edges according to Step 1.

4. If the ruffle forms a complete circle, stitch the short end together either before or after hemming based on your design, how it will be sewn to the garment, and the type of fabric. For excess length, it's often easier to join the short ends once the ruffle is attached to the garment.

Gathering the Ruffle (D)

5. Replace the regular thread on the bobbin of your sewing machine with heavy-duty thread or buttonhole twist.

6. Turn the ruffle strip wrong side down and run a line of machine basting (6 stitches to the inch) ⅝″ (1.6 cm) from the unhemmed edge. Leave about 4″ (10.2 cm) of loose thread at each end of the stitching.

7. For ruffle strips several yards long, the gathering you make will be easier to adjust, and the gathering threads less likely to break if you divide the line of basting into several segments. Stop basting about every 2 yds (1.8 m). Go back a few stitches and start a new line of basting as close to the first line as possible.

8. Run a second line of machine basting ⅜″ (0.9 cm) from the unhemmed edge. If you divided the first line of basting, make sure to divide the second line at the same points. Again, leave about 4″ (10.2 cm) of loose thread ends.

9. Grasp one pair of the heavier loose bobbin threads with one hand and use the other hand to gather the ruffle strip by pushing the fabric away from the hand holding the threads. Repeat at the other end of the same pair of bobbin threads. Continue with the remaining pairs of bobbin threads until the ruffle is the desired length. Distribute the gathers of the ruffle evenly.

10. Attach to your garment as desired either in the hem, on top of the hem, in a seam line, under a facing, between two garment pieces, layer ruffles of the same or different width, or however your design dictates.

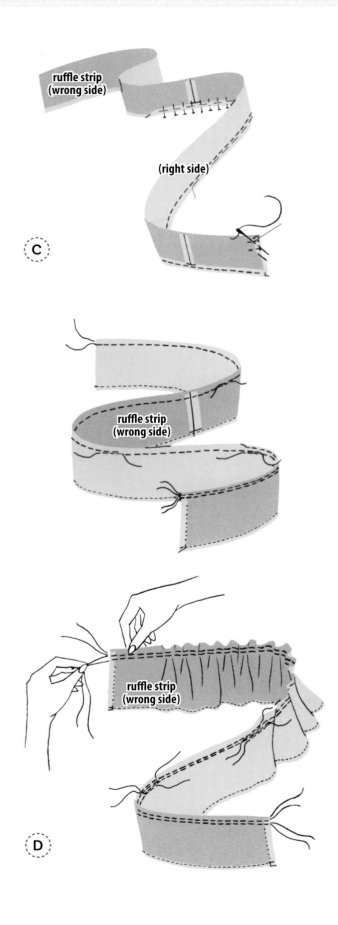

ruffle strip (wrong side)

(right side)

C

ruffle strip (wrong side)

ruffle strip (wrong side)

D

CHAPTER 8

PUTTING IT TOGETHER

ASSEMBLING ALL YOUR BUILDING BLOCKS INTO COMPLETE PROJECTS

Sewing is all about learning skills and then putting them to practice. In this chapter, we will combine selected techniques featured throughout this book to create complete, yet seemingly complex projects. Think about sewing in terms of layering different techniques, like building blocks.

By breaking down our projects into smaller steps that are then joined to the next one, we can assemble a whole, finished project by adding different techniques to its individual parts. You will find that a sequence of masterfully executed steps will enhance both your project and enjoyment.

For example, it is much more rewarding when you not only know how to sew a bound buttonhole, how to edge-finish with your favorite stitch, or how to pattern a new neckline closure, but also how to artfully apply them to specific garments or projects. What is your favorite skill or "building block?" Create the featured projects as illustrated or change them up to your own unique creation.

ALL-SEASON CARDIGAN

Perfect for any season and fabric, the All-Season Cardigan features a dropped shoulder and easy-to-fit full cut sleeve. Finished cardigans may be beaded, embroidered, or embellished with many techniques featured earlier in this book based on the fabric type and style you create. Your cardigan may be lengthened or shortened to your preference, styled with an embellished open front, or incorporate a front button closure. Change the fit by contouring the side seam to make an hourglass fit or change the neckline with creative pattern design. This pattern was designed to feature a variety of wool, knit, and sweater knit fabrics, but you're not limited to these.

Before you begin sewing, you will need to download the pattern, determine your size, and follow the fabric cutting and pre-sewing instructions. The downloadable pattern for the All-Season Cardigan is available in the online store at www.designerjoi.com. If you're using a similar style pattern, the instructions may vary slightly from those illustrated here, but you can apply all the same techniques and core skills featured in the previous chapters. Remember to reference Chapter 5 for tips on sewing wool, knits, lace, and other specialty fabrics. Adjust your seams and stitches to match your fabric selection.

Try the following techniques on your cardigan:
Lined Appliqué Pocket, Chapter 1
Button Closures, Chapter 1
Edge Trimming, Chapter 2
Beading, Chapter 3
Extra Wide Seams, Chapter 4
Sewing Wool, Chapter 5
Sewing Knits, Chapter 5
Hand Monogramming, Chapter 6
Changing the Neckline, Chapter 7

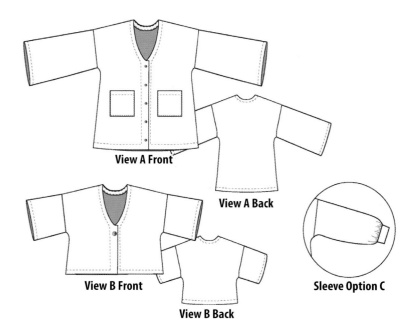

View A Front

View A Back

View B Front

View B Back

Sleeve Option C

Applying the Patch Pocket (A)

1. Apply the patch pocket to the front of the cardigan prior to assembling the garment. Fold under the top hem 1″ (2 cm), right sides together, and sew along the upper corners ⅝″ (1.6 cm). Clip corners, turn, and press. Following the seam allowance, fold along the side and bottom edges. Press. Attach to the front by machine or hand stitching. Reference page 33 for complete patch/appliqué pocket technique.

Sewing the Shoulder Seams (B)

2. With the right sides together, sew the shoulder seams of the cardigan. Make sure you stabilize your seam with twill tape or stay tape and apply seam techniques for your specific fabric (wool, page 137; knits, page 139).

Sewing the Sleeves (C)

3. With the right sides together, pin the sleeves to the arm opening.

> **Tip:** Pin the center of the sleeve to the shoulder seam first. Sew the sleeves to the body. With the right sides together, match the notches and stitch the underarm seam from top to bottom. Hem the sleeve or see the pattern for optional cuff instructions.

Sewing the Facing (D)

4. With the right sides together, match the neck and front edge facing to the garment lining up the notches and shoulder seams. Pin in place and sew at ⅝″ (1.6 cm). Clip curves and corners once the seam is sewn. Follow button instructions (page 19), or edge finish with a specialty trim (page 46).

Sewing the Hem (E)

5. Turn the lower edge under ¼″ (0.6 cm) and press. Turn under another ¼″ (0.6 cm) and stitch. You may modify the hem based on your fabric and embellishments. An alternate hem suggestion would be to apply an edge trimming (page 66), or a decorative edge hand stitch (page 146).

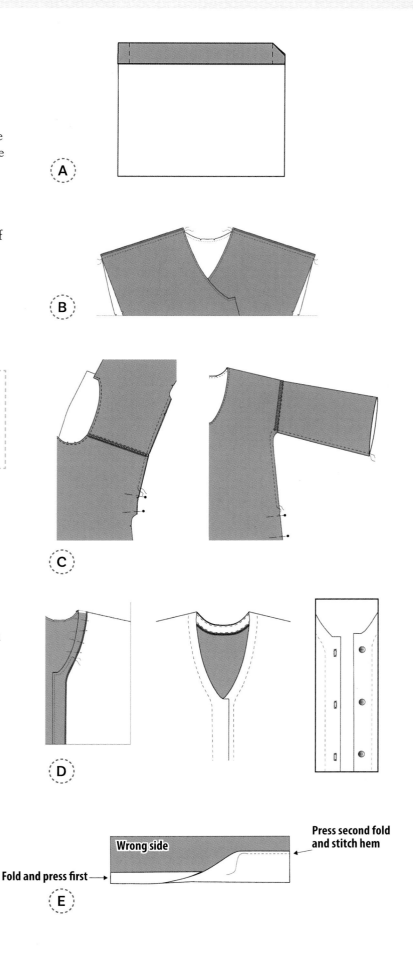

THE CAPSULE
WARDROBE KNIT TOP

Designed as a knit top to fill the need and popularity of easy-to-sew knit garments and the capsule wardrobe essential, this design is an ideal project for beginners with its simple pattern and ease of assembly. For the more experienced sewist, use this pattern as a base for your wardrobing and add stitches and a variety of finishes to display your skill mastery.

The pattern uses only three simple pattern pieces, and only requires 1–2 yards of fabric. By changing the style of knit fabric, this wardrobe staple will transition from everyday wear in a jersey knit to a surface design sweater knit for a classier look and feel. It will also transcend from one season to the next based on your fabric selections. Make and wear by itself or layer with a sweater, jacket, or wrap.

The Capsule Wardrobe Knit Top can be entirely hand sewn, machine sewn, or serged (optional) with an overlock machine, complete with decorative edge finishes. Even more versatility is added by using a quick, deconstructed sewing method featuring the raw edges of the knit fabric. The Capsule Pattern is designed to fit a ¾ to a ²⁶⁄₂₈ size range, with an easy-fit style. Of course, you can make the top as loose or snug as you desire.

The pattern featured here is available for download in the store at www.designerjoi.com. It features more details about selecting your knit fabric and some additional project details. This is the core breakdown of this style.

Try the following techniques on your Capsule Wardrobe Knit Top:
Elastic Casings, Chapter 1
Bias Bindings, Chapter 2
Crochet Edge Binding, Chapter 2
Sewing Beads, Chapter 3
Stabilizing a Seam, Chapter 4
Sewing Knits and Sweater Knits, Chapter 5
Creative Hand Stitches, Chapter 6
Adding Flair, Chapter 7
Changing the Neckline, Chapter 7

Preparing and Cutting the Pattern (A)

1. Select and download your pattern based on your measurements and desired fit. Cut out the pattern pieces on the dotted cutting line. The pattern pieces include a front, back, and sleeve.
2. Fold the fabric right sides together in half creating a fold on one long edge.
3. Place patterns on the fabric right side of the pattern facing up matching the edge marked place on fold to the fold of the fabric. Cut out the front and back. When cutting the patterns, make sure the most stretch of the fabric is positioned horizontally around the body rather than vertically up and down. Cut optional sleeves.

Sewing the Top (B)

4. With right sides together, pin the front to the back at the shoulders. Stitch using a straight stitch and a classic balanced seam (page 104). Finish the seam by stabilizing the seam (page 104), applying a bias binding (page 68), or edge finish with an overlock stitch or serger.
5. With right sides together, pin the front to back at the side seams using the straight stitch and finishes in Step 4. Although the fabric is stretched, it doesn't need the functional stretch on the shoulder seam or the vertical side seam. A straight stitch provides the stability, and the edge finish adds durability.

Adding Sleeves (C)

6. With right sides together, fold the sleeve in half and stitch the under-arm seam length using the same straight stitch as Step 4. Finish using a self-fabric bias binding or overlock stitch.

7. Turn the body of the top wrong side out. Insert the sleeve into the arm opening (the sleeve will be right side out), matching the center of the cap of the sleeve to the shoulder seam of the bodice. Ease the fullness of the cap and pin as needed. With right sides together stitch around the arm opening.

8. Serge or use a bias binding to finish off the armscye seam. The sleeve pattern for this design features a longer sleeve with a slight flair. For a more fitted sleeve, simply pin fit to the desired fullness around the arm and sew a narrower fit.

Finishing the Edges (D)

9. There are many options for edge finishing your capsule top. The simplest finish is to simply turn under the edge and topstitch with a lightening stitch or use an elastic thread for added stretch when putting the top on over the head, binding the edge with a stretch trim or bias binding (page 68). Those with a cover stitch machine or cover stitch on their machine can elevate the edge with these options.

10. If you like the deconstructed look seen in fashion, it's possible to omit any edge finish on the neck, arm, and hem area for most knits. Fabrics, like jersey, naturally roll to the front and create a rolled edge finish. Some knits will roll by simply stretching the length of the edge and creating a mechanical roll. To determine what is best for your fabric, test on a sample piece of fabric and decide what looks best for your design, the end use, and the fabric.

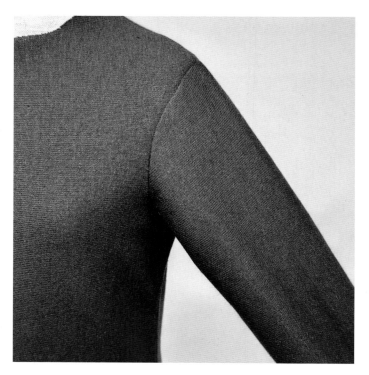

FLUTTERING SCARF TOP

Wrapped and tied snugly around the body, this fluttering blouse is made from four scarves in a matter of hours. The sleeves can be one design and the body another, but two should be related in style and color—small, all-over motifs work best. If the scarves have a border, its design becomes an element of the blouse.

The body front and back is cut from a pattern for a simple bodice back. All parts use the scarves finished edges, eliminating the need for hems unless you cut scarf-like pieces from a drapey lightweight fabric. If ordinary fabric is substituted for the scarves, cut four 28″ (71.1 cm) squares, and hem all edges.

The basic sloper pattern used for the front and back of this design is ideal with its simple lines and classic bust and waist darts. A version is available for download in the store at www.designerjoi.com if needed.

Try the following techniques on your Fluttering Scarf Top:
Inseam Pockets, Chapter 1
Silky Fringe, Chapter 2
Crochet Edge Binding, Chapter 2
Single Beads with a Lace Knot, Chapter 3
French Seams, Chapter 4
Sewing Delicate Fabrics, Chapter 5
Monograms, Chapter 6
Adding Flair, Chapter 7

Cutting Out the Back Bodice (A)

1. Eliminate any shoulder or neck darts from the bodice pattern by folding along the dart line and pin the dart closed. Do not close any waist darts.

2. Pin one scarf on a flat surface. Fold the wrong sides together; pin along the finished edges to prevent shifting.

3. Position the bodice back pattern on the scarf and align the center back line with the fold. If the center back line of your pattern is curved, place the high point of the curve on the fold of the scarf. Make sure the grain line arrow, if there is one on the pattern, is parallel to the fold.

4. To make the scarf top waist length, shift the pattern until the waistline marking at the center back is at 1″ (2.5 cm) above the bottom edge of the scarf. Pin the pattern to the scarf.

5. To draw a new side cutting line, first measure the pattern at the widest part, just below the armhole curve, and use a dressmaker's chalk to make a mark on the bottom edge of the scarf at the distance from the fold.

6. Make a second mark on the bottom edge 1″ (2.5 cm) inside the first one, removing the pins and turning away the bottom side corner of the pattern if necessary.

7. Draw a line to connect the mark made in the preceding step with the widest point of the pattern at the bustline.

8. Cut out the bodice back only along the new side cutting line and the original neck, shoulder, and armhole cutting lines of the pattern. Do not cut along the waistline cutting line and do not transfer any pattern markings to the scarf.

9. Remove the pattern and set it aside. Remove the pins around the edges of the scarf.

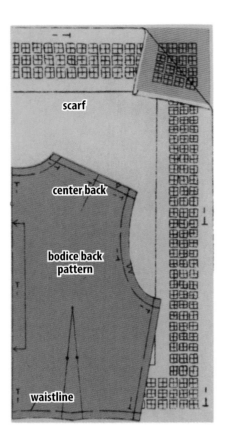

scarf

center back

bodice back pattern

waistline

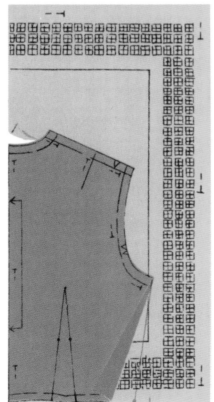

Cutting Out the Front Bodice Pieces (B)

10. Place the second scarf on the flat surface and fold the scarf in half diagonally, wrong sides together. Pin along the finished edges.

11. Measure the side of the bodice back along the cut edge and make a chalk mark on the open side edge if the scarf is at this distance from the bottom edge.

12. Place the pattern on the scarf with the bottom of the armhole curve on the chalk mark.

13. Shift the pattern until the center back line or the grain line is parallel to the side edge of the scarf. Pin the pattern to the scarf.

14. Cut out the bodice along only the armhole and shoulder cutting lines. If the neckline edge of the shoulder line does not reach the fold, cut straight out from the shoulder line through the fold.

15. Separate the front bodice into two pieces by cutting along the fold.

16. Remove the pattern and again set it aside; remove the pins around the edges of the scarf.

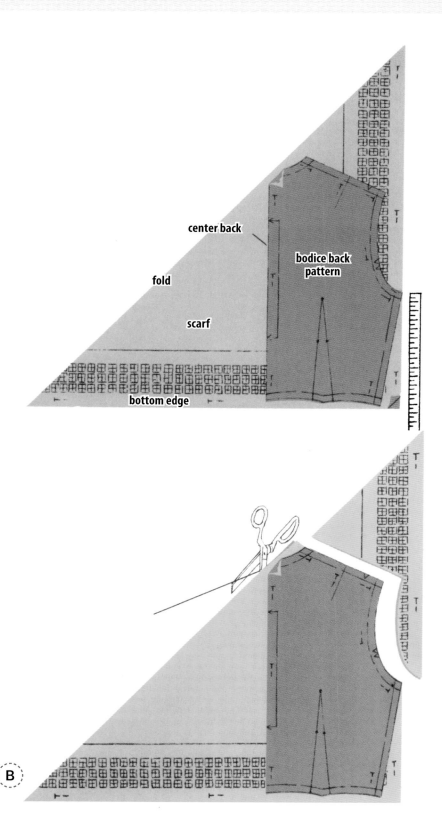

Cutting Out the Sleeves (C)

17. Place another scarf on the flat surface and fold the scarf in half, wrong sides out. Pin the corners together.
18. To cut out the armhole, set the bodice back pattern on the scarf and position the armhole at the middle of the folded side. Move the pattern sideways until the seam allowance at both ends of the armhole extends ¼″ (0.6 cm) beyond the fold. Pin only around the armhole.
19. Cut out the sleeve along only the armhole cutting line. Remove the pattern and the pins around the scarf.
20. To cut out the other sleeve, repeat Steps 17–19.

Assembling the Bodice (D)

21. Join the back and front bodice with French seams. To do this, first place the bodice back wrong sides up, and set one bodice front piece on top of it, wrong side down.
22. Align and pin the shoulder and side edges. If there's excess fabric at the neckline of the front piece, do not try to ease it into the shoulder seam. The excess will be trimmed off later.
23. Baste ½″ (1.3 cm) from the edges and remove the pins.
24. Machine stitch ⅜″ (0.9 cm) from the edges. Remove the basting.
25. Trim the seam to within ¼″ (0.6 cm) of the stitching.
26. To enclose the seam allowance inside the shoulder and side seams, turn the bodice inside out and roll the seamed edges of the shoulder and side between your fingers to bring the stitching to the edges. Press.
27. Machine stitch ⅜″ (0.9 cm) from the pressed edges.
28. Spread out the bodice, wrong side up, and press the seams flat toward the bodice back.
29. To attach the other half of the bodice front, repeat Steps 21–28.

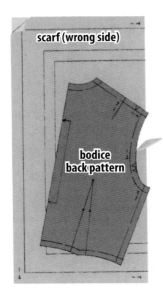

C

scarf (wrong side)

bodice back pattern

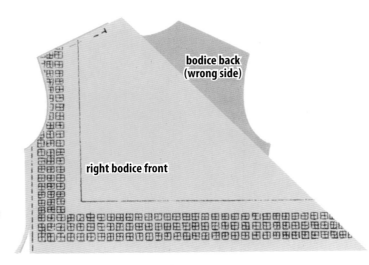

bodice back (wrong side)

right bodice front

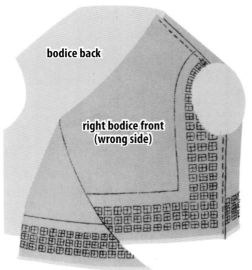

D

bodice back

right bodice front (wrong side)

Attaching the Sleeves (E)

30. Attach the sleeves to the bodice with French seams. To do this, first spread out the bodice, wrong side up, on the flat surface. Position one sleeve wrong side out on the bodice back and align the pieces at one armhole. Make sure the deeper end of the armhole curve of the sleeve is toward the bottom of the bodice.

31. Turn the bodice front over the sleeve.

32. Starting at the top of the armhole, pin the bodice and sleeve together around the armhole, aligning the edges and easing in the sleeve.

33. Baste ½″ (1.3 cm) from the edges. Remove the pins.

34. Machine stitch ⅜″ (0.9 cm) from the edges. Remove the basting.

35. Trim the seam to within ¼″ (0.6 cm) of the stitching.

36. To enclose the seam allowances inside the sleeve seam, first reach through the armhole and pull out the sleeve through the hole.

37. Turn the bodice wrong side out and roll the armhole seam edge between your fingers to bring the stitching to the edge. Press.

38. Baste ¼″ (0.6 cm) from the edge.

39. Machine stitch ⅜″ (0.9 cm) from the edge. Remove the basting.

40. To attach the other sleeve to the bodice, repeat Steps 30–39.

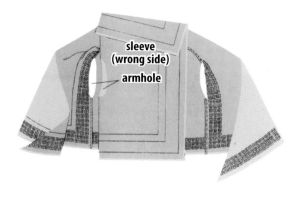

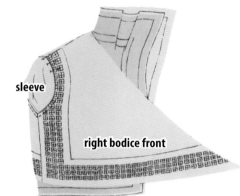

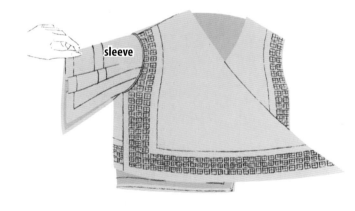

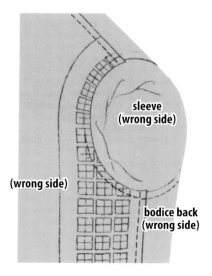

Finishing the Front and Neck Opening (F)

41. Turn the garment right side out. Trim off any excess fabric at the neckline of the front bodice.
42. Pin a strip of ½" (1.3 cm) seam tape over the edge all around the front and neck opening, attaching the tape so it extends ⅛" (3.2 mm) outside the edge. Make sure to ease the tape around the curving neckline. Cut off the excess tape.
43. Baste and remove the pins.
44. To conceal the raw ends of the tape at the bottom corners of the opening, first flip one corner back so the wrong side of the garment faces up.
45. Fold back the corner at a right angle to the bottom edge and baste along the fold.
46. Repeat Steps 44 and 45 on the other bottom corner.
47. From the right side of the garment, machine stitch along the inside edge of the tape. Remove all the basting.
48. To conceal the tape, fold the opening to the wrong side ¾" (1.9 cm) and press.
49. Secure the bottom corners of the opening with a hemming stitch.

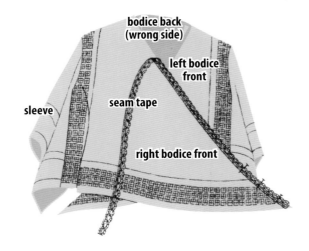

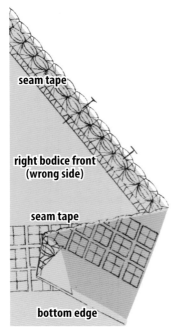

CONTOURED FABRIC-COVERED BELT

There are many ways for a garment to encircle the waist. Some designs simply join the bodice to the skirt with a waist seam, others contour to the body using the vertical seam lines, yet others abruptly stop at the waist. In all cases, the bodice should be fitted perfectly to your figure to enhance your silhouette and avoid the pitfalls of a waist that falls in the wrong location, or droops or puckers because of an ill fit. When styling the figure with a belt, the placement must be impeccable.

A contoured belt is designed to follow the contours of the waist and hipline and can add interest to any dress, shorts, or ensemble, with or without a waistline seam. The key to achieving the proper shape for the contour belt is hidden within it: the shaping is the result of many curved lines of parallel machine stitching that fuse together two pieces of interfacing, as shown on the following pages. These lines add the structure needed for a classy finish to the waistline.

The pattern featured here for the Contoured Fabric-Covered Belt is available as a free download in the store at www.designerjoi.com. The interfacings are also available in the store. You can draft your own pattern to use with this project as well.

Try the following techniques on your Contoured Fabric-Covered Belt:
Shaped Waistbands, Chapter 1
Decorative Edge Trimming, Chapter 2
Bias Binding, Chapter 2
Creating an Elaborate Design, Chapter 3
Classic Balanced Seam, Chapter 4
Sewing Wool and Heavy Fabrics, Chapter 5
Monogram Stitches, Chapter 6
Decorative Stitches, Chapter 6

Preparing the Interfacing (A)

1. Using the pattern piece provided for the contour belt, cut out two identical pieces of garment fabric—one for the outer belt and one for the belt facing—and two identical pieces of special interfacing fabric.

2. Join the two pieces of interfacing, matching the seam lines, the center front lines, and the center back line.

3. Pin the interfacing pieces together and baste ⅛″ (3.2 mm) inside the seam lines. Remove the pins. Machine stitch between the basting and seam lines.

4. Trim the seam allowance along the seam lines and remove the basting.

5. Machine stitch a series of parallel lines ¼″ (0.6 cm) apart from one end of the interfacing to the other, stitching through both layers. Trim loose machine threads at both ends.

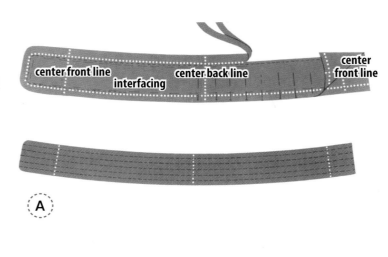

Interfacing the Outer Belt (B)

6. Unless you have already done so, run a line of basting stitches on the outer belt section along the pattern markings for the center front and center back.

7. With the outer belt wrong side up, run a line of machine stitching ¼″ (0.6 cm) outside the top and bottom seam lines, starting at the straight end of the belt (at right in this drawing) and stopping ½″ (1.3 cm) from the curved end.

8. Set the machine at six stitches per inch and continue to sew around the curved end, connecting the lines of stitching made in Step 7. Leave 4″ (10.2 cm) of loose thread at the beginning and end.

9. Center the interfacing between the seam lines of the outer belt, matching the center back and the center front markings. Place pins at these points, then add more pins at 1½″ (3.8 cm) intervals all around the interfacing.

10. Baste the interfacing to the outer belt, sewing ⅛″ (3.2 mm) in from the edge of the interfacing. Remove the pins.

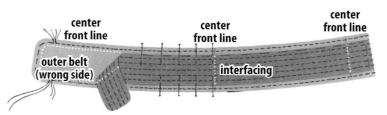

Attaching the Interfacing (C)

11. Fold the upper and lower edges of the outer belt over the interfacing and pin at 1″ (2.5 cm) intervals.
12. At the curved end (at left in this drawing), fold the edge over in tucks. Distribute the excess fabric evenly by gently pulling one end of the loose threads stitched in Step 8, then the other. Make little tucks around the curve and pin.
13. Baste the folded edges ⅛″ (3.2 mm) from the fold all around except at the squared end (at right). Remove the pins.
14. Press the folded edges of the belt to flatten out the seam allowances and press the fullness at the curved end to smooth the tucks.
15. Trim the basted seam allowance to ⅜″ (0.9 cm).
16. Hand stitch the trimmed seam allowance to the interfacing, using a catch stitch (page 242). Space the stitches more closely together around the curved end than along the upper and lower edges. Remove the bastings.

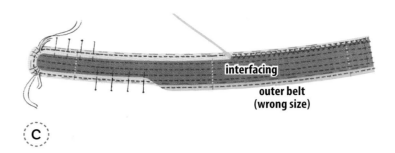

Preparing the Facing (D)

17. Unless you have already done so, run a line of basting stitches on the facing along the pattern markings for the center front and center back lines.
18. Machine stitch a line along the upper and lower seam lines of the facing, then run a line of stitches around the curved end at right in this drawing, following the directions in Step 8.
19. Fold over the upper and lower edges ⅛″ (3.2 mm) beyond the seam lines on the upper and lower sides of the facing. Pin at 1″ (2.5 cm) intervals and baste.
20. At the curved end, fold the edge over in tucks, distributing the excess fabric evenly and pin, baste, and press as in Steps 12–14.
21. Trim the seam allowance all around the facing to ¼″ (0.6 cm).

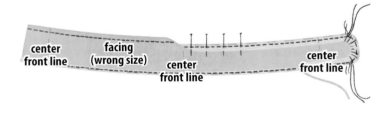

Attaching the Facing to the Outer Belt (E)

22. Place the facing wrong side down, over the interfaced side of the outer belt, matching the center front and back lines on the two pieces. Pin at 1″ (2.5 cm) intervals.
23. Baste all around the belt except at the squared end. Remove the pins.
24. Slip stitch (page 244) the facing to the folded seam allowance of the outer belt.
25. Remove all bastings except those marking the two center front lines. Press both sides of the belt.

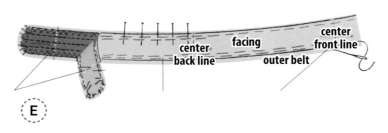

Attaching a Slide Buckle (F)

26. With the belt facing wrong side up, run a line of machine stitching between the upper and lower edges ¼″ (0.6 cm) in from the squared end.
27. Finish the raw edge at the squared end with overcast stitches (page 243).
28. Turn the belt wrong side down. Place the buckle wrong side down and slip the overcast end of the belt through one side of the buckle. Slip it over the center bar and down through the other side.
29. Turn the belt and buckle wrong side up and pull the belt through until the center front line is at the side of the center bar farthest from the rest of the belt. Fold the belt down along the center front line.
30. Pin the squared end to the main part of the belt and baste between the machine stitching made in Step 26 and the straight edge. Remove the pins.
31. Fasten the squared end to the main part of the belt with a hemming stitch. Remove all bastings.

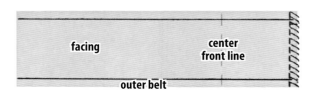

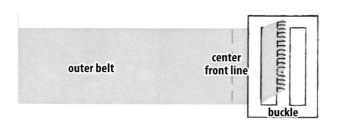

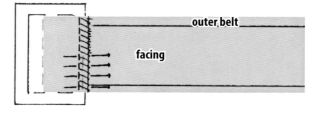

Try the following techniques on your Decorative Yoyo Inset Sleeve:
Fashion Yoyo, Chapter 2
Bias Binding, Chapter 2
Single Bead with Lace Knot, Chapter 3
Self-Bound Seam, Chapter 4
Changing the Neckline, Chapter 7
Sleeve Slash and Spread, Chapter 7
Adding Flair, Chapter 7

Note: The inserted row of yoyos (Suffolk patches) offers a homespun, peek-a-boo effect on a classic back-button blouse. Guest project by Amelia Johanson.

DECORATIVE YOYO INSET SLEEVE

Yoyos (also called a Suffolk patch) are gathered fabric circles, which were made popular from the 1920s through the 1940s and used primarily to embellish bedding. In a recent issue of *Vogue Magazine*, a gorgeous silk satin cape was featured made entirely of overlapping yoyos, showing just how fashionable this technique is in garment sewing. Featured here is a less daunting application illustrating how to add these vintage rosettes to wearables. Using a basic button back blouse pattern with a short sleeve, they are joined together and to the sleeve with an easy machine technique.

The sleeve inserted here with a ⅝″ (1.6 cm) seam finishes approximately 8½″ (21.6 cm) long. The unfinished pattern piece is approximately 10″ (25.4 cm) long (including the 1″ or 2.5 cm hem allowance). The yoyos start at the seam allowance and finish where the sleeve edge would finish.

These yoyos each started with a 3½″ (8.9 cm) circle, and finished yoyos ended up 1⅝″ (4.1 cm)—approximately half as large as the starting circle. Smaller circles will yield smaller yoyos, and larger circles, larger yoyos. Once joined together, five down and two across the panel finished approximately 8¼″ (21 cm) long, which was perfect for the length of the sleeve pattern. Refer to Photo 1.

Note: Some length is lost when you join the yoyos together due to the tiny seam allowances. For a longer sleeve, you'll need to add yoyos or start with a slightly larger circle, depending on how much additional length you need.

Creating Your Sleeve

1. Place your yoyo panel centered on your pattern piece. Make sure its ends are at the bottom hemline and top seam line.

2. Determine how much fabric you will need on either side of the yoyo panel in order to cut out your sleeve. Your fabric is doubled on each side, folded in half with the fold butting up against the sides of the yoyo panel. For the sleeve shown, the panels were cut 11 deep by 14″ (35.6 cm) wide and folded to 7″ (17.8 cm) wide.

3. Position the folded panels next to the yoyo panels so the bottom raw edges of all are flush. Double check you've accounted for the hem allowance.

4. Working one side at a time, place the yoyo panel face down on the left side fabric, pinning the right edge of the yoyos to the fold of the fabric as shown.

5. As for the single yoyo, set your machine for a narrow zigzag (2 width; 0.6 length). Pierce the center edge of the yoyo and through the fabric. Take four or five stitches of the fabric and back on the fabric, fixing your stitching as you begin and finish.

6. Continue stitching each yoyo to the fabric edge in the same manner.

7. Fold open so the left side of the sleeve block is created.

8. Repeat for the right-side panel, making sure that the yoyo and panels are aligned and pinned straight across. Repeat to make a second sleeve block.

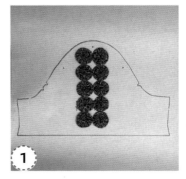

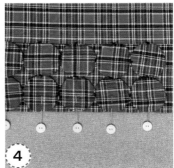

9. Place your pattern over your sleeve block, making sure the bottom of the sleeve aligns with the hem fold line and you have adequate seam allowance at the top. Trace off a right sleeve and a left sleeve, one from each block. Note that your sleeves will have an open area at the top between the top yoyos. Stay stitch on the seam allowance before cutting out to keep the fabric layers aligned and create a stitch line for the open area. You can stitch over an iron-away stabilizer in the open are if desired. Cut out your sleeves.

10. Cut two fabric strips of 1⅜″ (3.5 cm) wide and slightly longer than the lower edge of your sleeves. Make bias trim by folding the strip in half, then folding each raw edge in to meet the center fold, then pressing in half. Starch and press for a crisp finish, but don't stretch.

11. Using a glue stick or other fabric glue, insert the bottom edge of the sleeve into the bias tape and press to secure. Make sure the edge of the sleeve is against the inside fold of the bias tape. Do not stitch at this time.

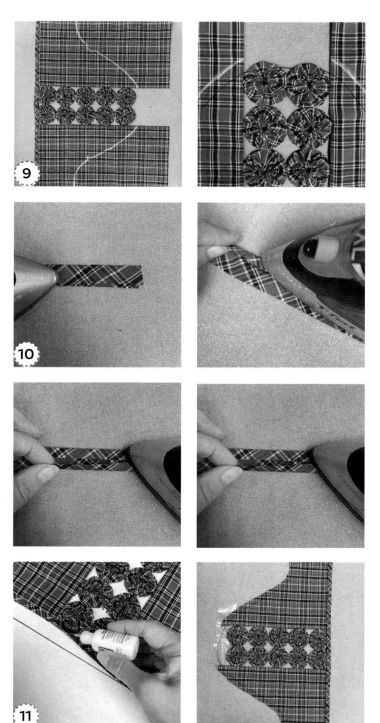

12. Construct the body of the blouse to the point of joining and finishing shoulder seams. Run two rows of gathering stitches on the sleeves. Wrong sides together, pin the sleeve into the armscye, making sure the yoyos at the top are approximately ¼" (0.6 cm) beyond the stitch line. Ease and stitch the sleeve into the garment making sure to catch the top of the yoyos. Serge to finish the seam.

13. Carefully detach the bias tape from the wrong side of the sleeve edge so that you'll be able to stitch ⅝" (1.6 cm) seam. Make sure the front of the bias tape is still glued to the sleeve edge.

14. Pin and stitch the sides of the garment from hem of the blouse to the edge of the sleeve. Finish with a serger. Fold the bias tape back over and adhere with glue if needed.

15. From the right side of the sleeve, edge stitch the bias tape in place.

QUILTED REVERSIBLE COAT

Combine the popularity of a quilted garment and this all-purpose, go-anywhere patterned coat, and you'll have the satisfaction of creating a functional and fashionable item within your wardrobe in a variety of fabrics that's easy to dress up or down for any occasion. The two sides sandwich an optional light layer of quilt batting to make the coat warm enough for a chilly evening. Ties, rather than buttons, make a neat closure, but buttons are also an option for making a neat closure whichever way the coat is worn.

The basis of the coat is a simple jacket pattern—no collar or front overlap, and classic straight sleeves combined with some basic pattern enhancements to lengthen, slightly flair, and add extra inseam pockets. Begin with a coat pattern that's oversized for your body to allow for padding and a casual fit.

The pattern featured here to create the reversible style is the Coat for All Seasons Design, available as a download in the store at www.designerjoi.com. The bodice front, back, and sleeve will be used. The interfacings featured are also available in the store.

Fabric requirements will vary based on the finished length and width of your design. This coat will use approximately 3–5 yds (2.7–4.6 m) of two cuts of fabric, one for each side. Additionally, a single layer yardage of interfacing, fusible web, or batting to match will be necessary for inner structure based on your fabric and design specifications. Pockets will use a scrap of lining or self-fabric. It is suggested that you measure all pattern pieces after they are made to determine the exact yardage. Read the assembly instructions prior to cutting your inner fabrics to determine what you will need for your design. When using batting, adding a fusible web is suggested to join the layers together.

Try the following techniques on your Quilted Reversible Coat:
Bound Buttonholes, Chapter 1
Corded Buttonholes, Chapter 1
Inseam Pocket, Chapter 1
Appliqué Patch Pocket, Chapter 1
Corded Tubing and Chinese Ball, Chapter 2
Beading, Chapter 3
Quilted Seam, Chapter 4
Monograms, Chapter 6
Decorative Stitches, Chapter 6
Designing with Dart Rotations, Chapter 7
Sleeve Slash and Spread, Chapter 7

Taking Your Measurements (A)

1. To determine the desired length for the finished coat, measure from the protruding bone at the back of your neck to the point slightly below your knees where you want the hem to fall.

2. Measure your bustline around the fullest part to get your overall full bust. Measure the front and back separately. Measure the front from the center front over to the side seam in line with the full bust; this is half of the front full bust. Measure the back from the center back over to the side seam in line with the full bust; this is half of the full back bustline. If you add these together and multiply by two, it should equal the overall full bust measurement.

3. To determine the placement for the inseam pockets, first tie a string around your waist. Then, place your hand several inches below your hip at a comfortable position for a pocket and measure from the string to the top of your hand. For the sleeve, measure from the shoulder point down the arm to the desired finished length of the sleeve on the body.

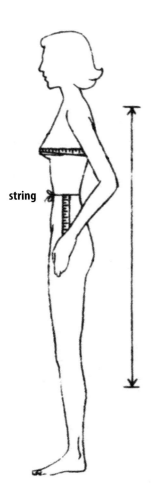

string

A

Adjusting the Length and Width of the Front and Back Pattern (B)

4. Place pieces of pattern paper under the side and bottom edges of the jacket back pattern. Secure the edges with tape.

5. To make the jacket pattern coat length, measure down the center back line of the pattern from the neck edge a distance equal to the desired length determined in Step 1. Extend the length on the paper.

6. Measure the added distance from the waistline of the pattern piece to the new length.

7. Using the distance determined in the preceding step, make pencil marks at intervals below the pattern waistline to lengthen the entire pattern piece.

8. Draw a new hemline by connecting the pencil marks.

9. To adjust the width of the coat at the bustline, measure from the center back to the side seam line at the level of the bust, just below the armhole seam line. Then, measure the front pattern at the bust level from the center front to the side seam line. Compare these measurements to the ones taken in Step 2. The coat pattern should measure at least your body measurements. If the pattern is smaller, increase at the side seams so your design begins with your right proportion. Ease will be added in the next step.

10. If you have a fuller abdomen or hip, you will want to take full waist and hip measurements across the front and also the back. Compare to the patterns before adding ease and extend the design outward to match your body proportion. You can connect the side seam from the underarm to hem with a ruler. Ease will be added in the next step.

11. Add 1½″ (3.8 cm) for ease to your front bust measurement, and 1½″ (3.8 cm) for ease to your back bust measurement. (Step 2).

12. At the armhole seam line, measure out the distance determined in the preceding step from the side seam line and make a pencil mark.

13. At the hemline marking on the pattern, measure out 1½″ (3.8 cm) from the side seam line and make a mark.

14. To make the new side seam line, draw a diagonal line from the bustline mark (Step 11) through the hemline mark (Step 12) and down to the new hemline.

15. Draw cutting lines ⅝″ (1.6 cm) outside the new side seam line and 1″ (2.5 cm) below the new hemline. This adds the seam allowance.

16. Transfer the waist dot to the new side seam line and any notches to the new cutting line if you choose.

17. Place a dot or marking below the waistline at the location of the top of the pocket. Cut out the back pattern. Repeat Steps 4–16 to adjust the length and width of the front pattern. Once the front and back have been adjusted, line up the side seams to make sure they match in length. If using a front pattern that has a built in facing, simply trim off the facing and convert the front neckline to feature a simple line.

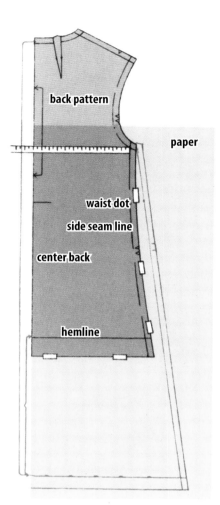

B

Adjusting the Sleeve Pattern and Armhole (C)

18. Using the sleeve length measurement taken in Step 3, measure from the shoulder point down the sleeve and length or shorten to match. Leave a 1″ (2.5 cm) hem allowance beyond the hem placement line.

19. If extra width was added at the underarm on the bodice in Step 9, extend the upper edge of the sleeve seam outward to match and make a mark. Further extend outward the ease amount of 1½″ (3.8 cm) at the underarm.

Making the Inseam Pocket Pattern (D)

20. Follow the instructions on page 35 for adding an inseam pocket. A free downloadable pocket template is available in the pattern section of the store at www.designerjoi.com.

21. Cut out the pocket pattern.

22. If using a patch pocket, follow the instructions on page 33.

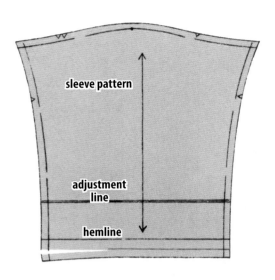

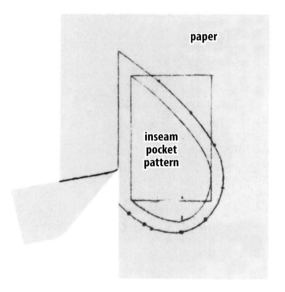

Cutting and Marking the Coat (E)

23. Fold the first coat fabric half lengthwise with the selvage edges together and the wrong sides facing out. If adding batting, the first coat fabric will be padded, so do not use a water repellent fabric for this layer.

24. Pin the pattern pieces to the fabric, following the layout determined in Step 22. If you plan to make a patch pocket on this layer of the coat, also pin the patch pocket pattern to the fabric.

    Cut around the pattern pieces. Then, if the front ties will be made from this fabric, use the larger scraps of fabric to cut out six 16 x 2″ (40.6 x 6.4 cm) front ties for the coat.

25. Use dressmaker's carbon and a tracing wheel to transfer the shoulder darts and the pocket opening markings to the wrong side of the fabric sections. Remove the pattern pieces.

26. Repeat Steps 23–25 to cut out the second coat fabric. Cut out the patch pocket and ties if you didn't cut them from the first fabric.

27. Transfer all pattern markings to the wrong side of each fabric section with dressmaker's carbon and a tracing wheel, using the new lines where adjustments were made. Remove the pattern pieces.

28. To cut out the inseam pockets and patch pocket lining, place the lining fabric wrong side down; fold over one side 10″ (25.4 cm).

29. Fold down the facing on the patch pocket pattern.

30. Pin the two pocket patterns to the double fabric thickness, keeping the grain line arrow of the patch pocket and the side seam line of the inseam pocket parallel to the fold.

31. Cut around the pocket patterns. Then, transfer the seam line markings to the wrong side of the lining pieces with dressmaker's carbon and a tracing wheel. Remove the pattern pieces.

32. Fold the remaining lining fabric and cut out two more inseam pocket sections, following Steps 30 and 31.

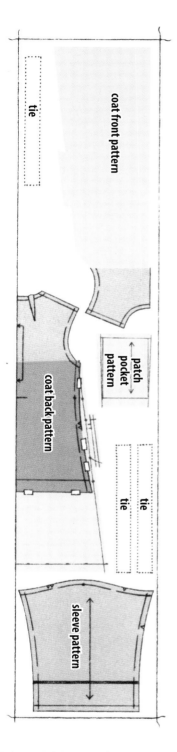

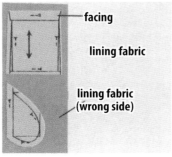

facing

lining fabric

lining fabric (wrong side)

Assembling the Coat (A)

Padding the Coat

Instructions for adding the batting are included featuring either machine quilting, fusible web, or a combination of both. It's suggested for a machine quilted coat to be cut a size larger, allowing for shrinking during the quilting process and wait to trim away the excess batting until the pieces are quilted. Extra-fine batting or cotton muslin is recommended for extra-fine fabric. Experiment with samples of your fabrics to find the perfect combination prior to sewing.

1. Stitch the shoulder darts on the coat back that you cut out of the first fabric. (Do not pad a waterproof fabric.) Then, clip the darts and press them flat.

2. Lay the batting on a flat surface. If the full width is unmanageable, cut off a section that's at least 2″ (5.1 cm) wider all around than the coat back.

3. When fusing the layers together, cover the batting with sheets of fusible web, butting the edges of the sheets.

4. Place the coat back wrong side down on top of the batting and pin the layers of fabric, optional web, and batting together. If machine quilting, hand basting is also an option for tacking the layers together.

5. Fold back the top edge of the fabric even with the bottoms of the darts. Cut out the darts in the batting and the web to reduce bulk.

6. Butt the cut edges of the batting and web darts together and fold the top edge of fabric back into place. Insert a pin at each dart to keep it closed and hold the layers together.

7. For fusible web joining of the layers, baste the three layers together all around the outer edge 1″ (2.5 cm) from the raw edges to prevent the batting from slipping. Remove the pins.

8. Fuse the fabric, web, and batting together, following the instructions for the fusible web. Try out both the dry iron and steam iron methods on a sample of the three layers to determine which method works best for the fabric you're using.

9. Machine quilt the pattern piece in any quilting pattern you desire. Quilting doesn't need to be overly complex or heavy for the coat, but experiment with patterns that will accent your fabric and not compete with it. Trim around the outer edge of the pattern piece and remove the excess batting and web if you haven't done so already.

10. Repeat Steps 2–8 to pad the coat front and sleeve sections that you cut out of the first fabric with the fusible web.

Note: If adding a patch pocket to either fashion side of the coat, attach them to the front pieces according to the instructions for Appliqué Patch Pocket on page 33.

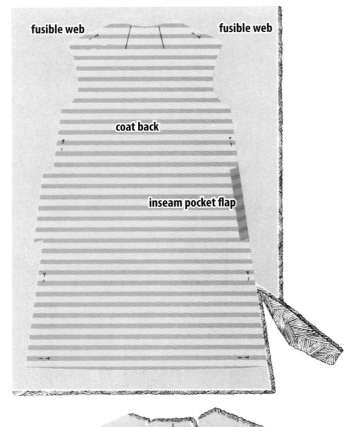

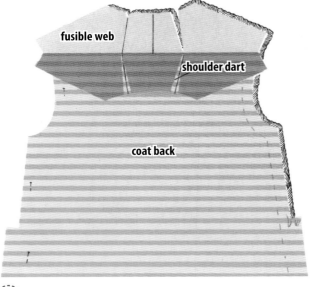

Finishing the Padded Layer of the Coat (B)

11. Place the padded coat back wrong side down; pin one inseam pocket section wrong side up to one pocket opening where marked. Add another pocket section to the pocket opening on the other side of the coat back similarly.

12. Stitch along the pocket side seam lines, removing the pins as you go, making sure to leave the upper and bottom edge unsewn ⅝" (1.6 cm) from the edge.

13. Place the coat front sections in the other fabric wrong side down; repeat Steps 11 and 12 to attach the other two pocket sections to the coat front pocket openings.

14. Press the seam allowances toward the pocket.

15. Pin the padded coat back and coat front sections together along the side seams, wrong sides out. Pin the pocket front and back sections together along the curved seam lines.

16. Machine stitch ⅝" (1.6 cm) from the raw edges; remove the pins as you go. Use the guide on the throat plate to keep the line of stitching straight. Start at the hem edge and stitch to the bottom pocket opening mark; pivot and stitch around the pocket to the top pocket opening mark. Pivot again; continue stitching up the side seam line to the armhole.

17. Clip the coat back seam allowances above and below the pockets.

18. Trim away the batting that extends beyond the seams, cutting just outside the stitching. Remove all bastings.

19. Press the seam allowances open above and below the clips made in Step 17.

20. Stitch the coat fronts and back together at the shoulder seams with right sides together; insert the sleeves, following your pattern instructions. Use the throat plate guide to keep the line of stitching straight. Trim away the batting from the seam allowances; press them flat. Press the sleeve seam allowances toward the inside of the sleeve.

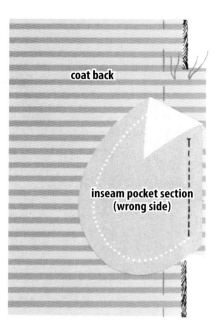

coat back

inseam pocket section
(wrong side)

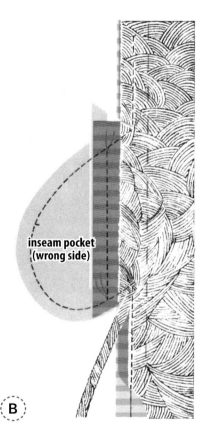

inseam pocket
(wrong side)

B

Attaching the Ties (C)

21. Fold one tie in half lengthwise, wrong sides out.

22. Set your machine at 10 stitches to the inch and starting at the fold, stitch across one end ¼″ (0.6 cm) from the edge. Pivot and stitch down the side. Clip the corners diagonally up to, but not into, the machine stitching.

23. Repeat Steps 21 and 22 to make the other five ties.

24. Turn the ties right side out, pulling out the corners with a pin. Then, press them flat.

25. Set your machine at six to eight stitches to the inch and topstitch just inside the edges of each tie. Starting at the open end of each tie, stitch up one long side, across the short end, and down the other side, pivoting at the corners.

26. Pin the unstitched end of one tie to one of the unpadded coat fronts at the neck seam line. Align the raw edges of the tie with the raw edge of the coat front.

27. Pin a second tie to the neck seam line of the other coat front. Pin on the other ties 6–8″ (15.3–20.3 cm) apart. Machine baste across each tie within the seam allowance. Remove the pins.

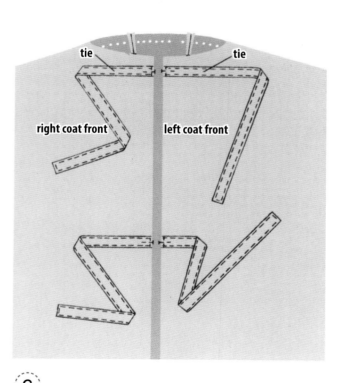

Finishing the Coat (D)

28. On both fabrics to keep the neckline from stretching, stay stitch around the neckline ½″ (1.3 cm) from the edge. Clip the neck at 1″ (2.5 cm) intervals up to, but not into, the stay stitching.

29. With the wrong sides facing out, pin the two layers of the coat together around the neckline and down the front edges. Baste and remove the pins.

30. Set your machine at 10 stitches to the inch and machine stitch the two layers together ⅝″ (1.6 cm) inside the raw edges. With the unpadded layer facing up, stitch along the seam allowance markings starting at one hem edge.

31. Trim the seam allowances around the neckline to ⅜″ (0.9 cm) and clip the corners diagonally.

32. Cut the batting out of the seams, close to the stitching.

33. Remove all bastings.

34. Turn the coat right side out through the hem opening, making sure to insert the sleeve of the inner layer into the outer sleeve. Press.

35. Turn under the hem of the unpadded layer 1″ (2.5 cm) and press the fold. Turn under the hem of the padded layer even with the unpadded layer.

36. Pin the hem edges together.

37. Baste around the hem and around the front and neckline of the coat. Remove the pins.

38. Try on the coat, pulling the sleeves down until there isn't any bunching under the arm.

39. Turn up the sleeve hem in the top layer of the coat 1″ (2.5 cm) and press the fold. Turn up the sleeve hem in the inner layer of the coat and press the fold.

40. Pin the folded sleeve hems together. Baste and remove the pins.

41. Set your machine at six to eight stitches to the inch and topstitch just inside the folds of the sleeve hem. Make three more rows at 1″ (2.5 cm) intervals around the hems of the sleeves.

42. Following the instructions in Step 41, make four rows of topstitching along the folded edges of the bottom hem, front, and neckline of the coat. Remove all bastings.

> **Optional:** Quilting stitches or blind hand stitching may be used to join the hem edges together.

More complex quilting of the fabric can be applied prior to cutting the fabric (you can repurpose a family quilt—just test the pattern fit prior to cutting and avoid treasured family heirlooms) or using pre-quilted panels are all ways to add more traditional hand or machine quilting to this design.

Embellish your reversible coat with decorative trim from page 66, monograms from page 146, buttons and button closures from page 19, add a custom flower from page 75, or add a creative neckline from page 99. Regardless of what you design, each version of your reversible coat will add enjoyment to your wardrobe.

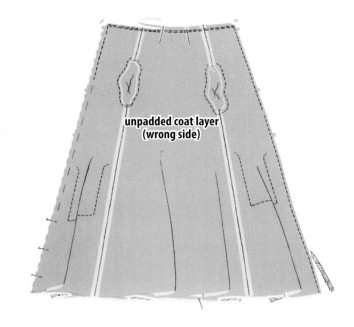

unpadded coat layer (wrong side)

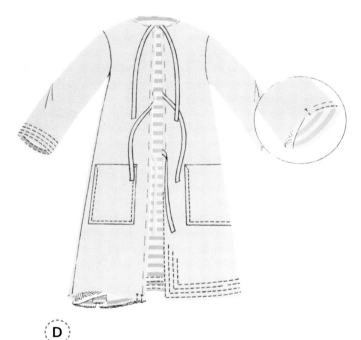

D

CHAPTER 9

REDESIGNING READY-TO-WEAR

ACCENTS THAT MAKE THE DIFFERENCE

The slightest addition of a trim or embellishment can create a dramatic transition from plain to striking in your wardrobe. If time is lacking, rather than creating an entire garment from pattern to completion, instead repurpose items that are already in your wardrobe. With the popularity of recycling, resale shops, and conserving resources, these accents are a great way to use forgotten materials and add new life into a plain garment.

A classic skirt is turned fashionable by adding a zippered inset in a complementing material. The new shape adds additional ease and flair for fashion and function. A plain pair of pants is transformed into a fashionable item when recutting the leg to feature a cuff or a contrasting bias band at the hemline edge. How about adding a pop of color? One sure-fire way to draw attention is to wear a bold print or color as featured in re-trimming a shirt. An almost unlimited supply of fabrics and combinations of fabric will bring your ready-to-wear or patterns to life and make clothing that is distinctly yours.

CREATIVE HEMMING: CONTOURED FACED HEM

This design features a store-bought trouser pant revived from the back of the closet. By tracing out a new hem shape, this pant takes on a whole new look. The length can be shortened to ankle length or ¾-length to further accentuate the new shape. The process for redesigning the hem involves a simple tracing of the new shape and then making a facing to finish off the edge. An additional contrasting band may be applied to the outside of the pant when adding a contrasting facing band. This same technique can be used on the cuff of a jacket sleeve or even the neckline of many garments. It's important to stabilize the edge prior to cutting it open to avoid stretch on any area that may feature bias. Of course, this technique can also be applied to your commercial sewing patterns. You will redesign the pattern prior to cutting out the pattern pieces and sewing. Additional techniques can be added and layered to this design such as adding a zipper or buttons.

Try the following techniques on your Contoured Faced Hem:
Invisible Zipper, Chapter 1
Buttonhole Loops, Chapter 1
Mitered Corners, Chapter 1
Decorative Edge Trimming, Chapter 2
Creative Hand Stitches, Chapter 6
Changing the Neckline, Chapter 7
Adding Flair, Chapter 7

Making the Hem Template (A)

1. With basting thread or chalk, plot out the new shape of the hem on the pant. For narrow pants, keep the shape to a minimum, such as a single scallop rather than multiples. If the pant has a fuller leg, then the design may be repeated if desired. Shapes that work well for the hem include a single curved edge toward the outseam, a mitered point near the outseam, or a simple v-opening near the outseam.

2. To make a paper template, measure the length around the bottom edge of the pant hem. Take a piece of pattern paper a few inches longer and taller than the hem area of the pant. Draw a horizontal line the length of the hem on the paper. Mark one side the inseam and the other the outseam.

3. Determine the height of the new shape. Because the pant leg is wider as it goes up the leg, measure around the pant leg at the height of the new opening. Measure up from the hem and place this width on the paper pattern. The edges of the seam will angle outward to accommodate the transition in the leg.

4. Plot out the shape of the new hem edge.

5. Mark a ⅝″ (1.6 cm) hem allowance around all edges of the pattern.

6. To make a fabric template, cut a piece of cotton muslin a little longer and taller than the hem area of the pant. Pin it to the pant and trace the width at the hem, trace around the upper edge of the new hem shape, and mark the inseam and outseam.

7. Remove the muslin fabric.

8. Plot out the shape of the new hem edge on the muslin.

9. Mark a ⅝″ (1.6 cm) hem allowance around all edges of the pattern.

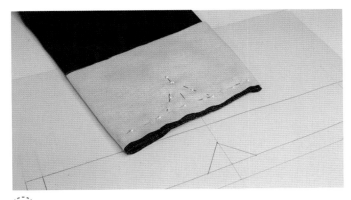

Prepping the Pant (B)

10. If the new shape is close to the current hem, remove the current hem stitches with a seam ripper and press the hem allowance flat, being careful not to remove any chalk marks.

> **Optional:** Place the pattern template on the pant and retrace the new shape with the polished pattern.

11. Baste around the pant leg marking the new edge of the hem. The basting will help stabilize the fabric. If the pant has a very loose weave, is a knit, or it may stretch, apply some interfacing to the underside of the pant to reinforce the fabric.

12. Mark a ⅝″ (1.6 cm) hem allowance on the pant and trim away the excess.

13. On the inside of the pant reinforce the seam lines by stitching on the seam allowance approximately 1″ (2.5 cm) above the new stitching line. This will prevent the side seams from unraveling.

Sewing the Facing (C)

14. With the wrong side of the fabric facing up, place the template on the fabric being used for the facing. Cut two facings, one for each leg.
15. With right sides together, sew the inseam and/or outseam of the facing.
16. With right sides together, line up the bottom edge of the facing to the bottom edge of the pant, matching seams and any new contoured shapes.
17. Stitch around the hem on the new edge/stitching line. Clip any curves or points and turn the facing to the inside of the pant. You may decide to trim down any excess fabric as needed. Press.
18. Finish the top edge of the facing with hem tape, bias binding, or an overlock stitch based on the weight of the fabric.
19. Tack the facing to the side seam allowance of the pant to anchor it in place, or topstitch from the outside of the pant.

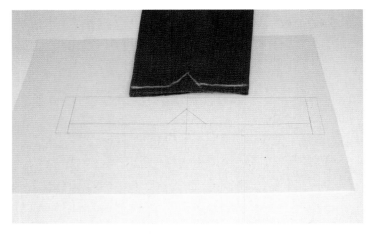

CREATIVE HEMMING: CONTRASTING BAND FACED HEM

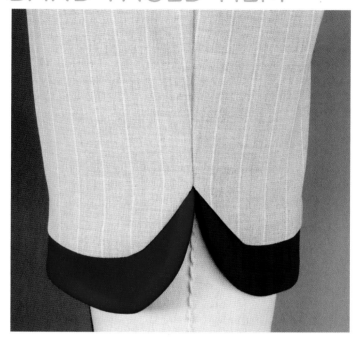

The Contrasting Band Faced Hem is an attractive hem that features a visible band of fabric outlining the shape of the hem on the outside of the pant hemline. This is the next step in elevating your sewing and creating an attractive hemline.

Making the Pattern (A)

1. To make the hem template, follow the previous Steps 1–9 for marking the hem and making a plain faced hem pattern, omitting the ⅝″ (1.6 cm) seam allowance in Steps 5 and 9 based on either the paper or muslin fabric template.
2. Once you have the hem plotted out on your pattern paper, determine how wide you want the accent band.
3. Trace outward from the lower hem line the width of the contrasting band and pattern the shape.
4. Add ⅝″ (1.6 cm) seam allowance on the top and bottom edge of the pattern.
5. If the new shape is close to the current hem, remove the current hem stitches with a seam ripper and press the hem allowance flat, being careful not to remove any chalk marks.

Optional: Place the pattern template on the pant and retrace the new shape with the polished pattern.

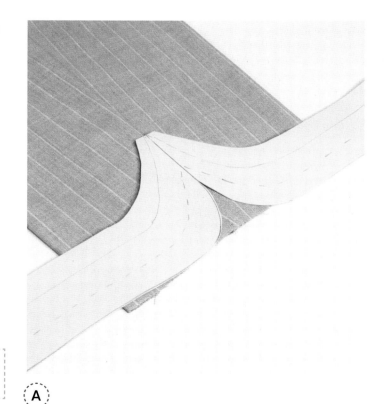

(A)

Prepping the Pant (B)

6. Baste around the pant leg marking the new edge of the hem. The basting will help stabilize the fabric. If the pant has a very loose weave, is a knit, or it may stretch, apply some interfacing to the underside of the pant to reinforce the fabric.

7. Mark a ⅝″ (1.6 cm) hem allowance on the pant and trim away the excess.

8. On the inside of the pant open the side seam allowance approximately 2″ (5.1 cm) above the new hemline. This will leave an opening for the band to blend into the seam allowance and the seam will be sewn shut after it is applied.

Making the Contrasting Band (C)

9. With the right side of the fabric facing up, place the template on the fabric being used for the contrasting band. Cut two bands—one for each leg.

10. With right sides together, sew the inseam and/or outseam of the facing.

11. Using the same pattern, cut an additional set of bands, but cut this set with the fabric wrong side up. This will be the inside facing to the contrasting band. Set this set aside and make sure not to mix them up.

12. With right sides together, take two bands and sew around the bottom edge, clip, and turn right side out. Baste across the top.

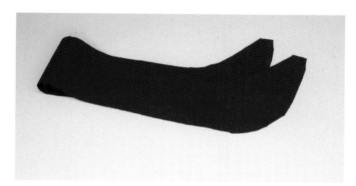

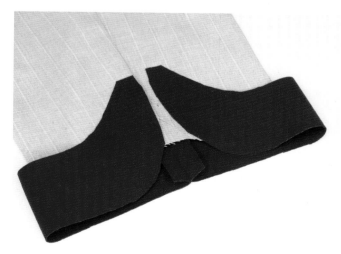

C

Sewing the Band to the Hemline (D)

13. If any part of the design features a right angle or square shape, reinforce the corner on the pant and the facing. Clip to the corner to allow for pivoting the fabric when stitching.

14. With right sides together, match the unfinished edge of the band to the bottom edge of the pant, matching seams and any new contoured shapes.

> **Tip:** For contrast with right angles, put the needle down and pivot to stitch the sharp corner. For bands with curve, it may be difficult to pin the contour. To help with the curve, clip the seam allowance or rotate the curve as you're sewing to achieve the shape.

15. Stitch around the hem on the new edge/stitching line. Clip any curves or points while sewing. Press the contrasting band flat and away from the pant. Press the seam allowance to the inside of the pant away from the contrasting band.

16. Finish the top edge of the facing with hem tape, bias binding, or an overlock stitch based on the weight of the fabric.

17. Tack the facing to the side seam allowance of the pant to anchor it in place, or topstitch from the outside of the pant.

18. On the inside of the pant, stitch the opening in the side seam to catch the contrasting band and close up the seam.

19. Embellish the outside of the band with beads, couture passementerie, Chinese ball buttons, or any other embellishment of your choice.

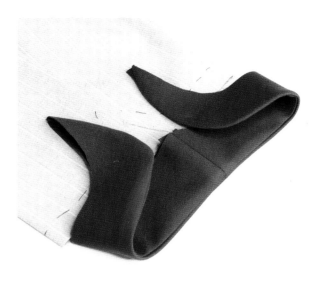

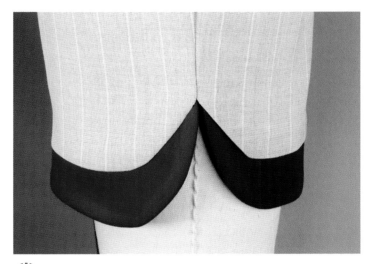

D

Take any button down shirt and give it new life by adding fresh, new details.

CONTRASTING ELEMENTS: RE-TRIMMING A SHIRT

Another creative way to add eye-catching details to a ready-to-wear garment or a plain shirt pattern—a new collar and a band of contrasting fabric have replaced the original ones. The shirt tails have been replaced by a tie belt, the sleeves have been cut short, and sporty new cuffs have been added. This clever application of simple, clean lines and design details layered with carefully selected complementary or contrasting fabrics, once again, changes up a plain, traditional shirt to fit your look. From classy and sporty to crafty and whimsical, what a fun way to utilize limited fabric yardage or smaller cuts of those designer fabrics that may not fit into your budget with garments needing large yardage requirements.

Try the following techniques on your Re-Trimmed Shirt:
Corded Buttonholes, Chapter 1
Stabilizing a Seam, Chapter 4
French Seam, Chapter 4
Sewing Delicate Fabrics, Chapter 5
Sewing Knits and Sweater Knits, Chapter 5
Changing the Neckline, Chapter 7
Front Closure with Button, Chapter 7

Preparing the Shirt (A)

1. Try the shirt on and make a pin mark 2–3″ (5.1–7.6 cm) below your natural waistline.
2. Make a pin mark 2–3″ (5.1–7.6 cm) above your elbow on one sleeve.
3. Measure the distance from the bottom edge of the shirt to the pin. Mark this distance with a chalk line all around the edge of the shirt.
4. Trim the bottom of the shirt along the chalk line.
5. Using a ruler, draw a chalk line at right angles to the folded edge of the sleeve at the point marked with a pin in Step 2. Then, trim the sleeve along this line.
6. Pin the cutoff sleeve on top of the other sleeve, aligning the shoulder seams; trim the second sleeve.
7. Remove the original collar from the shirt, using a seam ripper and working from the center back of the collar toward the center front. Save this collar as a pattern for cutting the new collar of a contrasting color.
8. Remove the tab from the right-hand side of the shirt front along the inner edge using a seam ripper.
9. Trim the right-hand side of the shirt front ¼″ (0.6 cm) outside the line of stitching that held the tab to the shirt.
10. Trim the left-hand side of the shirt front, taking the same amount as from the right-hand side.
11. Mark a new stitching line ¼″ (0.6 cm) in from the cut edge on the left-hand side of the shirt.
12. To enable you to center the new collar and waistband on the shirt correctly later, mark the center back of the shirt at the neck edge and at the bottom edge with a few running stitches.

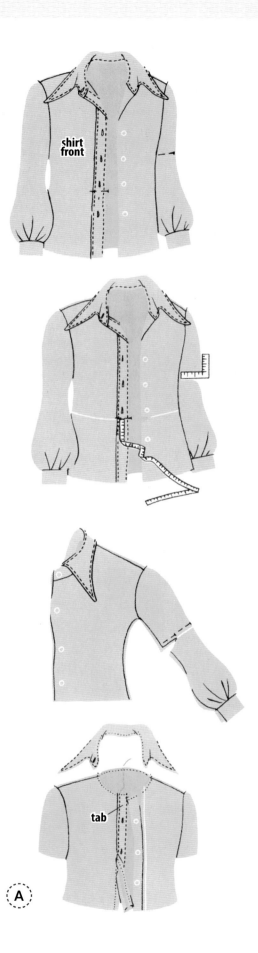

Cutting Out a New Waistband, Cuff, Tab, and Collar (B)

13. Fold the new fabric in half lengthwise.

14. To cut out the new waistband and tie, first measure parallel to the selvage edge and then mark with chalk a length equal to one half your waist measurement, plus 2″ (5.1 cm) (for wearing ease). Add 16″ (40.6 cm) for the tie ends, then measure and mark with chalk a width equal to twice the width of the old tab.

15. Draw a cutting line ¼″ (0.6 cm) outside all four edges.

16. To cut out the new cuffs, measure and mark a rectangle with a bottom edge equal to the circumference of the raw edge of the cut sleeve. Then, measure and mark a top edge equal to the circumference of the sleeve 2″ or 2½″ (5.1 cm or 6.4 cm) above the cut edge.

17. Draw a new cutting line ¼″ (0.6 cm) outside all four edges.

18. To cut out the new tabs, use the old tab as a pattern and place it lengthwise on the fabric. Pin in place and draw an outline twice the size of the tab.

19. Draw a cutting line ¼″ (0.6 cm) outside the edge of the tab on all four sides: then draw another line down the center.

20. To cut out the new collar, use the old collar as a pattern and place it on the fabric so the center of the collar falls on the fold line. Pin in place and draw an outline of the collar.

21. Draw a cutting line ¼″ (0.6 cm) outside the edges of the collar.

22. Repeat Steps 20 and 21 to cut out the undercollar.

23. Cut out each new piece in turn. Transfer all seam line markings to the other side of each pattern piece, using a tracing wheel.

24. To cut out a new interfacing for the collar, use the old collar as a pattern and repeat Steps 20 and 21.

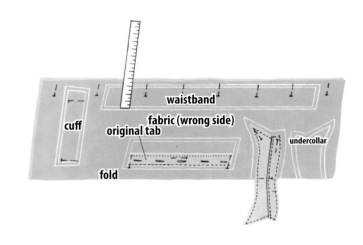

B

Attaching the Tab to the Shirt (C)

25. Turn the shirt wrong side out.
26. Pin the new tabs wrong side up to both shirt fronts. Baste and remove the pins.
27. Machine stitch and remove the basting.
28. Fold over the raw edge of the tab ¼″ (0.6 cm) and press.
29. Turn the shirt right side out. Press the seam allowances of both shirt and tab toward the tab.
30. With the wrong side facing out, fold the bottom end of the tab in half and machine stitch ¼″ (0.6 cm) in from the edge. Make a small clip into the seam allowances at the shirt edge as shown. Then, turn the tab right side out and push out the bottom corners using blunt scissors.
31. Pin the folded edge of the tab to the shirt, just covering the line of stitching made in Step 27.
32. Baste along the pinned edge and along the folded edge. Remove the pins.
33. Machine stitch ⅛″ (3.2 mm) in from both edges of the tab. Remove the basting.

Making the New Collar (D)

34. Pin and baste the collar interfacing to the wrong side of the collar. Remove the pins.
35. Turn the collar over so the interfacing lies face down on the table and the right side of the collar—the side that will show when the garment is finished—faces up.
36. Place the undercollar wrong side up on top of the collar. Pin and baste the undercollar to the collar along three sides, leaving the neck edge open. Remove the pins.
37. Machine stitch and remove the basting.
38. Trim the points diagonally. Clip into the seam allowances along the curved edges.
39. Turn the assembled collar right side out and push out the points using blunt scissors. Then, pull the points out farther from the outside with a pin. Press.

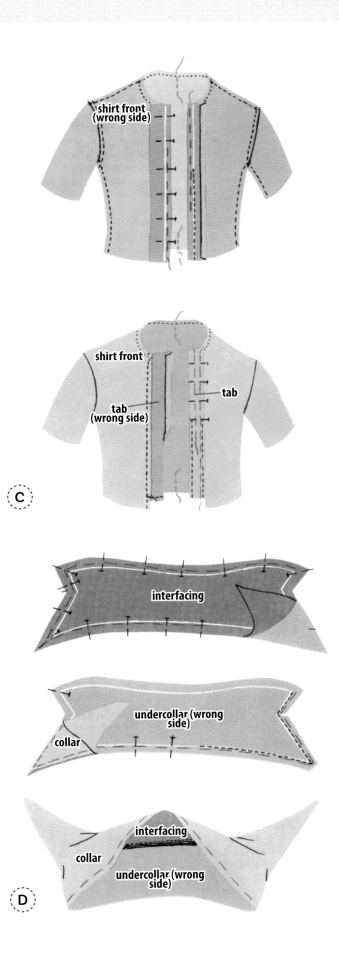

Attaching the Collar to the Shirt (E)

40. Lay the shirt on a flat surface, wrong side up.

41. Pin the collar to the wrong side of the shirt along the neck edge. Begin pinning at the center back and work toward the front. Baste and remove the pins.

42. Machine stitch and remove the basting.

43. Turn the shirt right side out. Press the seam allowances of the collar and shirt up toward the collar.

44. Pin and baste the undercollar to the shirt, covering the stitches made in Step 42. Remove the pins.

45. Machine stitch as close to the bottom edges of the collar as possible. Remove the basting.

46. Topstitch by running a line of machine stitching ⅛″ (3.2 mm) from the edge of the collar.

Making the Cuffs (F)

47. Fold the cuffs in half with the wrong sides facing out. Pin and machine stitch along the ends.

48. Remove the pins and press the seam open.

49. Fold over the wider edge of the cuff ¼″ (0.6 cm) and press.

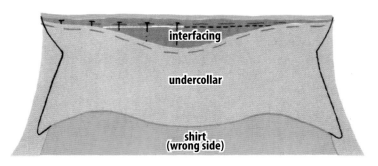

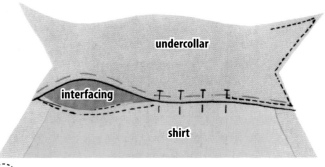

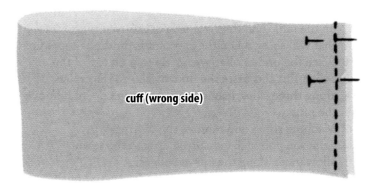

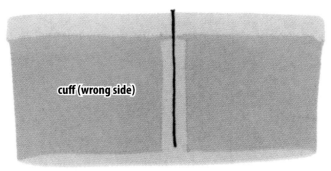

Attaching the Cuffs to the Shirt (G)

50. Turn the shirt wrong side out.
51. Pin the cuffs to the sleeves with the wrong side facing out, making sure the cuff seam is aligned with the underarm sleeve seam. Baste and remove the pins.
52. Machine stitch and remove the basting.
53. Turn the shirt right side out.
54. Press the seam allowances of the cuff and the sleeve up toward the sleeve.
55. Fold the cuff up along the seam line, keeping the seam ¹⁄₁₆″ (1.6 mm) to the inside, so it doesn't show on the outside.
56. Pin and baste the upper cuff edge of the sleeve. Remove the pins.
57. Topstitch by running a line of machine stitching ⅛″ (3.2 mm) inside the upper and lower cuff edges. Remove the basting.

Making the Waistband (H)

58. Machine stitch the two band sections together at one end. Press the seam open.
59. Fold the band in half lengthwise and press. Then, measure in 16″ (40.6 cm) from either end and make two small clips. These clips indicate where the tie ends will begin.

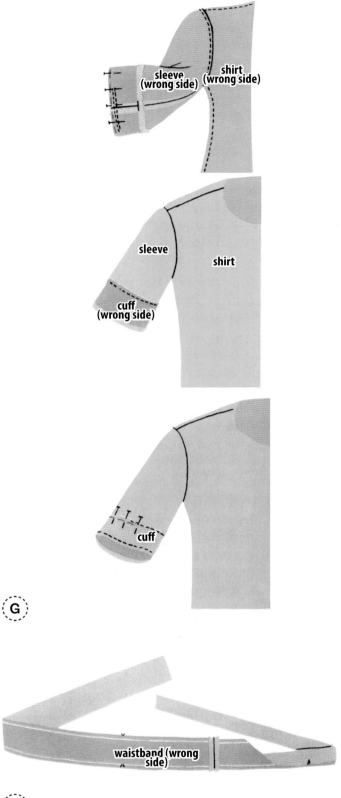

Attaching the Waistband (I)

60. Run two rows of machine basting stitches (six to 10 stitches to the inch) ½″ (1.3 cm) and ⅜″ (0.9 cm) from the bottom edge of the shirt. Gently pull the loose threads of the bastings on the underside (the threads that came from the machine's bobbin instead of the needle), in order to gather in the fullness at the lower edge of the shirt until it's approximately the same size as the waistline part of the band.

61. Place the shirt on a flat surface wrong side up.

62. With right sides together, pin one edge of the band to the bottom edge of the shirt. Make sure to match the band seam to the center back. Place the band wrong side down underneath the shirt and pin the band to the shirt, being sure to match the band seam to the center back mark on the shirt. Match the clip marks on the band made in Step 59 to the center front edges and pin. Add pins at ½″ (1.3 cm) intervals and adjust the gathers evenly.

63. Baste the band to the shirt ½″ (1.3 cm) in from the edge. Remove the pins.

64. Machine stitch the band to the shirt. Remove the bastings and press the shirt and band seam allowances down toward the band.

Finishing the Waistband (J)

65. Fold the ends of the band that extend beyond the shirt in half lengthwise with the wrong sides facing out.

66. Pin and baste ¼″ (0.6 cm) in from the edge. Remove the pins.

67. Machine stitch, starting at the point where the clip marks appear on the band and working out toward the ends of the band.

68. Trim the corners of the band diagonally.

69. Turn the ties right side out and press.

70. Turn under the remaining loose edge of the band ¼″ (0.6 cm) and press. Pin and baste the band to the shirt, covering the stitches made in Step 64. Remove the pins.

71. Topstitch the band by running a line of machine stitching ⅛″ (3.2 mm) in from all edges. Remove the bastings.

Adding Buttonholes and Buttons (K)

72. Mark the position for the new buttonholes, using the old tab as a guide for placement. Stitch the buttonholes by hand or machine and sew on new buttons.

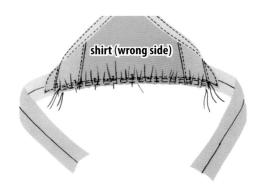

I

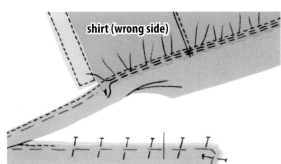

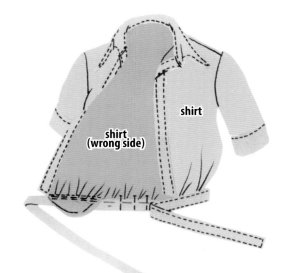

J

K

PANTS REMODEL: FROM PLAIN BOTTOMS TO CUFFS

Old pants that are too narrow, too short, or out of fashion in silhouette can be cleverly revived using a variety of techniques to elevate your sewing. Many techniques featured in this book can be applied to pants. Redesign a waistband by adding a self-fabric or contrasting fabric contoured waistband (page 201), open the side seam of your shorts or pants and add a matching or contrasting fabric flair (page 174), and decorative edge finishes can be inserted into seams or applied on top along with monograms, patch pockets, or button closures. Select your modification to complement the pair of pants you are working with. Baggy pants might transition into a pair of shorts with a gathered hem and bias band, while a trouser might feature hand stitches and an accent of fabric flair more appropriately. This project features shortening the trouser pants and adding a classic cuff.

Try the following techniques on your Pants Remodel:
Flat Welt Pockets, Chapter 1
Shaped Waistbands, Chapter 1
Decorative Edge Trimming, Chapter 2
Beading a Design, Chapter 3
Self-Bound French Seam, Chapter 4
Sewing Wool and Heavy Fabrics, Chapter 5
Piecing on the Bias, Chapter 7
Adding Flair, Chapter 7

Cutting and Marking the Pants Legs (A)

1. Try on the pants you want to convert into shorts and insert a pin across the crease of one leg where you want the lower edge of the cuff to be.
2. Remove the pants and place them on a table with the outer side seam of the pinned leg facing you. Keep the fabric flat, with the creased edges straight and the hemmed edges aligned.
3. Starting from the pin at the crease, insert pins across the pants leg, making sure the pins run parallel to the hem and that they go through both layers of fabric.
4. Measure down and draw a chalk line ½″ (1.3 cm) from the pins.
5. Cut off the lower portion of the pants leg along the chalk line. Remove the pins.
6. Run a line of basting stitches ½″ (1.3 cm) above the cut edge to mark a seam line.

Cutting Out the Cuff (B)

7. To determine how long the cuff should be, measure around the pants leg along the basted seam line and add 1″ (2.5 cm) for seam allowances.
8. Place the cutoff lower portion of the pants leg on a table. Keep the fabric flat with the creased edges straight and the cut edges and the hemmed edges aligned.
9. Starting at the cut edge, measure the distance you determined in Step 7 along one of the creases and mark with a chalk line at a right angle to the crease.
10. Decide how wide you want the finished cuff to be and add ½″ (1.3 cm) for seam allowance.
11. Measure in from the crease the same distance you determined in Step 10 and draw a chalk line parallel to the crease, from the cut edge to the chalk line made in Step 9.
12. Pin both layers of fabric together at 1″ (2.5 cm) intervals.
13. Cut the cuff out along the chalk lines. Remove the pins.

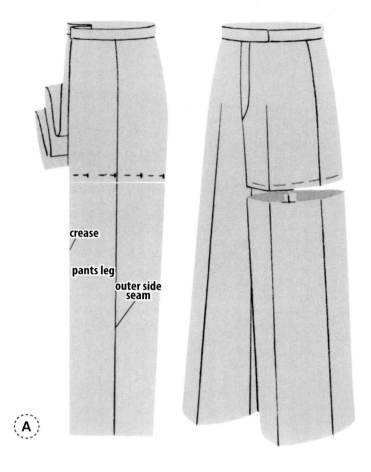

A

crease

pants leg

outer side seam

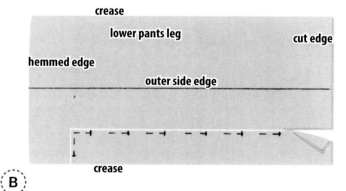

B

crease

lower pants leg

cut edge

hemmed edge

outer side edge

crease

Preparing the Cuff (C)

14. Open the cutout cuff so the wrong side is up.
15. Draw chalk lines, which will be your seam lines, ½″ (1.3 cm) in from and parallel to the two short edges.
16. Fold the cuff in half so the wrong sides are out and the seam lines are aligned.
17. Pin the ends of the cuff together at ½″ (1.3 cm) intervals.
18. Baste just outside the seam line and remove the pins.
19. Machine stitch along the seam line and remove the basting.
20. Press the seam open and trim to ¼″ (0.6 cm).
21. Fold the band in half along the original crease, wrong sides together; mark a seam line ½″ (1.3 cm) from the cut edge and parallel to it with basting stitches. Sew through both layers of fabric.

Attaching the Cuff to the Pants Leg (D)

22. Turn the pants leg wrong side out and position the pants so the bottom of the leg is facing up.
23. Place the cuff around the leg with the seam in the cuff aligned with the inner seam of the leg.
24. Align the basted seam lines and pin at 1″ (2.5 cm) intervals, going through all three layers of fabric.
25. Baste and remove the pins.
26. Turn the pants leg right side out with the cuff inside the leg.
27. Machine stitch the cuff to the leg along the basted seam line as shown. Remove all bastings.
28. Trim the leg seam allowance to ⅜″ (0.9 cm).
29. Trim the cuff seam allowance to ¼″ (0.6 cm).

Finishing the Cuff (E)

30. Turn the cuff away from the leg.
31. Press the trimmed seam allowances flat against the leg.
32. Turn the cuff up against the right side of the pants leg—the visible side when the garment is finished—so the seam is ¼″ (0.6 cm) inside the leg. Press.
33. At the inner seam of the pants leg, turn down the folded edge of the cuff slightly. Using a doubled thread knotted at the end, make a stitch in the leg about ¼″ (0.6 cm) inside the cuff; draw the needle through and pick up a few threads of the underlayer of the cuff. Repeat two or three times in the same place, ending with a backstitch. Tack the cuff down at the outer side seam of the leg in the same manner.
34. Repeat on the other leg.

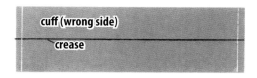

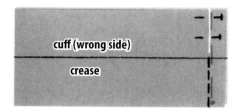

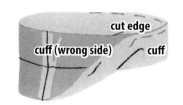

C

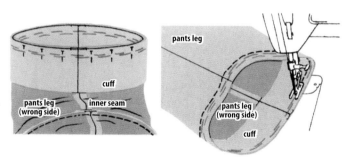

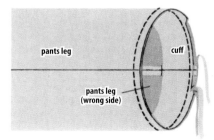

D

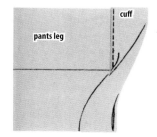
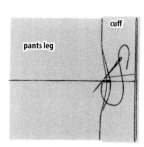

E

SKIRT REDESIGN: THE DECORATIVE ZIPPER GODET

A classic straight or A-line skirt is completely transformed by adding a decorative godet inset combined with a working zipper. The added fabric panel may hang straight, flair outward for added ease with a lavish triangular godet panel, or feature rows of pleating for even more contrasting emphasis. These variations are simple to add, since none require changing the waistband, center back zipper, or hip area of the original. Although, if using a skirt where the fit is slightly snug, the skirt may be made bigger by extending the panels further up into the body of the garment, creating more fitting ease.

Consider the weight of the fabric you're adding to your design. Avoid bulky fabrics; a lighter, drapey fabric will reduce bulk if adding pleats or excess fabric.

Try the following techniques on your Skirt Redesign:
Invisible Zipper, Chapter 1
Decorative Edge Trimming, Chapter 2
Bias Binding, Chapter 2
Reversible Seam, Chapter 4
Sewing Delicate Fabrics, Chapter 5
Adding Flair, Chapter 7

Marking and Preparing the Skirt (A)

1. Begin with a skirt that fits at the waistline. Determine the location for the zipper and godet inset.

For skirts with a seam line at the location of the new opening: (B)

2. Mark the location by basting or marking a vertical line from the hem up the length of the opening. Place a pin horizontally across the skirt at the location where the opening of the seam line ends.
3. Place an additional pin horizontally 1″ (2.5 cm) above the first marking.
4. Turn the skirt inside out and transfer both markings to the inside of the skirt by carefully placing an additional pin or chalk mark on the seam line. Remove the pins.
5. On the inside of the skirt, reinforce the seam line between the two chalk markings by stitching over top of the stitches already on the seam. This will prevent the seam from popping open above the new decorative opening.
6. Carefully open the seam using a seam ripper or by clipping a stitch below the anchor stitching and lightly pull the thread from the seam. Lightly press open the seam line, taking care not to press them out completely, as they will be needed later.

> **Note:** If there is an overlock stitch covering the seam, use a sewing blade to open the seam and scrape off the thread fibers. If there is a lining in the skirt, mark and open it the same way as the skirt, repeating Steps 1–6.

For skirts without a seam in the location of the new opening: (C)

7. Repeat Steps 1–4 to mark the opening.
8. Baste vertically up both sides of the marked opening approximately ⅛″ (3.2 mm) from the placement line.

> **Note:** It may be necessary to stitch or fuse a narrow strip of interfacing to the opening to help reinforce and prevent stretching. Use a ½–1″ (1.3–2.5 cm) wide piece of interfacing, making sure it's centered on the opening.

9. Cut the opening from the hem up toward the point where the opening stops. At the end of the opening, make a small ¼″ (0.6 cm) cut at a 45° angle on either side of the opening. Turn under the edges ½″ (1.3 cm) up the length of the opening and turn under the small triangle at the top of the opening.
10. Carefully, let down the hem on either side of the opening approximately 1–2″ (2.5–5.1 cm) on either side.

Making the Godet Insert (A)

1. For the plain godet, you will need fabric wide enough to create the look you envision and tall enough to fit into the length of the opening. The fabric style may dictate how large of an insert you can use; for example, if you're using a remnant.

2. Follow the steps on page 174 for Adding Flair and make the pattern the correct size for your garment. Repeat and make as many godets as needed for your garment if adding multiple inserts.

> **Note:** If you want the hem of the godet to hang separate from the hem of the skirt, then add the desired hem width and finish the hem edge prior to sewing to the skirt opening.

Attaching the Zipper (B)

3. Select a regular style zipper 2″ (5.1 cm) shorter than the opening. The zipper will be sewn in upside down so it opens from the hem upward.

4. With the top of the left side of the zipper and zipper pull 2″ (5.1 cm) from the hem, place one side of the zipper right sides together on the opening. Pin the zipper tape to the seam allowance or folded edge.

5. Using your zipper foot, stitch the length of the opening from the hem upward using a narrow seam allowance. Stop at the top and back stitch to anchor the zipper. Turn it outward and press.

6. Place the opposite side of the zipper tape to the opposite side of the long opening and repeat Steps 4 and 5.

7. Zip the zipper and make sure the opening lays flat and there are no puckers in the zipper.

> **Tip:** Baste the zipper in first to test the placement. The zipper teeth should be located so they face outward and are centered on the opening. When zipping the skirt, you will see a nice placement of the zipper. When it is unzipped, it will reveal the decorative godet.

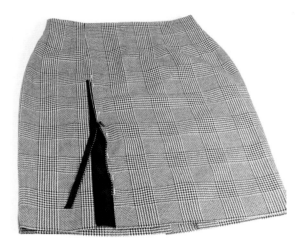

Attaching the Godet (C)

8. Unzip the zipper. The largest part of the godet and widest area of the triangular shape will be located near the hem. Place one side of the godet right sides together onto the zipper tape and seam allowance.

9. Stitch together and repeat on the opposite side.

10. Topstitch around zipper, making sure to reinforce the top of the opening for skirts with no seam allowance.

Hemming the Skirt (D)

11. Turn the skirt right side out.

12. To hem the skirt with the plain godet, turn up the bottom edge along the old hemline or 1½″ (3.8 cm) from the bottom and pin. Baste ¼″ (0.6 cm) from the edge of the tape and remove the pins. Hand stitch the tape to the skirt using a hemming stitch. Remove the basting and press.

13. To hem the skirt with a lining, turn under the lining seam allowance and pin to each side of the opening seam allowance. Or, cut a piece of lining the size of the godet and with right sides together, attach to the lining. Hem the lining and let it hang free, or attach to the hem of the skirt.

C

D

APPENDIX
MONOGRAM ALPHABET

This monogram is a fun combination of needlepoint and embroidery. To make a monogram from this alphabet, first enlarge and trace the letters on a 14-mesh canvas or stable fabric. Next, with six-strand embroidery floss and a size 5 to 10 crewel needle, make the white contour lines and the black shadows in padded satin stitch, using plain satin stitch for filler. Then, fill in the colored areas, working from the largest to the smallest and adding the black edging last. Follow the stitch guide for each letter, and the instructions on pages 242–244. Finally, complete the needlepoint background in a straight Gobelin stitch with a Size 20 blunt tapestry needle and three-strand Persian yarn.

White contour lines of letter and black shadows: padded satin stitch edged with split stitch. **Solid white area:** tent stitch. **Black design motif:** satin stitch. **Black interior contour lines:** chain stitch.

White kidney shapes, pointed ovals, and black shadows: padded satin stitch edged with split stitch. **Black dots:** French knots. **Black shade lines:** outline stitch. **Black and white stripes:** anchored couching.

Outermost white contour line of letter and black shadows: padded satin stitch edged with split stitch. **Black and white interior contour lines:** outline stitch.

White contour line of letter, white oval shapes and black shadows: padded satin stitch edged with split stitch. **Solid white areas:** tent stitch. **Black interior, contour and shade lines:** split stitch.

White contour line and black shadows: padded satin stitch edged with split stitch. **Solid white area:** tent stitch. **Leaves:** satin stitch. **Black vines and swirl shapes:** outline stitch. **Black dots:** French knots.

White contour line and center ring and black shadows: padded satin stitch edged with split stitch. **Black band and circles:** tent stitch. **Leaves:** satin stitch edged with chain stitch. **Flowers:** French knots.

White contour line of letter, white leaf designs and black shadows: padded satin stitch edged with split stitch. **Solid white areas:** tent stitch. **Black dots:** French knots. **Black shade lines:** split stitch.

White contour line and black shadows: padded satin stitch edged with split stitch. **Solid black area:** flame stitch. **White triangles:** satin stitch. **Circles:** padded satin stitch edged with anchored couching.

Outermost white line, white band and egg shapes, and black shadows and crescents: padded satin stitch edged with split stitch. **Black shade lines and black and white interior contour lines:** outline stitch.

White contour line and black shadows: padded satin stitch edged with split stitch. **Solid black areas:** padded satin stitch. **White dashes:** French knots. **Black and white interior contour lines:** split stitch.

White contour line, black shadows, and black design motifs: padded satin stitch edged with split stitch. **Solid white area:** tent stitch. **Black interior contour lines:** outline stitch. **Black dots:** French knots.

White contour line of letter, black shadows and black half-moons and circles: padded satin stitch edged with split stitch. **Black and white interior lines and stripes:** split stitch. **White band and rings:** tent stitch.

 White swirls and ovals: tent stitch. Black shadows, crescents, and stars: padded satin stitch. Shadow edges and black interior lines: split stitch. Black shade lines: stem stitch. Dots: French knots.

 White and black swirls and black shadows and diamonds: padded satin stitch edged with split stitch. Black interior contour lines: outline stitch. White dots: French knots.

 White contour lines and black shadows and circles: padded satin stitch edged with split stitch. Interior stripes: straight Gobelin stitch. White rings: chain stitch. White flowers and dots: French knots.

 White contour line and ovals, black shadows, and circles: padded satin stitch edged with split stitch. Black and white stripes: outline stitch. Black shade lines: stem stitch. White dots: French knots.

 White contour line of letter and black shadows: padded satin stitch edged with split stitch. Interior area: brick stitch.

 White contour line of letter and black shadows: padded satin stitch edged with split stitch. Solid black area: tent stitch. White pointed oval shapes: padded satin stitch. White dots: French knots.

 White contour lines and black shadows, black and white crescents, and ovals: padded satin stitch edged with split stitch. Interior lines: outline stitch. Black and white dots and broken white lines: French knots.

 White contour line of letter and black shadows and circles: padded satin stitch edged with split stitch. White band: tent stitch edged with outline stitch. Black and white interior contour lines: chain stitch.

 White contour line and flowers, black shadows and circles: padded satin stitch edged with split stitch. White motif: tent stitch. Stripes: straight Gobelin stitch. Black interior lines: outline stitch.

 White contour line of letter, black shadows, bricks, diamonds and star: padded satin stitch edged with split stitch. White bands: tent stitch. Black shade lines: split stitch. Black and white dots: French knots.

 White contour line of letter, white ovals, white and black clover leaves, black shadows and crescents: padded satin stitch edged with split stitch. Stripes: outline stitch. Shade lines: anchored couching.

 White swirl shapes, circles and ring and black shadows: padded satin stitch edged with split stitch. Solid black interior areas: tent stitch. White flower: French knots. Black interior lines: split stitch.

 White contour lines of letter, white ovals, and black shadows: padded satin stitch edged with split stitch. Stripes: straight Gobelin stitch. Black swirls, contour, and shade lines: split stitch.

 White contour line, leaves and ring, and black shadows: padded satin stitch edged with split stitch. Black oval: tent stitch. White flower and black dots: French knots. Stripes: outline stitch.

BASIC STITCHES

Arrowhead Stitch (A)

1. Mark the guidelines on the fabric by making two parallel rows of basting stitches separated by a distance equal to the desired length of the stitches. Then, using knotted thread, bring the needle up from the wrong side of the fabric at the righthand end of the upper guideline. Pull the thread through.

2. Insert the needle on the lower guideline one stitch length to the left of the hole made in Step 1. Bring the needle up on the upper guideline one stitch length to the left of the point at which the needle was inserted. Pull the thread through to form a diagonal stitch.

3. Insert the needle on the lower guideline, just to the lower of the bottom of the diagonal stitch. Pull the thread through to the wrong side of the fabric to complete the arrowhead shape.

4. To make the next stitch, bring the needle up on the upper guideline just to the left of the previous stitch, as shown. Repeat Steps 2 and 3.

5. Make similar stitches from right to left until you reach the lefthand end of the guidelines. Complete the last stitch as shown in Step 3; pull the thread through to the wrong side of the fabric.

6. End off on the wrong side of the fabric by slipping the needle underneath the nearest stitch and sliding the thread under the needle as shown. Then, pull the thread through tightly, creating a small knot. Clip the excess thread and remove the basted guidelines.

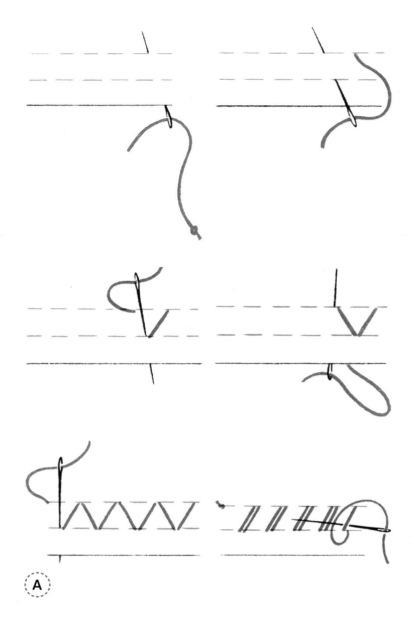

A

Catch Stitch (B)

1. Working from left to right, anchor the first stitch with a knot inside the hem ¼″ (0.6 cm) down from the edge. Point the needle to the left and pick up one or two threads on the garment directly above the hem, then pull the thread through. Take a small stitch in the hem only (not the garment), ¼″ (0.6 cm) down from the edge and ¼″ (0.6 cm) to the right of the previous stitch. End with a fastening stitch.

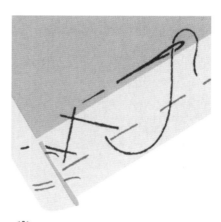

B

Ending Off (C)

1. On the wrong side of the material, slide the needle underneath the nearest 3 or 4 consecutive stitches and pull it through. Snip off the excess thread.

Fastening Stitch (D)

1. To end a row with a fastening stitch, insert the needle back ¼″ (0.6 cm) and bring it out at the point at which the needle last emerged. Make another stitch through these same points for extra firmness. To begin a row with a fastening stitch, leave a 4″ (10.2 cm) loose end and make the initial stitch the same way as an ending stitch.

Overcast Stitch (E)

1. Draw the needle with knotted thread through from the wrong side of the fabric ⅛–¼″ (0.3–0.6 cm) down from the top edge. With the thread to the right, insert the needle under the fabric from the wrong side ⅛–¼″ (0.3–0.6 cm) to the left of the first stitch. Continue to make evenly spaced stitches over the fabric edge and end with a fastening stitch.

Prick Stitch (F)

1. Using a knotted thread, draw the needle up from the bottom layer of fabric and pull it through. Insert the needle to the right three or four threads and bring it out ¼–⅜″ (0.6–0.9 cm) to the left of where it last emerged. Continue the process, ending with a fastening stitch on the bottom layer of fabric.

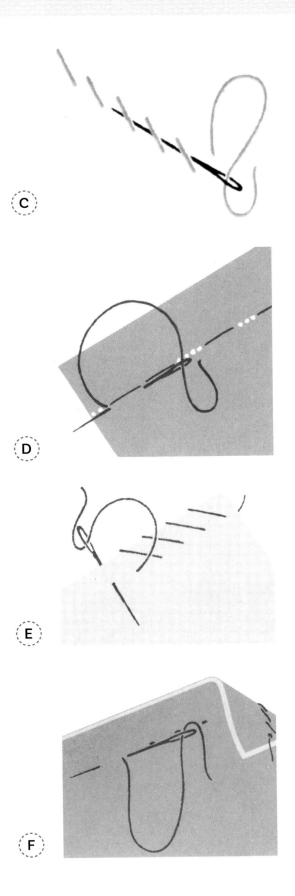

Satin Stitch (G)

1. Using a knotted thread, bring the needle up from the wrong side of the material held in the hoop. Then, at the angle desired, insert it down to the wrong side at a point diagonally across the design.
2. Bring the needle straight up from the wrong side just above the first hole and insert it above the hole made in Step 1.
3. Repeat Step 2 until the top is filled. Then, bring the needle from the wrong side just below the filled part and make diagonal stitches until the bottom is filled. Secure the last stitch on the wrong side ending off.

Slip Stitch (H)

1. Fold under the hem edge and anchor the first stitch with a knot inside the fold. Point the needle to the left. Pick up one or two threads of the garment fabric close to the hem edge, directly below the first stitch, and slide the needle horizontally through the folded edge of the hem ⅛″ (3.2 mm) to the left of the previous stitch. Continue across in the same manner and end with a fastening stitch.

Tailor Tacks (I)

1. Using a double strand of unknotted thread, take a short stitch through the point to be marked, picking up the pattern piece and one or two layers of fabric, depending on whether or not the fabric is doubled. Leave 2″ (5.1 cm) long loose ends. Take another stitch through the same point, leaving a 2″ (5.1 cm) loop on top of the pattern. End with at least 2″ (5.1 cm) of loose thread.

Whipstitch (J)

1. Using a knotted thread, draw the needle up from the bottom layer of fabric about ¹⁄₁₆″ (1.6 mm) from the edge. Reinsert the needle, again from the bottom layer of fabric, about ¹⁄₁₆″ (1.6 mm) to the left of the point from which the thread emerged, making sure the needle is at a right angle to the edge. Continue to make tiny, slanted, even stitches over the fabric edge. End with a fastening stitch.

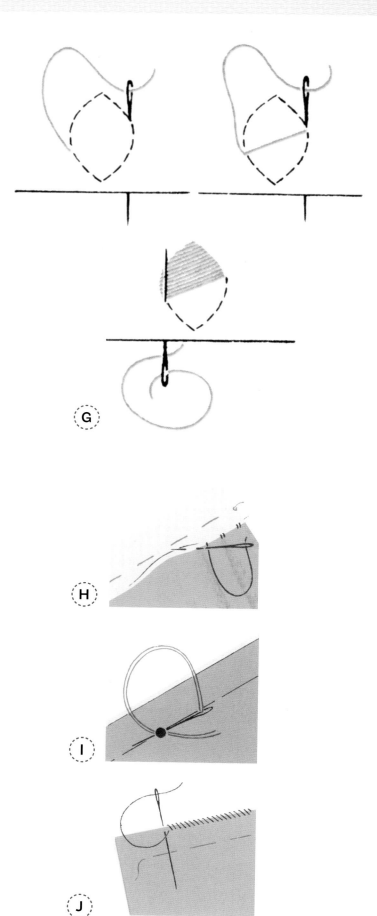

ABOUT WRITING A SEWING BOOK

I would like to thank my editor, Amelia, who came to me with the idea for this book after my last book, *The Ultimate Illustrated Guide to Sewing Clothes*, was published. I have found that writing a book to teach these advanced sewing techniques has challenged me to continue to refine and hone my own personal sewing skills. I believe this process is how learning sewing should be for everyone and reflects my own experience since the first day I picked up a needle and thread. No matter your experience or skill level, you always have room to improve, which is what I think makes sewing both challenging and enjoyable. It is truly the art of becoming a sewing master.

ABOUT THE AUTHOR

Joi Mahon is the owner of The Sewing Factory in Sioux City, Iowa and has been designing, fitting, and teaching sewing for over 25 years. She began sewing at a young age, transitioned into 4-H in the 6th grade, and was working as an assistant to a tailor at the age of 15. Joi has a degree in apparel design, merchandising, and production from Iowa State University and she treasures all of her training and experiences both from the tailor shop and her mentors in the classroom. She describes herself as a fashion entrepreneur with a wide array of sewing interests and endeavors. She has been featured in numerous sewing and craft magazines and online programs, and has hosted Nancy's Notions Wardrobe Builder, *Threads* Magazine Complete Course on Interfacing, and Perfect Pattern and Fit Club.

Joi is a McCall's licensed pattern designer, Craftsy instructor (Fast Track Fitting and Fast Track Fitting in the Details), brand ambassador for Mettler Thread since 2011, and brand ambassador for OESD.

She is part of the BERNINA Sewing Industry Alliance, and travels to various stores and events to teach sewing, along with holding regular retreats in her onsite classroom at the Sewing Factory Location.

Her first book, *Create the Perfect Fit*, was published by F+W Media and was followed by Designer Joi's Fashion Sewing Workshop. The *Ultimate Illustrated Guide to Sewing Clothes* (March 2022, Fox Chapel Publishing), repurposed from the Time Life series and combined with her pants content, has been very well received.

Joi says, "The joy of sewing and design is that you have unlimited choices in what you make and how you make it. You also have the control to change the look, fit, and fabric when customizing your wardrobe. These options are not available in ready to wear so this freedom is refreshing and exciting."

Joi has a line of patterns, fabrics, and resources available on her website, and teaches free lessons every week on the Sewing Time Live program on the Designer Joi Mahon Facebook page.

Website: www.dressformsdesign.com
Facebook: DesignerJoiMahon
X: @DesignerJoi
Instagram: @DesignerJoi

INDEX